BEST FRIENDS FOR LIFE

Books by Michael Phillips

Best Friends for Life (with Judy Phillips)
George MacDonald: Scotland's Beloved Storyteller
A God to Call Father†

THE HIGHLAND COLLECTION*

    Jamie MacLeod: Highland Lass   *Robbie Taggart: Highland Sailor*

THE JOURNALS OF CORRIE BELLE HOLLISTER

    *My Father's World**   *Sea to Shining Sea*
    *Daughter of Grace**   *Into the Long Dark Night*
    On the Trail of the Truth   *Land of the Brave and the Free*
    A Place in the Sun   *A Home for the Heart*

Grayfox (Zack's story)

THE JOURNALS OF CORRIE & CHRISTOPHER

    The Braxtons of Miracle Springs *A New Beginning*

MERCY AND EAGLEFLIGHT†

    Mercy and Eagleflight   *Goodness and Mercy*
    A Dangerous Love

THE RUSSIANS*

    The Crown and the Crucible   *Travail and Triumph*
    A House Divided

THE SECRET OF THE ROSE†

    The Eleventh Hour   *Escape to Freedom*
    A Rose Remembered   *Dawn of Liberty*

THE STONEWYCKE TRILOGY*

    The Heather Hills of Stonewycke *Lady of Stonewycke*
    Flight From Stonewycke

THE STONEWYCKE LEGACY*

    Stranger at Stonewycke   *Treasure of Stonewycke*
    Shadows Over Stonewycke

*with Judith Pella   †Tyndale House

BEST FRIENDS FOR LIFE

MICHAEL & JUDY
PHILLIPS

BETHANY HOUSE PUBLISHERS
MINNEAPOLIS, MINNESOTA 55438

Published by Bethany House Publishers
A Ministry of Bethany Fellowship, Inc.
11300 Hampshire Avenue South
Minneapolis, Minnesota 55438

Printed in the United States of America.

Library of Congress Cataloging-in-Publication Data

Phillips, Michael R., 1946–
    Best friends for life / Michael & Judy Phillips.
        p. cm.
    ISBN 1–55661–943-X
    1. Mate selection. 2. Mate selection—Religious aspects—Christianity.
3. Friendship. 4. Friendship in adolescence.
I. Phillips, Judy. II. Title.
HQ801.P48 1997
306.82—dc21   96–45910
                                                                    CIP

Dedicated to a new generation of young men and women everywhere who are determined to form good and lasting "best-friend marriages."

A TRIBUTE FROM JUDY PHILLIPS

This is the first time my name has been on the cover of a book, and since this opportunity may never come my way again, I want to also offer my own dedication. This in no way detracts from the sincerity of our joint dedication on the previous page. I think Mike's loyal readers will understand.

Many of you have responded to Mike's books by writing to him. Your letters are a great encouragement and often arrive at just the right time, when encouragement is most needed. But another aspect of the letters is that you readers want to make contact. You want to share with him what the Lord is doing in your lives and how his stories and characters have helped you grow. You feel that he would listen and understand. I think you feel somehow that you know him.

This is very similar to how Mike and I feel about George MacDonald. His stories and characters have enriched our lives as Christians, and if he were alive we would love to make contact with him—to thank him, to share with him, to know him. But over the years, through our reading and research, we have found that to know MacDonald's characters is to know *him*. He has become our friend. We have turned to him through his stories for help. As Jesus' desire was to show us the Father, we feel MacDonald's desire was to point us to the Father through Jesus, His Son.

Those of you who have read the bulk of Mike's stories do know him. For his characters are very representative of the real Michael Phillips. Surrounded by a shell of shyness (and a great propensity for being misunderstood!) is the wisdom of the Baron, the gentleness of Pa, the strength of character of Christopher, the dying to self of Robbie Taggart, the romance of Matthew, the practical faith of Zeke Simmons, the courage of Dieder Palacki, and on and on. Mike is a man who can be trusted. And his greatest desire in life is to tell others of God's infinite goodness and to try to live the commands of Jesus Christ. His greatest prayer is that Christians will learn to live in unity.

Mike has not led a charmed life. Circumstances have thrown him (and me) many curves. We have been repeatedly challenged in the very areas about which he writes. Many of the sufferings of his characters sound real because they are very real in Mike's life. We have had to cope with much. Our own humanness has often overwhelmed us, our weaknesses far outweighing our strengths. But through it all we have been there for each other. And that is why I want to take this time to say to you, his good friends:

Here is a man whom I honor.
He is indeed a man among men.
I give to you
Mike Phillips
my best friend for life.

CONTENTS

INTRODUCTION

We were married twenty-five years ago. We recently celebrated our silver anniversary.

It seems such a short time to look back on. Yet the entire climate of relationships and the state of marriage itself was altogether different then.

It was *so* different that it feels as if a century has passed rather than just twenty-five years. At that time a certain value structure prevailed throughout society that guided young people such as ourselves into adulthood, governing us in many ways we were not even aware of.

True, it was a value structure already crumbling. Yet when the two of us were getting to know each other as the decade of the sixties drew to a close, and then prepared for marriage as the seventies dawned, there remained a shadow of what might be called an old Victorian virtue and morality still shakily in place, with mores and absolutes that kept a good many young people, Christian young people especially, more or less on track relationally and ethically.

Everything has now changed.

The cracks in that "moral system"—a moral equation of truth where right did not equal wrong—came to represent a *new* outlook where values were *no longer* determined as before by absolute standards but now by individuals as each saw fit. Such an outlook began to be seen in the 1950s and accelerated rapidly through the 1960s. Then through the '70s, '80s, and '90s, the values of previous generations finally crumbled beyond recognition.

Right and wrong have been shaken loose from centuries-old foundations. Whatever definitions you choose to attach to "right" or to "wrong" are up for grabs. Morality has become a yard-sale clothing bazaar. Take whatever you like. Mix and match. Everything's cheap and comes with no strings attached. If you don't like it, you can always trade it in somewhere else next week. Call the end result truth or right. Call it whatever you like. It hardly matters, because your wardrobe is different from everyone else's anyway, and there is nothing left to define the way anyone *ought* to dress.

The standards that once defined virtue and relational absolutes are afloat on the waves of a sea, without any rock-hard land on which to sink an anchor.

The world *looks* the same. People look the same. Yet ethically and relationally, we who live in this declining Western culture of the United States and Europe are walking about on C. S. Lewis's floating island of Perelandra. We are floundering on a constantly varying surface, disconnected from solid underpinnings of morality beneath us.

An ethical *terra firma* no longer exists under our feet. There is no place we can secure a firm footing to be able to say, *"This* is true, *this* is right . . . these are the solid standards upon which the world and truth are based and by which *everyone* should live."

No wonder establishing permanent marriages is harder than ever. Society is ethically adrift. There are no foundational *rocks* to which marriage can be attached. Men and women are not merely building relationships on *sand* these days, they're building them on *quicksand!*

We are writing this book to address this problem.

We write both to young people and to parents, hoping to provide solid principles that will help young men and women establish the kinds of "best-friend friendships" that will be capable of undergirding good, fulfilling, lifelong marriages. (We had originally included the word "happy" in that last sentence, but after some thought removed it. "Happy" has become a word nearly as romanticized as "love." Most of us tend to associate it with a Hollywood-style definition, and therefore its usefulness has almost been lost. True happiness and love do indeed emerge from good marriages. However, as we will discover later, having *happiness* as one's primary goal does not always contribute to a strong marital foundation.)

We will emphasize the term "friendship" throughout this discussion. There was a time when a marriage could survive without a man and woman being friends. They could be lovers, social companions, partners, and co-workers to sustain the family business or farm—such practical aspects of the relationship were often enough. A man had *his* friends, a woman had *hers*. The existing moral framework kept most couples intact even if friendship occupied no vital element in the marital bond. Happiness may not always have been present either. But men and women—some happy, some not, some in love, some not—persevered together because the fabric of marriage and family was strong and made to last.

But as we have said, ours is a changed society. The fabric of marriage that held society together has decayed. We live in a busy, fragmented, truth-starved, tight-packed, and affluent world. The hardworking, sometimes harsh, and largely rural social conditions that once bound most marriages together have disappeared. We now live in a social milieu that *encourages* multiple romantic attachments, and as a result the state of marriage has paid a terrible price. Short-term,

Hollywood-image "love" has replaced lifelong commitment as the central ingredient of relationships between men and women.

Because of this titanic shift, friendship has now become, in our opinion, *the most important component* in determining whether a marriage will be strong and lasting—more important even than happiness, being in love, or financial security. Friends are always there for you. You can talk and share openly with friends. Friends stick together through the down times. Friends remain loyal through disagreements and frustrations. Friends don't allow emotional ups and downs to define their friendship. Even when life is bumpy, friendship proves steady. Friends like each other and would rather be with each other just about any time and under any circumstances than with anyone else. When things go wrong and discouragements arise, it is always to your *best* friend you want to turn first of all.

It is vital that a married couple be there for each other too. They must be able to talk and share openly . . . and all the rest. A man and woman have to *like* each other to sustain being together every day for thirty or forty years—or longer, until death finally parts them.

That is friendship!

Many of today's young people, however, are thrust so early into the dating game that they cheat themselves out of the opportunity to learn what comprises good and lasting friendship. Romance enters the relational matrix so early that friendships with the opposite sex rarely have the chance to develop and mature.

Romance and *friendship* ought not to be mutually exclusive. But the sad fact is that in the teen years the former easily squeezes out the latter. That is why we are writing to young people and their parents—to help them discover how to nurture *both*, each at the right time.

This book has grown out of the flood of correspondence we have received, particularly in response to our two series of novels, *The Journals of Corrie Belle Hollister* and *The Secret of the Rose*. The principles we will here discuss first arose in a fictional format in these series. In particular, the book *A Home for the Heart* generated such an outpouring of response and questions—on the part of both young people and parents—that we felt the necessity to respond in more depth and to explain our "best-friends-for-life" principles more fully.

The mail we receive comes almost equally from young people and parents—from young men *and* young women, from fathers *and* mothers.

This is a crucial point. *We are writing to entire families!* Very little we propose will work without a partnership between sons and daughters and their parents.

We will return to this theme continually: What we propose is a *partnership*. One that takes *time, trust,* and *prayer.* It is our prayer that young people will read what follows and will take it to their parents and say, "Hey, Mom, Dad . . . check this out! This book has some cool ideas I'd like to try. Will you help? Will you be part of it with me?"

Equally we hope parents will say to their sons and daughters, "Wow, look at this. These are some interesting suggestions. We haven't talked much about or planned for this stage of your life. Perhaps we ought to. Would you read this and let us know what you think? Then let's talk about it. Maybe we can work together on some of this."

Partnership! That's how solid marital foundations are formed.

Foundations are the first part of any structure to be laid down. Before foundations can be established, plans—good and detailed plans—need to be drawn up to help you know what kind of foundation you hope to build—and what kind of structure you plan to build on that base. Once you're living in a house, it's too late to think about foundations.

Isn't marriage far more important than a building? Shouldn't we take at least as much time to plan and secure the proper relational foundation that enables us to build lifelong marriages?

The following prophecy from the lips of Isaiah will serve to focus the challenge before us all: "Your people will rebuild the ancient ruins and will raise up the age-old foundations" (Isaiah 58:12).

This will not primarily be, therefore, a book about how to make *marriage* work. There are hundreds of such resources already, many offering excellent help. This is about *foundations* for marriage. We will address the dilemma young people face *before* they walk down the aisle: the decision *whom* to marry.

This single question sits squarely in the middle of nearly every young person's mind at some time or another: *Who will I marry?*

Other issues included in this one large question are:

- How do I *find* the right husband or wife?
- How do I *know* whether the relationship I've started is going to last?
- What *kind* of relationship is worth building a marriage on?
- Is dating the best method for "getting to know" someone?
- What is this thing called "courtship" all about anyway?

We will look at all these questions. And we will introduce you to several true-life young people who have gone about the process of finding husbands and wives very differently, and let you see what you think of their methods. We will talk about how you can establish the sorts of relationships from which to choose your own particular lifelong partner that will insure that *you* make a wise decision. We will continually return to the three foundational elements in wise marital preparation—time, trust, and prayer.

For every topic of concern about which someone seeks guidance and help and counsel, there are *many* books, *many* ideas, *many* perspectives advocated. Pat answers are easy to spout but more difficult to apply. The truth is, everyone has to individualize the counsel they receive and apply it as wisely as they can to their *own* personal situation.

We cannot lay out a program that if followed is guaranteed to work for one and all in every situation, that will automatically insure happy and utopian marriages for all those who follow it.

Let's face it, life throws us curves. With God's help we do our best. Time was when the odds worked in most people's favor. Ninety percent of marriages (with or without friendship as a vital ingredient) endured. But now the odds are against us. Less than half of marriages survive, and that statistic becomes more grim every year. The fact is, we need to be more careful and thoughtful than ever about this life decision.

Life is a smorgasbord of principles, some more meaningful for some than for others. Picture yourself at a church potluck. Everyone brings a different dish to the table. As you walk through the line, looking over your options, you decide what to take—a little of this, a little more of that, something else you'll skip, and that odd-looking pasta concoction over there you'll taste to see if you might want more later. You find familiar recipes alongside casseroles you don't recognize.

This book may be like one of those odd concoctions you haven't seen before. We will offer some options about establishing wise and sensible relationships that we believe will lead to a sound marriage. We are putting our "dish" on the table for you to examine and ponder. Hopefully many of our ideas will be useful to you and will turn out to be ones you will want to try.

Any parent with more than one child knows well enough that parenting techniques do not work for all children in exactly the same way. That's why so many books on child-rearing are written. And on the "marriage potluck" table, as we said, there are already hundreds of books full of ideas and traditions and customs to choose from.

Why add another dish to an already crowded buffet?

Because we think we've cooked up a stew about premarriage relationships that is interesting and just a little unique. Most won't have sampled quite this combination before. You may not altogether like the taste at first read. At the same time, some of our ingredients may give you ideas on how to plan ahead for your own marriage.

We hope you'll find it worth a few nibbles . . . and will want to come back for more!

Michael and Judy Phillips

PART I

A BATTLE CRY FOR CHANGE

A true friend is a gift of God, and He only who made hearts can unite them.

—Robert South

Bill and Candi

It was a bright Sunday morning in early September.

Eighteen-year-old Candi Pickering slipped into the pew at First Evangelical Church with her two friends and waited for the song service to begin. It was a quarter till eleven—a day she would never forget.

The three chatted in whispers as a guitarist announced the first chorus. One of Candi's friends glanced about, informing her two companions of the presence of any promising young men in the congregation.

Suddenly her voice stopped. Candi glanced over to see the gaze of her friend riveted to the rear of the church where people continued to file in.

Unconsciously Candi turned to follow the other's expression of astonishment. Instantly she detected its cause.

"Who's the **dreamboat**!" whispered her friend.

By now, however, Candi was too busy watching the handsome newcomer to reply. The young fellow glanced about a bit nervously, then began walking down the aisle toward them. Candi tried not to be obvious, but she couldn't keep her eyes off him.

"He's coming this way!" came a frantic whisper in Candi's ear.

Closer and closer he came . . . he was right alongside them now! Candi could feel her neck getting warm. What if he noticed them staring at him!

He glanced about. His eyes paused momentarily as he saw the three girls. Was that an attempt at a nervous smile?

Now he slid into the vacant pew right in front of them!

A deep blush crept over Candi's whole face. Both friends were whispering

*in her ears and giggling. She was getting red, but she couldn't help it—he was
so good looking! And there he was so close she could reach out and touch his
shoulder!*

*How would she ever make it through the service without positively dying of
embarrassment and distraction!*

*Candi was relieved when the song service began. At least she had something
to do other than stare at the back of the newcomer.*

*Bill Stanley had been in Redsdale less than two weeks. He'd moved here
from out of the area to attend the junior college.*

*He had been raised in a strong Christian environment. Back at his home
church, his own parents and siblings were active in a full slate of church activities. He had a strong faith for his nineteen years, and therefore it was natural
for him when he moved north to college to find an active church to become a
part of. Last week he had attended Community Baptist Fellowship, but had not
been particularly impressed. He'd asked around, and someone told him about
First Evangelical. Today was his first time in attendance.*

Neither was it a day he would soon forget.

*The worship service was great—very much like at home. They sang lots of
contemporary choruses and people had a friendly spirit. Bill noticed in the bul-
letin an announcement for a college-age group that met at six on Sunday evenings. He would try it tonight.*

*The evening proved even more eventful than that morning's service. Bill
walked into the social hall about five till six. Already twenty or thirty college-
aged young people were milling about. In one corner several guys were tuning
guitars. The group looked promising.*

*"Hi," said a bouncy female voice as Bill glanced about trying to get his bear-
ings.*

*Bill turned and found himself face-to-face with one of the prettiest young
women he'd ever seen.*

*"Oh . . . hi," he said. "I'm . . . uh, new—I guess you can tell that," he
laughed.*

*The girl laughed lightly too—almost a musical laugh. "Then let me wel-
come you," she said. "I'm Candi Pickering."*

"Hi. My name's Bill Stanley."

*"I saw you this morning," said Candi. "I was going to say something, but—
you know." She smiled and looked away coyly.*

"Yeah. That's okay. I saw you too."

"Is it your first time here?"

"Yeah. I'm going to the JC."

"Oh, me too. Come on, I'll introduce you to the others."

*Bill followed his new acquaintance into the room, knowing already his
search for a new church was over.*

1 | IT'S A MESS ... BUT WHAT CAN WE DO?

We are all travelers in the wilderness of this world, and the best that we find in our travels is an honest friend.

—Robert Louis Stevenson

It should come as no surprise to you reading these words that the present state of the ancient, historic, holy institution of *marriage* is being assaulted as never before. Anyone who is paying attention to the world around him is aware that the family is under serious and unrelenting attack.

TRENDS IN SOCIETY

The signs of change exist everywhere and are visible to us all.

Divorce is positively rampant in society and not that much less prevalent in the Church. When we were growing up, divorce was unusual and almost unheard of among serious Christians. Then we began to hear "one marriage in four ends in divorce." Before long it was one in three. A few years ago it was one in two. And now a staggering *six in ten* marriages break up, and we seem to be headed toward the day when it will be two out of three. It is a cultural plague that seriously threatens society and the family as we know it.

In his booklet *Marriage and Divorce*, noted English pastor and teacher John Stott writes that in 1980 "in Britain, there were 409,000 marriages (35 percent of which were remarriages) and 159,000 divorces. The British divorce rate has increased by 600 percent during the last twenty-five years. In the United Kingdom, one in every three marriages breaks up. In the United States it is more than one in every two." This was sixteen years ago—and the situation has only deteriorated since then.

Sexual promiscuity is so widespread that it is openly discussed among young people without guilt, without raised eyebrows, without embarrassment, literally everywhere—including church youth groups and Christian colleges. It is not merely discussed, premarital sex is *practiced* by young people (including those who consider themselves Christians) to an alarming degree. How can this fact do other than contribute to and accelerate the downfall of scripturally solid marriage as the cornerstone of the family?

Homosexuality is rapidly becoming accepted as a viable lifestyle "option," and this acceptance is subtly infiltrating the Church as well. "Goals 2000" mandates that schools offer programs for young people of gay persuasion to help them feel good about themselves. Homosexuals are now gaining legal grounds to call their relationships "marriages" (whatever that means!) Many Christian young people, as well as married couples, are being blinded to scriptural truth concerning homosexuality by the pervasive permissive outlook abroad in the land as well as by the attitude of "acceptance" that has become so prevalent in our times.

Television contains overt visual references to sex almost nonstop from morning till night. Many sitcoms and commercial advertisements center a large portion of their themes around sexual activities. Many talk-show programs are based on sex. These trends are watched by Christian young people and Christian parents along with the rest of the public.

Discipline is no longer widely practiced in the home as a component of child-rearing and has been effectively removed from the public school system. In fact, discipline in the home is outlawed in some countries, and we move closer every year to that kind of legislation in the United States.

Children are taking their parents to court for the "crime" of exercising parental authority. What the Bible calls discipline is often termed *abuse* and a *violation of rights* in the courts, and children are winning their lawsuits. Youngsters barely in their teens have been granted "divorces" from their parents (whatever *that* means!) Children are routinely taken away from their parents by government-run social agencies on no more grounds than what three or four decades ago would have been considered common parental discipline.

Today, in some states, children anticipating a spanking, or having already had one, can call 911 to report their parents and the youngsters will be removed from the home. As the adopted daughter of acquaintances of ours grew, any attempt to discipline her or curb what proved her growing rebellion only succeeded in inciting her anger. At one point, not being allowed to have her way, she retaliated by telling neighbors that her father had beaten her. Almost immediately the authorities were on the doorstep of this Christian home. Though the entire episode was based on the lie of an angry eight-year-old, the father was put in jail, their infant son placed in foster care, and their daughter taken away for more than a year. Such occurrences are an all too frequent product of today's liberal social atmosphere.

TRENDS IN THE CHURCH

Our humanistic and permissive "society" is not the only problem. Unbelievably, the *Church* has become part of the problem too.

Most churches sanction divorce on the most insignificant grounds, which often leads to an unscriptural sanctioning of remarriage as well. This has had widespread impact on the Church, leading to trends that would have appalled the apostle Paul and rendering many basic Christian tenets impotent—such as honor, respect, kindness, forgiveness, long-suffering, patience, graciousness, servanthood, and love, not to mention what it means to keep one's marriage vows.

Churches cater to the divorced and the single, closing their eyes to the breakdown of marriage and family rather than *combating* it. Paul's stringent New Testament teachings on the subject of divorce and remarriage are emphasized in very few churches today. Is it because these teachings prohibit what has become today's norm? Young people view this and conclude that being divorced or remarried or once-married-but-now-single are perfectly normal options if marriage "doesn't work out."

Pastors are not only willing but often eager to perform marriages between divorced Christians, conveying the unmistakable message to young people that marriage and promises are expendable and that marriage is not something to consider lasting a lifetime.

In some churches divorced men and women are not only allowed to teach and hold positions of church leadership, they are encouraged to do so.

Authority has become a word of contempt. All forms of authority and the exercise of it (whether biblical, masculine, governmental, or parental) are viewed as coming from a less enlightened time and therefore to be disregarded.

All these factors contribute in a direct cause-effect progression to the breakdown of family values, scriptural truth, and marital permanency. Do we need further convincing that the problems facing the institution of marriage are of epidemic proportions?

WATCHING THE SHIFT ENGULF US

We have operated a Christian bookstore for twenty-seven years. If you wandered through our store shortly after we began, you might have found a couple of books on marriage. Twenty years ago that number had increased manyfold, and with them on the Marriage and Family shelf you would also have found a few on the tragedy of divorce within the church. (At that time it was still considered a tragedy.)

Fifteen years ago books began to appear on how to reconcile marriage when breakups occurred within the church. By ten years ago many more books were in print about coping with divorce.

The "tragedy" showed signs of turning into an epidemic!

Five years ago pastors and books and conferences and singles groups were not just helping people cope, but encouraging remarriage! The tide had entirely shifted. Marital values have been turned almost completely upside down within evangelicalism in less than a generation.

Recently, a few voices have begun to be heard in this wilderness. They say that perhaps there should be a different response to such change. Maybe something should even be done *before* marriage to help young people avoid divorce.

Jonathan Lindvall of Bold Parenting Seminars was one of the first to begin trumpeting the need for a new perspective on these shifting interpretations of Scripture. Soon after, the Advanced Training Institute of America began advocating the concept of "courtship" in their seminars. And now a widespread campaign called "True Love Waits" encourages young people to abstain from sexual activity prior to marriage.

It pleases us to see such efforts. But it cannot be denied that a crisis still is upon us, and Christians on the whole seem unprepared to meet it.

Marriage today is in a sad state. The prospect for any new marriage to endure thirty or forty or fifty years is exceedingly slim. These dreadful societal shifts away from the biblical standards of faithfulness and permanency ought to alarm us. Yet as we have seen, Christians generally accept them with a shrug, and when the specifics of these trends intrude upon their own lives and families, *hope* for the best.

As a result, even what we call "Christian marriages" are more tenuous all the time. Every day beaming Christian brides walk down the aisle while family and friends watch the happy ceremony, and those most aware of the dangers sit with their fingers crossed and their lips moving in silent prayer, wondering how long the bliss will last.

Is that all we can do—*depend on luck, throw in a little last-minute prayer, and hope for the best?*

That is hardly a forceful and biblical strategy for meeting the enemy's attack on marriage and family—hoping for the best. Yet that is the first—and only—line of defense many families have.

A PARTNERSHIP RESPONSE

We happen to think Christian parents and young people *can* combat the decay of marital permanency more vigorously than simply "hoping for the best." We believe that concerned and serious Christian parents and their sons and daughters *can* stem this rising tide of marriage failure.

The odds are against those embarking on marriage today. It is time we who are their parents, and you young people who are directly involved in marital decisions and who are the Christian parents of the future, do something about it.

We need to help our sons and daughters. And you young adults need to help yourselves!

How?

By attacking the problem at the root—*before* marriage. We need to look at the foundation. We need to look at how we prepare for marriage.

We need to rethink the entire process of selecting future husbands and wives.

We need to address the epidemic of marriage impermanence by doing a better job *beforehand.* It is an assignment that involves both young people *and* their parents.

To accomplish these things, therefore, we need to form a partnership between parents and young people.

It is our conviction that there are ways to establish wise, sensible, and lasting marriages—marriages that will stand the test of time, marriages that will endure. We call them *best-friend marriages.* We think the prospects are exciting.

But building strong foundations will go against everything society teaches, against every trend promoted on television. It will probably be laughed at by your Christian friends as well. It will not even be widely accepted in many churches.

We are not deterred. We hope you will not be either.

So let's get to the business at hand. Let's see if those of us who take the principles of the Bible seriously cannot do something to stop the flood of marital failure that is engulfing Christian families along with all the others.

And if we cannot change the direction society is moving, at least we can do something to help *your* marriage be a best-friend marriage.

ESTABLISHING THE PARTNERSHIP—IT MIGHT NOT BE EASY!

What will it take to succeed?

We might as well tell you right from the start that it won't be easy. To succeed you may have to make sacrifices and learn to conduct your social life differently. It may not be comfortable at first.

- It will take young people working together *with* their parents—standing in unity against the subtle infiltration of secularism that is growing like a cancer within the Church.
- It will take trust on the part of young people toward their parents, greater trust than perhaps they have ever given their mothers and fathers before.
- It will take involvement on the part of parents in the lives of their sons and daughters to a greater and more sacrificial degree than perhaps they have ever exercised.
- It will take parents and young people rising above whatever petty squabbles may have separated them through the years.
- It will take young people putting behind them the independence of the teenage point of view and saying, "I am going to trust my parents to see things I cannot see. Even when we disagree I am going to listen to them and try to hear what they are really saying."
- It will take parents recognizing their sons and daughters as no longer children but adults, and saying, "I determine to view my sons and daughters as mature and equal beings in their own right. I will listen to them and try to hear what is genuinely on their heart."

It will take all those involved sitting down together—relinquishing pride, independence, self-centeredness . . . forgetting the past, old arguments and grievances . . . laying aside the desire to have one's own way . . . listening to one another and praying together to seek God's will—and saying with mutual resolve, "How can we best make this work?" In a partnership of this kind there are no "sides." Either both win or both lose. Whatever the outcome, it will have a lifelong effect on both parents and young people. "For lack of guidance a nation falls, but many advisers make victory sure" (Proverbs 11:14).

In short, it will take mothers and fathers and sons and daughters joining hands and committing themselves together to the truth that a solid marriage is worth fighting for before the fact.

Let us warn you, however, that some of the things we will propose may seem so outrageous that you may laugh out loud. When we first began home schooling seventeen years ago, many scoffed at what we were trying to do. But in the years since, hundreds of thousands of families have come to see the wisdom and necessity of wholly revamped educational priorities. Similarly, however outlandish some of the ideas of this book may strike you now, we believe these new priorities for marriage foundations will become the standard within the Christian church in the next decade.

We are in earnest here. We believe drastic measures are called for if we Christians who understand the biblical pattern are going to take a determinative leadership role in establishing strong marital foundations.

The Christian norms of our society are disappearing. Marriage as formerly defined is disappearing along with them. Therefore, unusual and nonconformist as some of these ideas may sound, we don't see hope for meeting this threat other than to attack it head on.

So we encourage you—young people and old, parents, sons, daughters, grandparents, singles—to put on your fighting gear and join us in the battle. We challenge you to be part of the attempt to win back the sanctity, the strength, the purity, and the longevity of marriage as God intended it.

Most of all, we want *your* marriage, or the marriage of *your* son or daughter, to be a great marriage. As we said, we are not trying to save society as much as we hope to give *you* the tools to establish a *best-friend marriage* for life. Of course, whenever enough young people make a like commitment, society *does* change. But it has to start with you.

Come with us on an adventure. Let us raise the battle cry together!

*There is nothing so great that I fear to do it for
my friend; nothing so small that I will disdain
to do it for him.*

—Sir Philip Sidney

Young and In Love

*Bill Stanley and Candi Pickering hit it off from their very first meeting.
First Evangelical fit Bill's tastes perfectly. It was vibrant and alive, with an
exciting youth and college program, contemporary music, outreach ministries,
and study and prayer groups for all ages. Bill loved it and was soon as active as
he had been in his home church.*

*Candi had lived in Redsdale all her life and had grown up in the church,
where her whole family was active. Her father had been an elder for eight years,
had been a youth leader even longer, and was recognized as one of the pillars
of the growing congregation. Her mother taught two women's Bible study
groups and, together with the pastor's wife, was involved in a good deal of counseling among the women.*

*Most of all, Bill's decision to stay with this church had to do with the young
lady he had met at the first college group meeting. To have called it love at first
sight might have been an exaggeration. But such would not be far from an
inaccurate assumption—on the part of either of the two young people.*

*Candi was a beautiful and vivacious young woman who would attract a
second look from any robust college man. She was one of the most dynamic
and popular young people in the church and was already making her presence
felt on the junior college campus as well. Before their first meeting had even
gotten underway, Bill knew she was someone special.*

*On Candi's part, she hardly thought of anything else, after first noticing Bill
in the morning service, than whether the handsome stranger might attend the*

college meeting that evening. When he walked in, she was ready.

She had dated regularly through high school and was well familiar with the young men of her church whom she might regard as potential beaux. But she had known most of them for years, and they bored her.

When she had followed her friend's gaze to the rear of the church and seen the visitor whom she would know before the day was out, Candi had immediately envisioned new possibilities on her personal horizon. He was good looking, three or four inches taller than she, and carried himself with poise. As she found out more about him, Candi discovered him to be both athletic and musical (he was already making plans to play on the JC basketball team, and on his third meeting he brought his guitar to the college Bible study). There was a spiritual dimension to Bill as well, and he wasn't afraid to speak his mind or pray out loud.

Very soon after their mutual introduction and first brief conversation, Candi's glances in Bill's direction, her coy smiles, and the flash of her eyes were accomplishing their purpose. The following week Bill and Candi sat next to each other at college group—neither trying to be too obvious, and yet it was clear both were more than moderately interested in each other. Within three weeks they were talking alone afterward, then moving slowing together along the corridor to the sanctuary for the evening service.

Finally Bill summoned the courage to ask Candi for a date.

"Hi, Candi," he said over the telephone, pausing for a quick swallow because his throat had suddenly gone dry. "This is Bill."

"Hi, Bill," she purred.

"I, uh . . . was wondering if you might like to go to the homecoming game . . . and the dance afterward with me. That is—" he added hastily, "if you aren't already going with someone else."

With more composure than her pounding heart felt, Candi quickly accepted, then put down the phone and ran to her room in giddy delight.

2 | WHOSE DECISION IS THIS?

A valuable friend is one who'll tell you what you should be told, even if it offends you.

—*Frank A. Clark*

What do you as a thirteen, sixteen, twenty, twenty-five, or thirty-year-old young man or young woman want more than anything else as you contemplate the rest of your life?

Don't you think first of all of a happy marriage?

And you concerned Christian parents—in addition to a growing and maturing walk with the Lord, isn't a good marriage right up at the top of your list of hopes and dreams for your son or daughter?

Clearly, then, the choice of *whom* to marry is probably the most important, practical life-decision facing young people as they make the transition into full adulthood. Upon this decision will the whole course of life's future be based.

It is not only an important decision . . . it is *the* important decision!

SIDELINE PARENTAL INVOLVEMENT

The first thing we need to look at, then, is simply this: How do young people and their families prepare for this vital and significant decision?

How is a future husband or wife chosen?

Most young people, without thinking the matter through in depth, assume they'll saunter through life until one day they meet someone with whom everything will click. In the process they'll get to know many young men and young women. They'll have lots of dates, perhaps any number of romances. But eventually the day will come when they will meet that special *someone*, and something called "love"—the real thing, this time—will either gradually or suddenly happen—like in the movies and romance novels.

As much as parents want their sons and daughters to marry well, and as concerned as they are that they establish solid marriages, for the most part parents are relegated to the sidelines throughout this entire process of dating and eventual choice of mate—offering advice here and there, mostly unsought and unwelcomed—while young people decide *on their own* whom to marry.

And then after being uninvolved in what has gone on for most of the game, the parents reappear again in the final stages. Finances are needed for the wedding. Suddenly *now* the two young people welcome parental involvement—when there are bills to pay.

In other words, parents are usually nonparticipants in the early stages of the process.

Is the Traditional Process Best?

Before going any further, let's pose a question that may come as a surprise. *Is this the right way and the best method?* Should young people be the only ones making this all-important lifetime decision?

Your response may well be, *Who else? They are the ones contemplating marriage. Who else would possibly decide whom to marry?*

You young men and women may be saying, *It's my life. Deciding whom to marry is obviously my decision. What could anyone else have to say or do with it—especially my parents!*

May we boldly suggest that perhaps they are supposed to have more to do with it than society has told you? May we further suggest that parents may not only have wisdom to give to the matter, they may even possess the God-given and scripturally mandated obligation to occupy a central role in the mate selection process? It can be argued, of course, that the parental involvement found in Scripture is merely cultural and that we may therefore ignore it. But the fact remains—in the Bible, parents *were* involved in marriage decisions. If the Bible is to be our pattern, that's a fact we must take into account.

God instructed Moses, "A matter must be established by the testimony of two or three witnesses" (Deuteronomy 19:15). We believe many Old Testament family patterns still have relevance today, not because we believe in a God of legalism but because God knew what was *best* and made that clear to his people. Throughout the Bible, *marriages involved parents*.

We will make it as clear as we know how. Parents who truly love God and their children do indeed possess the *right* and the *duty* and the *obligation* to occupy an integral role in the marriage decisions of their sons and daughters.

Not merely an *advisory* role . . . but a central, even determinative role.

Some of you young people may be shaking your heads, wondering what kind of a book you have picked up. Many of you parents likewise may already be laughing to yourselves and saying, "Forget it. If there's anything I *don't* want to do, it's get involved in that can of worms! Let them decide whom to marry for themselves. Leave me out of it."

For those of you who are still with us, however, we hope you will continue reading with ears and heart open enough to ask yourselves, and to pray and ask God, if what we say doesn't make sense. Might wise, godly, experienced parental involvement indeed help establish wise, sensible, and lasting marriages?

DO WE NEED ANYBODY ELSE'S HELP?

We live in an age where the god independence rules.[1]

No one has the right to tell anyone *else* what to do. Because of the near complete collapse of authority in almost every sphere of life, the personal right to self-rule and self-determination have become fundamental principles in today's world. This is the loudest voice calling out from "Generation X" across the nation. The Bible, however, calls Jesus the chief cornerstone of the spiritual building that God is building. Clearly this spiritual structure is founded on *our* submission to *his* authority.

Unfortunately, *submission* is a hateful concept these days. The very sound of the word in the ears of this new age grates like fingernails across the blackboard of self. Modernism's cornerstone is something altogether different—*independence*.

Rather than be obedient to *parents'* wishes, young people today do whatever *they* want and expect parental approval in the process. When parents do not approve, teenage boys and girls cry foul, falling back on that weakest of arguments— their parents don't accept them as they are (another of modernism's most revered creeds). On the other hand, when parents do give their approval, society commends them for being capable of maintaining healthy relationships within the family. In both cases, however, young people have set the tone and dictated the

---

[1]We here use the word "independence" in its spiritually negative sense, to denote the spirit determined to "do its own thing," the spirit of self-rule and self-determination. The independent spirit is one that resents authority and is loathe to submit to anyone, man or woman.

It is one of the unfortunate characteristics of language, however, that sometimes the same word is used for two very different things. In the discussion that follows, we will also be talking about independence in a good and positive sense, having nothing to do with a negative spiritual attitude, but rather with that healthy quality of maturity capable of wise judgment and sound decisions.

Along with this, we will use the word to note that societal position where one is "on one's own," financially supporting himself or herself, and fully out from under the parental wings, so to speak. We will try to clarify these three very distinct definitions—one harmful, two healthy and positive— of "independence" as we go along.

outcome. Respect for parental authority and wisdom is rarely part of the relational equation.

This is neither a book about independence nor authority. We will not, therefore, attempt to bolster this point with further discussion and take away from the point we want to make, which is simply this: In the economy of God's kingdom, if you want to know and do God's will, if you want your life to be founded on God's principles, and if you want to succeed in what you do, then independence—*making decisions for yourself*—is often *not* the best means by which to achieve these goals.

There are times when we need other people's help. Sometimes that help might even come from your parents!

We realize those nine words may sound like blasphemy to some teen ears. *What!* you say. You think *I* need help? *From my parents!* No way! I'm seventeen . . . I'm twenty-two . . . I'm twenty-six years old. I'm an adult. I don't need *anybody's* help!

No doubt many of you feel this way, and there's probably not much we can do to convince you otherwise.

But hear us out. We happen to believe that parents have the right and the solemn responsibility to assist their sons and daughters in the selection process of a husband or a wife.

Why should they help? Only because they have the right to? That alone may be a good enough reason. But let's look at the thing practically. Their help makes sense. There are no guarantees, of course, but we are convinced a parent's help will *greatly* increase the likelihood, not merely of a long and enduring marriage, but of a good and happy and fruitful one—and even one that is more financially successful.

It simply makes good sense to get all the help you can for a decision of this magnitude.

Josh Harris writes, "What does it mean to be a grown-up? At the end of this year I turn twenty-one years old. As I approach this symbolic birthday, I realize my ideas about adulthood have been mixed up.

"Even though a big part of growing up is being able to stand on your own feet, a focus on achieving independence and self-sufficiency can crowd out gratitude. Young adults often see the journey to adulthood as a process of shedding dependence on their parents. But I'm beginning to realize that true maturity isn't measured in the dependency we can throw off, but in the responsibility we can take on. We mistakenly believe that maturity is not needing others, when in fact maturity is responding as servants. . . ."[2]

---

[2]"Practical Homeschooling" (Dec. 1995/ Jan. 1996), p. 96.

If you are a young person reading these words, think of it this way: If you go at it alone, you might have about a 40 percent chance of having a marriage that lasts and about a 20 percent chance of having a happy one. However, if you bring your parents into the process with you and ask for their help in making many of the decisions concerning marriage—whom to marry, when to marry, and so on—those percentages change dramatically. With their involvement in the process, you might have a 75 percent chance of having a marriage that lasts and an 80 percent chance of your marriage being a happy and fulfilling one.

It's just plain smart to go with those odds!

"Plans fail for lack of counsel, but with many advisers they succeed" (Proverbs 15:22).

*Oblige with all your soul that friend who has
made a present of his own.*

—Socrates

All a Parent Could Hope For

*The homecoming football game and dance was just the beginning for Bill
Stanley and Candi Pickering.*

*Throughout the winter they dated nearly every weekend. By the time Bill
made the basketball team several months later, the two were scarcely apart—
either at school or at church.*

It was obvious they were in love.

*What made the match so perfect, especially in the eyes of Candi's parents,
was the apparent spiritual component of the relationship. Though the Pickerings were dedicated Christians, they had not shared with any of their friends
the fact that they had been more than a little concerned about Candi during
her last two years of high school.*

*Mrs. Pickering's assessment in response to the increasing number of boys
hanging around Candi in her junior year had been: "She's too attractive for her
own good."*

*If the parents had had their way, they would have discouraged Candi's re-
lationships with more than half the boys she dated, most of them, as far as they
knew, were not even Christians. They were uncomfortable with the attention
their daughter drew and the calls and dates that multiplied far too rapidly. Especially disturbing was the fact that Candi **knew** she was pretty and played it
to her advantage. To call her a flirt might have been an overstatement. But it
could truthfully be said that she knew the power of both her eyes and her smile
upon the opposite sex and used their subtle influence when it suited her.*

But Mr. and Mrs. Pickering had been reluctant to say much or to exercise too much parental authority for fear of alienating their daughter. At least she was still interested in church, they reasoned, and was not rebelling against them outright. The dating stage would pass, they hoped, without too much harm done.

Right from the start, therefore, the young, clean-cut, respectful Bill Stanley was an answer to their prayers. In their eyes, he seemed so different from most of the boys Candi had dated. When he and Candi were together they talked about the Lord, sang Christian songs, and centered most of their activities around church functions.

The Pickerings noticed almost immediately that Candi was taking a greater interest in spiritual things, and they could not have been more pleased. Following his first Sunday afternoon dinner at the Pickering home, Bill began to be a regular guest and hit it off with Mr. Pickering, an athletic coach at the high school, almost as much as he did with his daughter.

Simply put, the Pickerings **liked** Bill. He gave every indication of being a virtuous young man. His bearing was full of respect toward adults, and he always behaved as a perfect gentleman toward their daughter. His integrity was admirable. They never had so much as a remote concern for Candi's safety or honor whenever she was alone with him. Bill and Candi even prayed together on dates!

3 | WHY SHOULD PARENTS AND YOUNG PEOPLE WORK TOGETHER?

Friendship is the marriage of the soul.

—Voltaire

Why does it makes sense for young people and their parents to work together in preparing for marriage? Because adulthood is not as easily defined or as quickly reached as most young people would like to think. It is a process, like everything else in life, where help and mentoring can only benefit the success of the final outcome.

ADULTHOOD—A SLOWLY PROGRESSIVE ACHIEVEMENT

Historically, in most cultures and eras, what we call adulthood does not fully begin until marriage.

In our present Western society and particularly in the United States, *aspects* of adulthood begin much earlier. They begin, in fact, as early as ten and twelve years of age. At sixteen, young people are permitted to drive a car and have legally fulfilled their schooling requirements. Such "freedoms" indicate that adulthood is approaching by steadily increasing degrees.

At eighteen comes the vote and certain other components of legal independence. The ballot cast by an eighteen-year-old counts no less than that of the president of the United States. Politically, then, the age of eighteen signifies adult independent equality.

Does that make the age of eighteen a magic moment when full adulthood has suddenly arrived?

Of course not—only increasing aspects of it.

Most things in life are progressive. The gaining of adulthood is one of the slowest progressions of all. The age of twenty-one represents yet another milestone, a transition whereby one is no longer considered a "minor" or "under age." But overnight does the twenty-first birthday *now* make one a full-fledged "adult"? No. The process continues.

Let a twenty-four-year-old try to rent a car and see how "adult" he feels when he is turned down because he is not old enough. Once he turns twenty-five, however, in the eyes of Hertz, Avis, and Alamo, *now* he is an adult.

But even then the process is not over! What would be the response to a thirty-two-year-old who tried to file papers to run for the presidency? He or she would be told, "You are too young."

These milestones of chronological age are clearly societal in nature. Every historic era, every culture, every nation imposes its own such guidelines and legalities. Obviously, therefore, they are somewhat artificial in nature. The fact that one is *permitted* to drive does not mean one is capable of driving carefully or of exercising discretion in the use of the family car. The fact that one is *permitted* to vote does not mean one is capable of voting wisely. And the fact that one has reached the age of thirty-five does not imply that he is equipped to lead our country.

Therefore, many additional factors must be considered when we attempt to define how and when adulthood arrives, and what it means to be an adult in the first place.

MATURITY AND WISDOM MEAN MORE THAN CHRONOLOGICAL AGE

It is obvious—as much as young people *want* to be treated as adults at sixteen or eighteen or twenty-one—that there is more involved in maturity than mere age.

What about maturity of character—the capacity to *act and behave* in adult ways? Ought not *mature behavior* and *wise judgment* count more in the determination of adulthood than what happened to be one's most recent birthday?

Moreover, financial independence is a significant factor. Earning your own living, supporting yourself, being financially established to an extent capable of taking on the responsibility of marriage—these have always been regarded as key elements in determining when independence and adulthood have been reached.

The coming of adulthood, then, is a long, gradual process that extends over many years—generally between the ages of fifteen or sixteen and twenty-five or thirty, when financial stability is achieved and when character and demeanor progress the final steps toward a fully mature plane of attitude and behavior.

MARRIAGE—THE MOST SIGNIFICANT ELEMENT IN DEFINING ADULTHOOD

In many respects, perhaps more than any other single factor, marriage represents the point at which most of these progressive elements in the growing-up process culminate, or at least *ought* to culminate.

Marriage brings a unique independence: "For this reason a man will leave his father and mother and be united to his wife" (Genesis 2:24 and Ephesians 5:31). And with marriage generally comes a heightened degree of financial responsibility, which again signifies a dramatic leap out of youth into adulthood.

Marriage, however, is no more a magic moment of maturity than one's twenty-first birthday. Mary Queen of Scots succeeded to the Scottish throne at one week old and was married at the age of fifteen. Did these events make her capable of grown-up wisdom and discretion as either a queen *or* a wife? Marriage alone does not make one capable of behaving responsibly as an adult.

As much as society tells young people that they have the right to think and do anything they want, the fact is, until the moment marriage and/or financial independence are reached (and sometimes beyond), young men and women are supported and *mentored* into adulthood by their parents and teachers.[1]

It's part of the process. It's the way it is supposed to work. To get a driver's license requires first being instructed in the skills of driving and in the laws of the road. There is a training period that accompanies all increased responsibility, until the day of graduation finally arrives. Usually a parent drives his or her son or daughter in the family car to take a driver's test, in much the same way that a father walks his daughter down the aisle to give her away in marriage. These are moments when the reins are passed from one generation to another.

Preparing for marriage is a process, like driving, that also requires *mentoring*

---

[1]This represents a time when these principles and their application must be individualized. When we say that generally marriage and financial independence represent the culmination of the young-person-to-adult process, it is a statement obviously containing many variants. Under any and all circumstances, there is never a single *moment* when adulthood is attained.

Consider the seventeen-year-old who marries but who cannot yet vote. Clearly there is *an* adulthood and independence that has been reached, but neither are yet complete.

What about the thirty-five-year-old unmarried man or woman on his or her own and completely independent of daily parental influence and control? In such a case, certainly adulthood has been reached without marriage being a factor.

Consider a twenty-six-year-old married couple, both attending graduate school, living with one set of parents who are helping the couple financially. Even after marriage, there remains a dependency upon parents that postpones full adult independence.

and the guidance of wise adults, especially parents.

It is traditionally and scripturally vital that parents be the ones to guide their young people into the adult role of marriage, at which point, culminating this long process of growth, young men and women embark on the responsibility of adulthood—adding to it financial independence and maturity of outlook and character.

Young men, if you are wise you will heed the words of Peter, because he spoke them straight to you: "Young men, in the same way be submissive to those who are older. All of you, clothe yourselves with humility toward one another, because, 'God opposes the proud but gives grace to the humble' " (1 Peter 5:5).

It is significant of this parental hand in the process that a bride walks down the aisle *with her father*, who then symbolically *gives* his daughter to the groom. This tradition is a picture of the preparation that has gone into this culmination and the intrinsic parental role in it.

Young people were not meant to make decisions alone about marriage and the selection of a future husband or wife any more than they are meant to drive a car without proper preparation and training.

It will take a particularly mature outlook on the part of young people to recognize the value of Peter's words. We write to mature young men and women who possess a realistic outlook on the difficulties involved in making a marriage work, who are not too proud to say, "If anything can increase my chances of a good marriage, I'm all for it."

REGAINING THE RUDDER TOWARD TRUTH . . . TOGETHER

Mothers and fathers are *supposed* to help their sons and daughters make the decisions leading to marriage. It is inherent in what it means to be a parent. It represents the final and culminating phase of the parenting role.

Is all this an entirely new idea to you?

You may be shaking your head in disbelief at the notion of parents playing a pivotal role in the marriage decision. We confess that neither did we understand the importance of this principle twenty-five years ago. We chose to marry each other without input from either set of our parents. We did not ask whether they felt we were well suited for each other, nor whether they thought we were ready to marry when we did.

We made the decision ourselves, then told our parents about it. We knew no better. Neither, really, did they. This parental function we speak of has largely been lost to recent generations.

Does that mean we should continue to abandon it?

By no means! The fact that a truth has been lost makes it all the more important, once the error is recognized, that it be regained. Lost pearls of truth and wisdom should be searched for with vigor!

Most couples today were married under less than ideal conditions and without much parental oversight. Many who read these words will be from broken homes with less than ideal pasts. But this is not a book about looking *back* at what we or our parents might have done wrong, but about looking *ahead* to how future marriages—in a society of decaying values—can be strengthened.

We believe this absence of the parental role is one reason why marriage is in such trouble today. To right the lurching vessel called *marriage* requires grabbing on once again to the rudder that will help establish wise, sensible, and enduring marriages. That rudder is the partnership between parents and their sons and daughters.

Whose fault is it that the proper role of parents has been lost?

It is the fault of parents and young people together, and especially of Hollywood, of television producers, of authors, and of society in general.

Parents have abdicated their roles, assuming from society that they have no right to exert an influence over their children. And young people want to stand on their own two feet and make all their own decisions at a far younger age than God intends.

Neither have Christian leaders taught us to stand firmly against unscriptural societal trends. Indeed, most of today's churches embrace the music, dress, entertainment, and marital standards of the hippest aspects of society. Young people have grown up assuming all forms of independence are good, and considering the world's value structure benign. They have not as a rule been taught to be wary of its danger.

In fact, the self-seeking independence at the root of society's prevailing outlook is the most destructive mindset a man or a woman can bring into marriage, one almost guaranteed to lead ultimately to marital breakup.

Together, parents and young people must agree to remove marital decisions from the arena of nobody-will-tell-*me*-what-to-do independence, and bring them back where such decisions belong—*under the safety-umbrella of the home*.

Parents have the right, the duty, and the obligation to be involved in the process. Their involvement ensures safety, wisdom, and protection for their sons and daughters.

Wise young people ought to eagerly seek it.

"Honor your father and your mother, so that you may live long in the land the Lord your God is giving you" (Exodus 20:12).

To be trusted is a greater compliment than to be loved.

—George MacDonald

Dream of a Blissful Future

Mr. and Mrs. Pickering could not have been more delighted when midway through their daughter's sophomore year in college, about a year and a half after their first meeting, Bill and Candi came to them and told them of their engagement.

"Congratulations!" boomed Mr. Pickering, rising from his chair and giving Bill a hearty handshake.

Already Candi was in her mother's arms. There was laughing, more handshakes, and hugs and congratulations all around. The news was received with equal enthusiasm by the Stanleys when Bill and Candi traveled south to tell them of their plans.

Everyone at First Evangelical was as excited as their parents. When plans for the wedding were announced, everyone rejoiced. The whole church would likely attend. By now Bill was one of the most well-liked young men of his new congregation. He and Candi were on First Evangelical's worship team, which led singing every Sunday morning. Both were also popular on campus. At college, Bill had been voted all-league in basketball and recognized as one of the school's best athletes, and Candi was now a cheerleader.

A June date was set, immediately following their graduation from the junior college. Bill would be twenty-one, and Candi twenty.

It was a wedding to remember—one of the happiest in First Evangelical's history. Bill and Candi sang a duet they had written themselves, in which each sang a solo verse to the other expressing their love and promises of lifelong faithfulness and fidelity. Bill accompanied their song on guitar.

A bright sun shone through the stained-glass windows, almost as if a divine sanction of the marriage. Neither the mother of the bride nor the mother of the groom shed a tear, although it was noted Mr. Pickering wiped at his eyes for a moment upon taking his place at his wife's side after giving his daughter away. But generally the afternoon was too happy for tears. This was a day of rejoicing. It was what marriage was supposed to be all about!

When Pastor Keyes announced, "Ladies and gentlemen, may I have the honor of presenting to you . . . Mr. and Mrs. William Stanley!" the congregation beamed in happy optimism.

4 | IT TAKES TRUST
(A Chapter to Young People)

*Friendship is a strong and habitual inclination
in two persons to promote the good and
happiness of one another.*

—Eustace Budgell

We have been laying the groundwork for a bold
and daring—some might call it startling and revolutionary—alternative strategy
for choosing a husband or a wife and entering into a lifelong best-friend marriage.
By the time you get to the end of this book, believe us, you will have encountered
some proposals that will indeed seem revolutionary in the eyes of contemporary
society.

We happen to think, however you view them, that they are *exciting* ideas for
the plain and simple reason that they are practical . . . and they work!

We believe that following these proposals will dramatically reduce the likelihood that *you* will ever face divorce, even though statistics show that half of all
new marriages today will. You are sure to face marital difficulties and frustrations—everyone does. Even best friends have their ups and downs. But putting
into practice these best-friends-for-life principles will almost insure that *your*
downs won't become permanent.

There is a catch, however. To put these principles into practice requires something that may be extremely difficult for some young people to give.

A Partnership of Trust

To make all this work, a partnership is required—a partnership between a son
or daughter and his or her parents.

To implement the best-friends-for-life principles, a true friendship must develop. And we're not now talking about the friendship between husbands and
wives . . . but rather the friendship between parents and their sons and daughters.

To develop this friendship requires *trust*, and that's a difficult thing for many young persons to extend in the direction of their parents.

Have you been noticing the quotes on friendship we have interspersed throughout the book? As you read them, did you reflect upon the principles as describing your relationship with your parents?

"What?" you may say. "My parents aren't . . . my *friends*. They're, well, you know, like . . . parents."

In truth, your parents are the best friends you will ever have apart from your spouse. The sooner you figure that out the better. These are people you can *trust* . . . and *should* trust.

You may not always see eye to eye on music and clothes or a multitude of minor things—and yes, as big as these things may seem to you and your parents at this moment, they *are* minor. You will look back years from now and wonder how you could let such little disputes prevent you from entering into a trust-relationship during your wonderful teen years with the two people who care more for you than anyone else in the world. You will seldom find anyone who loves you as much, who would do more for you, who would sacrifice so much for you, and who so deeply want only the best for you as your father and mother.

Your parents may commit to all the principles, pray diligently, and do everything possible to wisely and lovingly exercise their love toward you, carrying out their parental role as properly and graciously as possible . . . but if you determine to make decisions independent of parental counsel, you are embarking on a long and perilous sea voyage aboard a ship without a rudder.

As we emphasized in the beginning, a partnership is required—a partnership of trust.

AN UNEQUAL PARTNERSHIP

The partnership we speak of is an unequal one. Believe it or not, it's one in which the inexperienced and younger half of the partnership carries the most weight.

It's you young people who wield the power to make it work or not. Your parents can do nothing, in a sense, without your authorization. *You* hold the keys that will determine whether this partnership succeeds. Young people, have you desired "power" and more "control" of your own destiny? Well, here you have it! *You* are in the driver's seat. Your parents can do nothing in this matter without *your* approval. You are, in a sense, *in charge* of how this partnership functions.

Parents these days have been beaten down, ridiculed, and rendered helpless in the lives of their young adult sons and daughters. Society has convinced young people that they need not heed what their parents say, that their mothers and fathers "just don't understand" and have no right to exert their influence. Society has tainted father-son and mother-daughter relationships with lies that young people have been all too quick to believe. As a result, many disheartened parents feel like mere signatures on a check, rubber-stamping their children's plans and finding themselves relegated to discouraged prayers as they struggle through tense family relationships. They hope merely to get through these years in one piece.

Only you young people can reverse these destructive trends by giving your parents your trust. By doing as the prophet Malachi spoke—*turning* your hearts in the direction of your mothers and fathers. "He will turn the hearts of the fathers to their children, and the hearts of the children to their fathers" (Malachi 4:6).

IT'S COMMON SENSE

Stop and think.

Does any parent want a *bad* marriage for their son or daughter? A parent wants nothing so much for his or her child as a good marriage!

It is common sense to listen to and trust your parents. Because of their own sometimes painful experiences, parents actually desire good and solid marriages *more* than do their sons and daughters. Young people tend to focus only on right now. That doesn't mean there's something wrong with you, it's just a fact of life— youth don't usually make decisions with the long range in view. It is sensible, therefore, to listen to those older and wiser in life's ways, however much society and your peers argue against it.

Your parents provide the perfect safety net. Even uninterested, less than conscientious parents want their children to avoid the mistakes they made and have a better marriage than they have. A common response of young people is, "But I want to make my *own* mistakes." Yet if you really stop to analyze it, such a statement reveals all the insight of someone who says, "But I *want* to keep hitting my head against this brick wall."

Both sides—parents and young people—must come together and jointly commit themselves to this plan. It will only work when young people recognize that working under the guidance of their parents' counsel offers the *best* likelihood of a long-lasting, productive, and happy marriage.

But no parent can *force* a son or daughter to comply with these or any other principles.

YOUNG MEN, YOUNG WOMEN—GO TO YOUR PARENTS

Here's how this partnership works.

You young people must go to your parents—father and mother, single mom or dad, or, if there are no parents in your life, then to a grandparent, aunt, uncle, lifelong mentor, pastor, or guardian who loves you—and say, "I *want* your help. I recognize that I will be more likely to have a strong, lasting marriage if I have someone guiding me through the process and helping me to make wise decisions. I recognize that your experienced and objective eyes will be capable of seeing things more accurately and clearly than my own when I think I am in love."

In doing so you will be fulfilling a hundred biblical commands at once, from the original commandments of God to Moses to Paul's words to the Ephesians: "Children, obey your parents in the Lord, for this is right. 'Honor your father and mother'—which is the first commandment with a promise—'that it may go well with you and that you may enjoy long life on the earth' " (Ephesians 6:1–3).

What a wonderful expression of trust to give your mom or dad! Even the mistakes a parent has made (and we have all made plenty!) will enable them to see certain things more clearly, oftentimes precisely *because* of those mistakes. Their pain is your gain.

If such a concept is as new to your parents as it is to you, or if you don't think they would even consider being involved, you must help them see that you truly *want* their involvement, and that such is part of their parenting role.

It is for your good and the ultimate strength of your marriage that they become part of this process with you.

And just a word to you parents, if you happen to be reading this chapter too: You must take hold of this exciting responsibility!

Young people, again we say—you must urge and encourage your parents to join you in this process. Your fathers and mothers must do their duty, but that will be impossible if you do not eagerly *invite* them to join this partnership of trust with you.

Flexibility, wisdom, and maturity—not legalism—is required in carrying out these ideas. The general principle involved here is that young people, because they *are* "young," will be better prepared in life by heeding counsel from wise elders. But there are clearly situations in which parents *cannot* be involved, and numerous situations where their counsel perhaps should *not* be afforded great weight. We do not want to bind sensitive and spiritually responsive young people to the advice of truly unsavory parents—for example, the emotionally unstable, or a spiritually abusive father or mother who lays down extreme expectations without giving the support to reach those expectations.

Not every parent has the capability of making wise choices or giving wise counsel. We recognize that there are certain situations where young people may be more spiritually mature in outlook than their parents. Especially in a family where the father has left the home for another woman, where a single mother is involved in multiple compromising relationships with men, where alcoholism, or other codependent relationships and "woundings" contribute heavily to the family environment, or in homes where abuse has taken place.

Young people should not take such exceptions as the above for license to shut parents out of the process, yet the recognition must be made that occasionally young people will have to seek alternate mentors and elders. With the high cost of divorce—financially, emotionally, and spiritually—and the lifelong regrets that result from impulsive youthful decisions, it behooves young men and women to seek wise counsel.

YOU CAN DECIDE TO TRUST YOUR PARENTS

So, even in the midst of falling head over heels in love, we beseech you young men and women to whom we have dedicated this book: Commit yourself to this partnership of trust with your parents or other trustworthy mentors.

Commit yourself to listen to them, even though they *may* tell you the relationship you are caught up in and excited about isn't right for you, or suggest that you wait. Remember, your future husband or wife will become part of *your parents'* family too, so they have a vested interest at stake as well.

In other words—*decide* to trust your parents. Decide that from now on you are going to view your mom and dad as your friends in the realm of dating, courtship, and preparation for marriage. Many of your peers may view their parents as adversaries. Are you strong enough to stand against this tide and accept yours as friends?

We hope so! Because a strong marriage can only result, which is what *we* want for you too!

Establish a partnership and friendship with your parents . . . then come along with us for the rest of this best-friends adventure!

"A cord of three strands is not quickly broken" (Ecclesiastes 5:8).

Part II

Finding Friendship Rather Than Seeking Romance

He that is thy friend indeed,
he will help thee in thy need;
If thou sorrow he will weep;
if thou wake he cannot sleep.

—William Shakespeare

Hal and Laurel

The relationship between Hal Gilbert and Laurel Willard progressed along
an entirely different path than that of Bill and Candi.

When Hal first walked into the Mervyn's department store, Laurel hardly
even noticed him. She had just finished ringing up a customer's purchase, then
glanced up to the next person in line. There stood Hal, who somewhat nervously
asked her where the offices were.

Laurel paid no particular attention to their brief exchange. By the time he
was out of sight, she was already ringing up the next sale and had already for-
gotten him. She did not even notice when he walked past as he left the store
ten minutes later, application in hand.

Hal started work a week later.

Still, Laurel paid him no more heed than she did the rest of her co-workers.
But either by coincidence or divine plan, the two young people usually found
themselves working overlapping afternoon and evening shifts at adjacent reg-
isters, and therefore, after regular nods and hi's and smiles, they gradually be-
came more and more friendly, chatting occasionally during slow times as they
straightened racks of clothes.

One day the manager called Hal to fill in during the late morning rush
period instead of working his normal evening hours. It happened that both he
and Laurel punched out at five o'clock that afternoon and found themselves

leaving the store at exactly the same moment. They exited the employee room together, chatting superficially about how busy it had been that day and laughing about the lady they had both spoken with who had occupied one of the dressing rooms for over an hour.

When they reached the door, Hal pushed it open, as naturally as if it had been second nature—which for him it was—allowing Laurel to walk through ahead of him.

"Thank you," she said, brushing against him as she emerged into the warm evening air.

Hal followed her through, then smiled. "Well, see you tomorrow," he said.

Both went their separate ways and walked to their cars.

It had been a simple enough gesture on Hal's part, but all the way home Laurel found herself thinking about Hal holding the door for her.

Hal is nice, she thought. He's a gentleman. Nicer than any of the other guys who work at Mervyn's, or even the guys at church. None of them would open a door for me.

Laurel had to admit she had felt a brief quickening of her pulse as she brushed against Hal on her way outside. She hadn't expected it, but then suddenly there it was. . . .

Had she been more experienced with boys, she probably would not have thought twice about such a simple encounter. But Laurel had rarely been around young men in social settings. Her rigid church background and her parents' old-fashioned views frowned upon unsupervised social interaction between teenage boys and girls. At eighteen, she had never so much as been on a date in her life. For Laurel Willard, therefore, this particular day proved a turning point.

All evening she was jittery, almost giddy. She tried to act normal, but at the dinner table kept finding herself giggling for no reason.

"What is wrong with you?" laughed Mrs. Willard at length. "You must have had a good day at work."

"That's it, Mother," replied Laurel. "I'm finally starting to enjoy myself at Mervyn's." She would have to tell them eventually, she thought, but not quite yet.

"Well, I'm glad to hear that," said Laurel's father. "I have been concerned about the atmosphere there for you."

"It's okay, Dad—really."

"Are you making friends?"

"A few."

"Are there any other Christians working there?"

"I think so . . . yes, I'm sure of it."

"Just be careful," added Mr. Willard. "You're out in the world now, Laurel. Satan's influence is everywhere."

Laurel did not answer. Her father was too worried that every little thing was worldly. She had long ago learned not to take his injunctions too seriously. Besides, it was not Satan who was on her mind at the moment, but one of her co-workers.

As Laurel got out of her car the following morning and walked toward the store, she was more nervous than she had been on her first day of work. What had come over her? Hal wouldn't even be there until three that afternoon!

It was with great difficulty that she kept her mind focused on her work. She tried to act natural as three o'clock approached, but she could feel herself beginning to feel warm. Then she began glancing out the front windows for his car.

Two-forty came . . . then two-fifty—there he was!

Oh, if only a customer would come to the register to occupy her! He was coming to the door. Suddenly, he was standing in front of her.

"Hi, Laurel!" he greeted her with a bright smile.

Laurel nearly melted.

5 | THE TEEN-ROMANCE MENTALITY

A "common friendship"—
who talks of a common friendship?
There is no such thing in the world.
On earth no word is more sublime.

—*Henry Drummond*

The prevailing point of view in our culture today is that teenage romance is a viable, even necessary part of learning to relate to the opposite sex and prepare for marriage. After all, feelings of attachment and love and romance are natural, and thus young people need to express and deal with them, don't they? Many can't imagine how adolescent development could progress without crushes, pairing off, dating, flirting, who-likes-who chatter, and all that goes with it.

We disagree.

The mindset and attitudes of teen romance—in fact, common dating practices, and the immodest way teens are allowed and even encouraged to express their budding feelings of attraction to the opposite sex—do more to contribute to unhappy marriages and divorce than any other single factor.

In saying this, we intend no blanket critique against dating. Surely many good relationships and marriages can and do result from it. It is our strong belief, however, that the dating system as widely accepted does not biblically prepare young people for marriage. "Success stories" do not mean there still might not be a better way.

Our society tends to make a god of anything that is perceived as "natural," without stopping to ask whether it leads to good or harmful results. The first questions to be asked, then, in evaluating a relational basis for marriage is the role romance should play in a teen's life and whether so-called natural feelings of attraction are given to young people to be expressed the instant they emerge within the human psyche.

"Above all else, guard your heart, for it is the wellspring of life" (Proverbs 4:23).

YIELDING TO NATURAL IMPULSES IS A CHARACTER WEAKNESS

In many respects, maturity can be seen as the ability to control and *not* do what one's natural impulses dictate. That's *self-control*. Yielding to everything "natural" is neither normal, beneficial, nor mature.

A toddler is recognized as growing up when he can *control* the natural impulse to go to the bathroom and can reserve that natural phenomenon for the proper time and place. As natural as it is, it is not to be spontaneously expressed.

An eight- or ten-year-old is recognized as growing up when he or she can *put aside* the natural impulse toward anger when the will is crossed and find calmer ways than yelling to express frustration. The anger may be natural, but he or she must learn to control it.

A teenager is recognized as approaching maturity when he or she can *lay down* the natural impulse to put oneself first in all things and begins to see value in putting others ahead of himself. Selfishness may be natural, but it is not desirable.

Young people of all ages desire independence. Such may be a "natural" impulse. But the independence of adulthood is not to be entered into for many years after the first desire for it is felt.

Clearly we could cite many more such examples. It is such an obvious and universally recognized principle that it hardly needs stating. Yet somehow when it comes to the so-called "natural" feelings of attraction toward the opposite sex that begin at ten, twelve, fourteen, or sixteen, society does not consider them in the same light as potty training, controlling anger or selfishness, and independence. At this point they say, "Ah, the hormones have kicked in, these are *natural* feelings, and we must let young people express them however and whenever they want."

How subtly destructive this error is! The result down the line is the disintegration of marriage.

Only the weak and immature yield to every natural impulse. The teen years provide the opportunity to learn to *control* our emotional and physical impulses and *not* to yield to the first stirrings of romantic feelings.

"It is God's will that . . . each of you should learn to *control* his own body in a way that is holy and honorable, not in passionate lust like the heathen" (1 Thessalonians 4:3–5).

"But the fruit of the Spirit is . . . patience . . . and *self-control*" (Galatians 5:22–23).

PREMATURE PREOCCUPATION WITH THE OPPOSITE SEX IS ALSO A CHARACTER WEAKNESS

Please hear us clearly. We are not merely discouraging touching, kissing, and all of what is called "going too far." Teenage *sexual* behavior is not the only problem. Far from it.

We are saying that the romantic mindset—*boy-likes-girl* and *girl-likes-boy*, and the gossip and flirting and "great date wait" that preoccupies many young people—does not foster a healthy preparation for marriage. The attraction leading to romance was *not* designed by the Creator for expression until marriage.

Hear us once again—we do not say it is necessarily wrong to *have* feelings of attraction. Perhaps for some it *is* natural.[1] We are saying, however, that it is inappropriate to *express* and *yield* to them and thus allow immodesty to gain a serious foothold.

Jonathan Lindvall comments: "Many of us have assumed that the typical pattern of American teenage dating is a necessary part of growing up and finding a mate. Christian young people experience an enormous pressure to be 'normal.' Being normal is somehow identified, during the teen years, as being romantically attached to someone of the opposite sex.

"In the typical Christian youth group, young people seek repeated romantic attachments. . . ."[2]

Many pastors and Christian counselors, and especially teen group leaders, will dismiss much of the above with a wave of the hand and contend that we are prude Victorians in our outlook. But we hope some of you young people will have

---

[1]There are valid questions about just how "natural" these romantic impulses of the twelve- or fourteen-year-old actually are. Actually we would contend that much of this early-teen romantic preoccupation is *learned*. That romantic impulses are *perceived* as natural by our society is unquestioned. How much of this, however, is the product of "Hollywood" and an urbanized affluent culture where young people see and read of idealized romance all day long and have leisure to indulge their every romantic fantasy is a question that has been insufficiently examined. Even an unnatural appetite can be made to appear "natural" if it is continually fed, as is the romance mentality by our society. That bodily and hormonal changes occur in the early teen years is not at issue. But do they really cause such an enormous preoccupation with things sexual and romantic? Jonathan Lindvall, for one, argues that this preoccupation is not natural at all. Our recognizing them to be not nearly so "natural" as society would tell us, and therefore not originating with God but man (the preoccupation, that is, not the hormonal changes) will perhaps make the contention that they are to be "controlled" easier to accept. Certain feelings begin gradually before marriage precisely to be stifled—though we will have the permissive psychologists down our throats for saying so. Far too much emphasis is placed on giving expression to whatever is natural, even in Christian circles.
[2]"The Teaching Home" (Dec. 1986/Jan. 1987).

the wisdom to see the truth that modesty and reticence are *virtues* of character, not weaknesses.

Simply put, it demonstrates a lack of maturity and self-control for a young person to yield to a preoccupation with the opposite sex. Giving in to natural attractions prematurely is a sign of character immaturity.

That may be a tough one for you to swallow. But it's true. A premature romantic preoccupation with guys (if you are a girl) or with girls (if you are a guy) reveals a *weakness* of character. It's not a sign that you have become a "real man" or a "real woman." Just the opposite. The "boy-crazy" girl and the "girl-crazy" boy are immature individuals.

Why? Because they are yielding to impulsive feelings and societal preoccupations rather than learning to control them and save romantic inclinations for later—namely, for marriage. A teenager cannot mature properly in the self-control that leads to wise adulthood if he or she does not resist the tendency forced upon him or her by the world to think about girls or guys all the time. Daniel's example ought to remain before the mind of godly youth: "Daniel resolved not to defile himself" (Daniel 1:8). Such defiling is not merely external. It is more a matter of the affections, motives, and priorities of the heart.

ROMANCE—NOT DESIGNED FOR THE EARLY OR MID-TEEN YEARS

No one disputes the fact that young people today grow up too fast. They are robbed of knowing the slow lazy days of childhood and youth, where friendships and family time and outings and shared experiences build deep roots of healthy relationships and loyalty. Television, movies, music, and novels (even many Christian romance novels) thrust young people far too early into a "boy-girl" environment. By the time they reach the teen years, young people assume romantic pairing off to be the acceptable and healthy norm for this stage of their life.

Nothing could be further from the truth!

Romance was given by God to humankind for marriage. That is its design and function. Romantic inclinations, however, begin with the human species sooner than our culture encourages marriage. Therefore, young people need to pass through a process of "romance training" to learn to properly control the feelings of romantic attraction and, when the time is right, to exercise them.

Lester Showalter explains: "Many teenagers allow themselves to be drawn into a boy-girl interest without *trying* to be disobedient or rebellious. They are simply following a natural, God-given attraction. But they follow this attraction without properly considering why God gave them [it] and what God wants them to do with [it]. God gave the attraction between men and women so that homes could be established."[3]

The common argument in favor of teen boy-girl "relationships," including pairing off into couples, is that young men and women need to be around one another and give vent and expression to the natural romantic feelings rising up within them. They need many relationships with girls and guys. They need to learn to chat and joke and bat their eyes and flex their muscles. Girls need to learn how to win over a guy, and guys need to learn how to impress a girl. If they are prevented from all this, and if these natural feelings are squelched, psychological damage will result and they will be ill-prepared for marriage. Such arguments contend that flirting and holding hands and boy-girl parties and pairing off in social occasions and dating and going steady are not only healthy but also necessary.

We might as well say that we ought to let toddlers give expression to their every physical impulse and let children express their tempers however they want and never try to teach them otherwise!

Showalter confirms: "Any misuse of the sacred attraction [between the sexes] is forbidden by Scripture. . . .

"When is the natural attraction between those of the opposite sex being misused? When it is pursued for any purpose other than the purpose of God: that is, to establish a home for the rearing of children.

"Cultivating a special boy-girl friendship is serious business and should never be played like a game or made into a joke . . . no school-age youth is mature enough to enter into that special relationship."[4]

THE TEEN-ROMANCE MENTALITY—A DETRIMENT TO MARRIAGE

As in many aspects of life, appearances are not what they seem.

In actual fact, the above teenage patterns (romantic preoccupation, boy-girl talk, hand-holding, pairing off, dating, romantic fantasizing and socializing, girl-guy gossip, parties, mall-walks, guy-watching, girl-watching, etc.) are actually *detrimental* to the future marriage relationship rather than beneficial to it. These activities, and the thought patterns behind them, *give in* to the natural rather than control it.

They therefore *deepen* weakness of character and lack of maturity and take the very young people who desire healthy relationships with the opposite sex

[3]*What About Boy-Girl Friendships*, pp. 17-18. Road and Staff Publishers, Crockett, Ky., 1982.
[4]*What About Boy-Girl Friendships*, pp. 18–19.

further from the capacity to develop those healthy relationships.

The very thing teens want so badly, romance-preoccupation and immodesty make impossible!

The more preoccupied with the opposite sex at an early age, the *less* equipped will a young person be for a sound marriage. To whatever extent the teen-romance mentality is *avoided*, and modesty and decorum worn rather than forwardness, the stronger will a young man or woman be as a future husband or wife. The reason is clear: they have exercised *strength* of character in properly training themselves not to let behavior be motivated by societal and peer pressures and budding feelings of attraction.

A moment's observation makes it quickly clear where preoccupations lie. A short time ago we were standing with a group of young women. Soon one broke away from the others to go talk with a young man who happened by. Almost from the first moment she had been glancing about, looking to see if there were any guys around. To her way of thinking, *any* guy held more fascination than a group of her girlfriends talking about boring girl things. The others remained talking among themselves, content in their mutual friendship, feeling no need to find "a guy" to talk to or to center their discussion about guys.

It is not difficult to recognize from which group the most mature future wives will come—from those who are *not* preoccupied with young men, but who have put those natural feelings on hold for *later* and are engaged now in learning to develop strong friendships.

For years we have worked with young people in a variety of settings—teaching in junior high, high school coaching, in youth groups, and giving music lessons. In all these environments our goal has been to encourage and challenge young people to excellence, both of character and in the particular activity in which we are involved together. It is exciting to bring young men and women to their full potential as musicians, as runners, as students.

Yet no matter what the setting, the distinction is abundantly clear between those who are focused and mature in personality and character, and those for whom a preoccupation with boys or girls outweighs most other interests. For these, what we call a "teen-romance mentality" (fluttering eyes, coy looks, who-likes-who, "isn't so-and-so cute," "I-want-to-ride-in-the-car-with . . . ," and a bold attention-getting demeanor in mixed group settings) colors their whole world.

All this sets a subtle pattern for later in life, when the contrast between level-headed and mature young people and those preoccupied with impressing and getting the attention of the opposite sex plays out on a stage where the consequences are anything but pleasant. When we think of the futures of these young people, we know that those who exercise the control that maturity of character brings will be stronger husbands and wives as a result. Those who yield to every whim of a fluttering heart will not have learned this vital life lesson—that self-control leads to maturity, while giving in to whatever is *natural* is a display of weakness.

It is hard to blame the latter group. Most of them have been reared by society and the influence of TV, their peers, and the golden calf of Hollywood's inverted moral structure to believe that the great end of womanhood is to beguile the opposite sex, and that for young men to impress the world of women represents the pinnacle of manhood.

What false values have been perpetuated upon our sons and daughters!

Christlikeness of character, sacrifice, servanthood, self-control, and the capacity to be a true friend—only these qualities will make a marriage strong.

"Flee the evil desires of youth, and pursue righteousness, faith, love and peace, along with those who call on the Lord out of a pure heart" (2 Timothy 2:22).

SENDING IMMODEST SIGNALS—IMMATURE DESIRE FOR ROMANTIC ATTENTION

Though perhaps subtle, young people continually give signals of either restraint or boldness to members of the opposite sex.

Besides the unmistakable signs of flirtatious or impressing behavior, immodesty is a clear indication that the romance mentality has become a destructive preoccupation. The behavior often is not even intentional, emerging simply out of personality, priorities, and underlying motives. But whether the individual recognizes it or not, the symptoms of this forwardness are as easy to interpret as a notice painted across his or her forehead: *I want to be noticed. Look at me!*

The attempt to look or act "appealing" and to attract notice is nothing more than a not-so-disguised desire for romantic attention. Young people send a hundred messages all day long with clothes, hairstyle, gait, jewelry, cologne, and ways of talking. A guy's or girl's whole demeanor and carriage contributes either to a modest, discreet, composed image of decorum and humility *or* to an immodest attempt to pull every eye toward oneself. How cool and hip a young person tries to be is a direct indicator of his or her IQ—immodesty quotient.

Johann Chrisop Arnold comments: "Flirting . . . has no place in the church. We have to reject it. . . . Hand in hand with flirting goes vanity. Dressing to draw attention to oneself or attract or impress someone is sin, plain and simple. It should not be tolerated. . . ."[5]

Modesty is one of the seriously overlooked traits of character in our day. Our

[5]"The Plough" (Feb./Mar. 1986), Plough Pub. Co., Ulster Park, N.Y.

culture thinks modesty is a character flaw. In reality, intentionally chosen modesty (in contrast to natural shyness) is a lost virtue and reveals a balanced sense of personhood, maturity, and humility. On the other hand, immodesty (and even shy persons can be immodest in their own quiet way) and its unquenchable desire for attention reveals insecurity, self-absorption, and weakness.

These immodesty signals come in a thousand subtle varieties other than a low-cut blouse, dyed hair, accentuated biceps, tight pants, flashy jewelry, or strong perfume. The whole way some young people interact (even in the absence of such external symbols) conveys the message, "Hey, world, look at me, I want to be noticed, I'm cute, I use the "in" lingo, I'm cool!" In addition they usually contain the not-so-subtle hint—"I'm available."

The demeanor and personal carriage of those with high MQs (modesty quotient), on the other hand, conveys an unpretentious and modest sense of decorum. Teens with high MQs are more interested in others than they are in turning every eye to themselves. They have a balanced outlook on life and their role in it and do not see themselves as the center of the universe.

Are these admonitions against flirting, immodesty, and romantic preoccupation only the warped opinion of a few ultraconservative old fogies like us?

Not according to the Bible. Scripture clearly considers forward, flirtatious, immodest behavior toward the opposite sex a sin. "Women should dress modestly, with decency and propriety, not with . . . gold or pearls or expensive clothes" (1 Timothy 2:9). We're sorry if this sounds offensive, but the Bible calls a girl or woman who sets out to *lure* and *charm* and *entice* nothing more or less than a prostitute. And what is flirting? A deliberate attempt to lure and charm and entice by looks and behavior. "My son, keep your father's commands . . . for these commands are a lamp, this teaching is a light . . . keeping you from the immoral woman. . . . Do not lust in your heart after her beauty or let her captivate you with her eyes . . ." (Proverbs 6:20, 23, 24–25).

What about men who try to impress, who look at women in a wrong way, whistling and cracking crude jokes among themselves—with smiles and jeers and raised eyebrows—men who focus on looks rather than character? What does the Bible call them? Nothing more or less than fools. "A fool's eyes wander . . . his lips are a snare. . . . Honor is not fitting for a fool" (Proverbs 17:24; 18:7; 26:1).

It does not matter that a young man may possess an "IQ" (as *society* judges it, not as we are using the letters here) of 145 or that a woman is not actually a prostitute—such behavior nevertheless draws the scriptural parallel. Do you want to behave *like* a fool or a prostitute?

Scripture considers immodesty a sin because of what sort of character it reveals. "Let us behave decently . . . do not think about how to gratify the desires of the sinful nature" (Romans 13:13–14).

In their book *It's a Lifestyle*, Nathaniel and Andrew Ryun write: "We are told that the works of the flesh include . . . licentiousness (Galatians 5:19, NKJV).

"According to *Webster's Dictionary*, licentiousness is 'the excessive indulgence of liberty; contempt for . . . morality, and decorum.' It is interesting that licentiousness is defined as a contempt for decorum.

"Similar to 'licentiousness' is 'lasciviousness,' which is 'the stirring up within yourself or another feelings and desires that cannot be righteously satisfied.' "[6]

Which kind of person would *you* rather have for a best friend, one with a high IQ (Immodesty Quotient) or a high MQ (Modesty Quotient)?

Once you have eyes to see more deeply into a man's or a woman's character, modesty is one of the most appealing and attractive of all virtues. A forward impropriety toward the opposite sex, even where surface beauty may be dazzling, is one of the ugliest signs of self-centeredness.

The beauty radiating from a modest, honest, humble face is beauty indeed!

ROMANCE MENTALITY IS DESTRUCTIVE TO LOYALTY

The teen-romance mentality undermines an understanding of loyalty and commitment.

We've all heard the expression that we live in a "throwaway society." Everything is temporary and passing.

Houses used to be built of stone and lasted hundreds of years. Today builders hope to get thirty or forty years out of a building before all the cheap materials begin to deteriorate. Both of us remember toasters our families used throughout our *entire* childhoods. We have gone through at least a half dozen during the years of raising our own sons! This book you are reading—a paperback—was unheard of a hundred years ago when *permanence* in bookmaking was considered standard.

In no area is this temporary mentality more visible than in romance relationships. *The* most permanent human relationship other than that between parent and child—marriage—is now looked upon as temporary. Many wedding vows, in fact, have eliminated the words *till death us do part*.

In large measure, we believe this sad fact originates with the teen-romance mentality we have been discussing. During adolescence especially, relationships are *never intended* to be anything but fleeting and passing. And because the teen-romance mentality is not seen for the destructive societal influence it is, and because many parents and teachers and youth leaders condone and even encourage it, patterns of impermanence take hold with the result that the underpinnings of marriage for an entire generation have been damaged.

---

[6] *It's a Lifestyle*, Silver Clarion Press, pp. 96–97.

Today's young people cannot fully comprehend how loyalty and commitment apply to friendship relationships if they allow themselves to be consumed by the romance mentality of their peers. If they want to escape its damage to their own thought patterns and attitudes, young people must commit themselves to a radically different perspective on teen relationships—one where *friendship* is emphasized to the complete exclusion of the temporary romance mentality.

Our generation of parents have not modeled a good example for our sons and daughters. Many men and women think nothing of casting off one spouse and falling in love with a new one. Many college students think nothing of living with someone of the opposite sex. Society encourages it. Co-ed dorms, so-called "partnerships" instead of "marriages" . . . our entire vocabulary of relationships now accepts the grim fact that romance between couples (we can't even say between men and women anymore) is temporary.

"What's the big deal?" society asks. "Haven't you seen the reruns of *Three's Company?* It's all just for fun and temporary gratification. So what if relationships are a round-robin sort of arrangement?"

High school girls have a crush on one boy this week and another the next. The activity of choice when junior high girls get together is to call boys on the phone or go to the mall to check out the boys hanging around in their girl-watching cliques. Who's-going-out-with-who changes at the high school or even at a church youth group from month to month. The "in" guys make the rounds of a half dozen girls in a year or two.

Undiscerning parents and relatives encourage this loyalty-less romance mentality from an early age, pumping their precocious kindergartners with questions about their *girlfriend* or *boyfriend*, thinking it's so cute—not realizing that in the process they are planting seeds that may sprout and bloom one day into marital failure.

A whole generation of young people is growing up that does not know how to form good and lasting friendships because of these false values we have given them and because of this romance mentality we have allowed to take over in our society.

Loyalty and commitment cannot be developed as intrinsic aspects of a relationship if friendships and associations change every week. You have to spend a long time in a relationship. Otherwise the true friendships out of which best-friend marriages will ultimately come simply *cannot* form.

Developing friendships takes time. Commitments ought not be made unless we intend to keep them.

In his *Life Purpose Commitment, Booklet 1*, Bill Gothard writes, "One of the great tragedies of our nation's method of dating is the discontentment and disloyalty it breeds. . . . Once marriage does occur . . . the relationship begins to cool off as the husband focuses on his business and the wife occupies herself with her own job or other activities.

"The couple soon encounters the inevitable conflicts that result when one or both partners neglect the responsibilities of marriage to enjoy the benefits of singleness. Through the deception of dating, Satan is able to reduce the fruitfulness of one's ministry both in singleness and in marriage."

Gothard encourages young people with the advice, "Save your first kiss for your wedding day." As a prescription for a "good marriage," we doubt there could be much better advice!

"Delight yourself in the Lord and he will give you the desires of your heart. Commit your way to the Lord; trust in him and he will do this" (Psalm 37:4–5).

MORE THAN ROMANCE

Many will vehemently disagree with our premise that giving way to these natural romantic tendencies reveals weakness—and can even be sinful. All we ask is that you examine the statistics. Look at the existing state of marriage and the prevailing methods by which teens "get to know one another." Ask yourself, "Is it working?"

We think radical measures are called for. We know this reoriented mentality toward relationships we are laying out *does* work. If you're satisfied with a less than 50 percent chance of the marriage of your son or daughter or your *own* marriage lasting, then ignore our premise and let the romance mentality continue to dictate your outlook.

But we *don't* think current methods are working.

It is really as simple as that. One may argue in favor of yielding to romance and putting on a fresh and forward manner around the opposite sex, justifying it because it is "natural." But the simple fact is this: it doesn't provide a solid foundation for marriage.

"For God did not call us to be impure, but to live a holy life. Therefore, he who rejects this instruction does not reject man but God, who gives you his Holy Spirit" (1 Thessalonians 4:7–8).

A WORD TO THE WISE

Finally, a few practical words to young people.

Young men, would you like to find a godly, mature, wise, self-controlled woman to be your wife? Be in no hurry to enter into a private relationship with a girl. Learn first what friendship means with other guys and in mixed group settings. Learn to be a loyal friend. Then, gradually, as time goes on and you move toward your later teen years, try to recognize *character* in the young women you meet rather than beauty or charm. Look beyond that young woman surrounded by a crowd of male admirers, whose eyelashes flutter, who well knows the power of her smile and bewitching expression and enjoys using it, whose eyes flash with flirtatious intent and who is caught up in the romantic feelings of her youth. Look instead to the girl at the edge of the crowd, perhaps not so pretty, who wears no heavy perfume or makeup, who does not flirt, but is loyal to her friends, and who can talk comfortably with guys and girls equally as *friends* without hint of turning on the feminine charm. She is one whose character is likely years ahead of the other. Perhaps she is one capable of a lifelong and best-friend marriage. She may be one to seek out—not for romance, but for a true friendship.

Young women, would you like to discover a godly, mature, self-controlled man to be your husband? Be in no hurry to enter into a private relationship with a guy. Learn first what friendship means with other girls and in mixed group settings. Learn to be a loyal friend. Then gradually, as time goes on and you move toward your later teen years, try to recognize *character* in the young men you meet rather than good looks or strength. Look beyond that dashing young man with broad shoulders and strong arms, whose wit and handsome face cause the hearts of all the girls in your school or church to melt, that athlete whose casual manner and captivating smile make him the object of the crushes of dozens of your friends. Look instead to him on the edge of the crowd, perhaps not so good looking, perhaps not such a great athlete, who shows no romantic interest in girls yet always treats them with kindness and respect, who can talk comfortably with anyone equally, girl or guy, but who never tries to impress. For he is one whose character is likely far ahead of the other. Perhaps he is one capable of a lifelong and best-friend marriage. He may be one to seek out—not for romance, but for a true friendship.

"Finally, brothers, whatever is true, whatever is noble, whatever is right, whatever is pure, whatever is lovely, whatever is admirable—if anything is excellent or praiseworthy—think about such things" (Philippians 4:8).

Friendship is the allay of our sorrows, the ease of our passions, the discharge of our oppressions, the sanctuary to our calamities, the counselor of our doubts, the clarity of our minds.

—Jeremy Taylor

A Courtship Engagement

Mr. Willard need not have worried about his daughter's non-Christian acquaintances. The person Laurel really cared about was from a Christian home and was the nicest, most gentlemanly, most responsible young man her father could have hoped for her to meet.

It was not long before Mr. and Mrs. Willard knew everything that Laurel did about her friend and fellow employee at Mervyn's department store, Hal Gilbert. Within a few weeks, Hal began attending their church on Sunday mornings.

Laurel had been home schooled all the way through high school graduation. Her parents believed strongly in shielding their children from the influences of the world. Laurel's father and mother were advocates of courtship and betrothal as representing the most scriptural and historically sound methods for entering into marriage. They had first encountered the idea at a Bill Gothard convention. Over the years they taught the concept of courtship to their four children. Laurel had reluctantly accepted that this would be the means by which she would enter into marriage, although she was well aware that guys sometimes looked at her in a way she liked. She had always secretly wanted a boyfriend.

At eighteen, her job at Mervyn's represented Laurel's first exposure to the world outside the church-and-family "greenhouse" her parents had provided her.

Hal had never heard the term courtship except as applied to pioneer times, or having to do with other cultures in past periods of history. He never dreamed anyone in **this** day and age, especially in the United States, actually practiced it.

But he was in for a surprise. When Hal asked Laurel out for a date, Laurel told him of her father's views—that no dating was allowed. Hal was so astonished he could scarcely speak.

"You don't date?" he repeated.

Laurel shook her head.

"Do you agree with your father?" he asked.

"I don't know—I guess so," Laurel replied with a shrug. "It's not as if I have a choice."

"I don't understand. Why not?"

"Because my folks will tell me who to be with. Who I will marry will be **their** decision."

"You mean . . . you can't . . ." Hal stammered, at a complete loss for words. He hadn't been thinking about anything serious, certainly not marriage. Laurel just struck him as someone he'd like to get to know better. "What if," he tried to go on, ". . . well, what if I want to spend some time with you? Do you mean you'd have to ask their permission?"

"Of course."

Hal shook his head in disbelief.

"But it wouldn't do any good anyway, because they don't believe in dating," said Laurel.

"Then how will you ever get to know someone well enough to know if you want to marry him?"

"By being courted," said Laurel, looking a bit embarrassed. "I . . . I really think you should talk to my father," she said, relieved that their break was over and that it was time to go back to work.

For the rest of the day, Hal found himself stewing over what Laurel had told him. He had been raised in a Christian home and had attended church all his life. But this was going too far. **How can Laurel's parents be so controlling?** he wondered. **What right do they have to dictate what Laurel does, who she sees, how she spends her time? Isn't eighteen old enough to decide for herself?** Hal didn't have the chance to do anything about Laurel's suggestion, for the very next day he answered the telephone at work to find himself speaking to Laurel's father.

"Hello, Hal," said Mr. Willard, introducing himself. "Laurel tells me you and she have spoken about dating."

"Uh, yeah . . . a little."

MICHAEL & JUDY PHILLIPS

"Did you ask her out for a date?"

"Not exactly—we were just talking about it, that's all."

"She told you, I believe," said Mr. Willard, "that we are opposed to dating."

"Yes, sir, she did."

"Well, Hal—the reason for my call is to find out what your intentions are."

"My, uh . . . intentions?"

*"Yes," replied Mr. Willard. "Are you **interested** in Laurel?"*

"I don't know—how do you mean, interested? I would like to get to know her better, that's all."

*"Then you **are** interested in pursuing a relationship with Laurel?"*

"Uh, yes, I guess I am."

"Then I think it is time you and I had a talk, Hal. Could you come over to our house for dinner after church this Sunday?"

"Uh, yes, that would be fine."

"Good. We'll see you then."

"All right—and thanks, Mr. Willard."

Hal put the phone down, letting out a breath of air. **Maybe Laurel's parents aren't so unreasonable after all**, Hal thought. Before meeting Laurel, Hal had not personally known anyone who had been home schooled. Now all of a sudden he found himself interested in someone who had never been to public school a day in her life, who had never been on a date, and whose parents would not allow her to go for a drive with a boy or even sit in church with one without a chaperone.

He'd been used to the normal girl-guy relationships of high school and had been in his share of situations and relationships where an undercurrent of romantic interest pervaded everything.

Now he felt as if he'd stepped into a time warp!

The following Sunday afternoon, Hal found out everything he had wanted to know about courting, and more. When dinner was over, Mr. Willard took him into the den and closed the door.

This was really much sooner than he had envisioned such a talk with a young man. Laurel was still far too young. But she was determined to have a boyfriend, and if he didn't take this step now, her father knew there was no telling what she might do.

"I'd like to talk with you man to man, Hal," Mr. Willard began, taking a seat opposite his guest.

"As you know," Mr. Willard went on, *"Laurel's mother and I believe in courtship as the proper means of finding a mate and preparing for marriage. I thought we should talk about it and clear up any questions you might have."*

"I really don't know much about what courtship is," said Hal, thinking it

best for now not to voice his objections. He liked Laurel, and if he could win over her heart through courtship instead of dating, he was willing to play along with the ancient custom. What harm could it do?

"Basically, courtship is an alternative to dating," Mr. Willard began. "A young man approaches a girl's father and states his wish to **court** his daughter. If the father has no objection, he gives his permission. The young man and young woman are then permitted to spend time together at the home of the young lady's parents in a supervised setting. As they gradually get to know each other, the boundaries widen. The end in view is, of course, marriage."

"Marriage?" Hal was incredulous. "So is courtship the same as engagement?" he asked, still more than a little perplexed and beginning to wonder if he had gotten in over his head.

"Not exactly," replied Mr. Willard, "although it is similar in that it leads ultimately to marriage."

"So, if I court Laurel, that does not make us **engaged**?"

"No. But if the courting works out, it will culminate in engagement and marriage. Courtship is like a trial period for you and Laurel to get to know each other and for us to get to know you. It also allows the two of you to decide whether you indeed want to follow through to marriage, and for us to decide whether we feel you are the husband God has selected for our daughter."

"So it is like a **trial engagement**?" suggested Hal.

"Something like that," agreed Mr. Willard.

By the time Hal Gilbert left the Willard home that afternoon, the announcement was made to the rest of the family that Hal Gilbert was officially courting Laurel Willard.

6 | CHOOSING FRIENDS OF CHARACTER

However rare true love is, true friendship is rarer.

—*La Rochefoucauld*

Most of us little realize how greatly the pervasive permissiveness of our society affects our thinking. It infiltrates us all, oftentimes where we least expect it. It is impossible to escape. Permissiveness makes up the very moral air we breathe.

Sometimes, however, we have to stand back and make a concerted effort to ask whether certain prevailing thought patterns and attitudes are in fact true and accurate and scriptural, even though we have perhaps long grown accustomed to them.

We live in an age where openness prohibits the drawing of moral lines. Nothing can be called "wrong" anymore. Relationally, no "sins" remain in our society—only a multitude of "lifestyle options." Any attempted recognition of fault or weakness is condemned as judgmental and non-accepting.

We, however, are going to dare to stand against that perspective and say that in the matter of choosing one's friends, circumspection is called for.

SHOULD FRIENDSHIPS JUST HAPPEN, OR SHOULD FRIENDS BE CHOSEN?

Even the phrase "choosing one's friends" is likely to raise eyebrows. Who are we to say that so-and-so is worthy of being a friend and someone else is not? The subtle tolerance of the age creeps in everywhere—as if we have no right to choose one individual over another as a friend.

In truth, most of us *don't* give much thought to the selection of our associations. Friends tend to come along more or less by accident of circumstance. Life's events throw people together, affiliations form, and from them friendships develop. It just . . . happens.

We also don't give much attention to the influence our so-called friends have on us. We're thinking neither of our own growth and character nor that of our friend. Unfortunately, friendships are founded more on the basis of fun, personality, common interests or dislikes, and shared activities than upon character.

But we *are* influenced. Character rubs off. We become more like those we are with. It can't be helped. "Don't be misled: 'Bad company corrupts good character' " (1 Corinthians 15:33). Ought we not, therefore, to surround ourselves with men and women of wisdom and character?

To do so requires that we remain on the lookout for quality people and that we consciously *choose* friendships from among them. This implies no judgment, no negativity toward everyone else. We can be courteous and kind and carry on conversations with all types of men and women. Everyone with whom we mix in school, at work, and in our neighborhoods will not be of sterling character, impeccable judgment, nor demonstrate maturity. We can learn and grow from all kinds of relationships. And we can love people as God does.

But when it comes to deep friendships, we need to be careful that we reserve those bonds for individuals who are going to lift us up, whose characters will exert a positive influence for good in our lives.

George Washington said, "Associate yourself with men of good quality if you esteem your own reputation, for 'tis better to be alone than in bad company.' "

The book of Proverbs is full of injunctions toward the same end. If Solomon's advice could be summed up in three words, they would probably be these: *Choose associations wisely!*

YOUNG PEOPLE DON'T OFTEN LOOK FOR CHARACTER IN FRIENDSHIPS

Young people can be oblivious to quality of character in their peers. They often are attracted first by looks alone (an absurd measure of friend-value, when you stop and think about it) and then by a fun and dynamic personality, as well as popularity among other young people. Unselfishness and Christlikeness nowhere appear on the measuring stick by which most teens evaluate one another.

One may hear a teen halfheartedly address the issue of character with the generally empty statement that someone is a "real neat person." What that usually means is that they have a crush on that individual. Being *neat* hardly defines character. You have to look deeper.

Common sense dictates that if you are talking about the kind of friendship that leads to a future marriage partner, unselfishness, kindness, graciousness, patience, and other such signs of maturity and character will only benefit *you* in the long run.

Do you want a popular, handsome guy for your husband, or a polite and considerate one? Graciousness and consideration will likely still be part of his makeup long after looks and high-school popularity have vanished. *You* will be the one who stands to lose if you don't, early in life, learn to identify the character qualities that will bear pleasant fruit later on.

Along with training yourself to look for friends among those not caught up in the romance-mentality trap, you must train yourselves to seek out *character* in your relationships and to make friends with people who have started early in life to put others ahead of themselves. Those individuals won't always be easy to find, for it is usually in the quiet corners of life, not in showiness, that true character reveals itself.

Character is one of those hidden mysteries of personality and individuality that must be skillfully and diligently *sought* if it is to be found.

But when you find a friend of depth and maturity, you have indeed made a priceless discovery. And looking for these qualities in others as well as developing them in your own life is the best preparation of all for a best-friend marriage.

Choose your friends, therefore, on the basis of character, not by who's *cute*, who's *hip*, and who's *in*. Usually (not always, but often) the person who is "cute," "hip," or "in" is weak in certain character virtues. The popularity to which these attributes often lead tends to the worship of oneself, and nothing destroys true character faster than that.

CHOOSING FRIENDSHIPS DOESN'T MEAN YOU'RE JUDGING OTHERS

We recently wrote to one of our sons away at college to give him some counsel along these lines.

He is a young man who values his friends above nearly everything in life. They are extremely important to him. That is an admirable priority. He realizes he is still in the process of learning, however, and is struggling with the notion of making some of these hard choices. Our letter came in response to an earlier discussion of the difficult necessity of scrutinizing friendships.

By encouraging him toward care in his associations, we did not mean to imply that all individuals do not have worth, or that by choosing a friend you are exalting one person over another. It simply recognizes the fact that all of us will have closer friendships with some individuals than with others. It therefore makes sense that your best friends be individuals of worth and character.

Here is what we wrote:

We would encourage you to give some prayerful thought to the kinds of people you seek to be around. As we tried to explain to you before, there is a difference between judging someone and wisely selecting good role models. You can love and accept someone and still recognize that possibly they're not the kind of person who is going to be a good influence toward Christlikeness of character.

D. C. used to be a very good friend. Really, one of our very best friends. When he told us he was going to divorce J., we said, "D., don't do this—it will change everything." And it did. Our paths have not crossed in the ten years since the divorce.

Now, were we "judging" him? Do we not "accept" him?

We don't see it that way. We simply realize that we are going to be influenced by the people we choose to be close to. We still love him, and we miss our friendship. But a Christian who has had multiple affairs and has been married three times is not the kind of individual who is going to raise us up, who is going to challenge us toward Christlikeness, who is going to further the one-marriage family values we stand for. If circumstances suddenly changed so that D. came around again, our home and our hearts would be wide open to him, and we would thank God for such an opportunity. There was never judgment toward him, only recognition of the fact that our relationship with him was bound to change by his unfaithfulness.

Again, being discriminating in your relationships is *not* the same as judging. There *is* such a thing as judging, and it is wrong. But you know us well enough to recognize how open we are to everyone we meet, and what a broad range of associations we have in our family. Yet in the midst of that wide circle of relationships, learning how to choose deep friendships is an element of maturity.

So when we meet a G. or J.Y. or a K.P. or a R.B. or a T.M. or a N.S. or a J.R., we lose no opportunity to expose ourselves to their influence, despite great distances, because we know they are seeking Christlikeness and purity and wisdom in their lives. You gradually learn to sense— among the hundreds of relationships that come and go in your life— which ones really count at the deep level of Christlikeness. Others come and go. You love the individuals involved, they are a part of your life for a while, but you simply recognize at a foundational level that the priority of Christlikeness is not one you share.

And it is usually *they* who drift away, just like D.C. did. He exited the relationship, we did not. Because friendship is so very important to you, we say to you again, choose your friends well. Get to know character, not just personality. Do they bring you up? Do they challenge you by their character to servanthood and sacrifice and love and forgiveness? Do they encourage you to be a better man?

YOUR PARTICULAR FRIENDSHIP REQUIREMENTS

How do you know whether or not someone you meet has the hidden qualities of character to lift you up, and to be for you a good friend?

What qualities are important to you in friendship?

This question is even more important as you begin thinking more specifically about your future husband or wife. So we're going to ask you to make a list of friendship qualities that you think would be important to *you* and would assist you in recognizing character in your future opposite-sex friendships.

We're not telling you to make out a Spouse Application Form! Yet as the Ryuns say, "Looking for character in a prospective mate is key. . . . Character is based upon an absolute standard of truth, which says there is a right and wrong for every situation. . . . What often muddles the issue of absolute truth is a justification of rationalizing relativism. Strong character versus strong will comes into play. Strong character is based on absolute truth. One who is of strong character knows the truth and acts on it."[1]

Be selective and be choosy as you focus your thoughts. Your friends will be people of character. People you can trust. Your list should reflect that.

Go ahead, write some things down.

Here is a suggested list of some things to think about in relation to a future husband or wife. If we were making a list, it might include

- someone who is from a Christian family
- someone who is from a single-marriage family
- someone in no hurry to date or marry
- someone with similar interests to mine
- someone who is a virgin
- someone who makes no attempt to be popular or "in"
- someone who's not up on every fashion and trend
- someone who doesn't cater to the most popular people
- someone who seeks to serve others
- someone who is not always at the center of attention
- someone with a tender and sympathetic spirit
- someone who enjoys the simple joys of nature
- someone who likes to read
- someone who likes classical music
- someone who treats everyone equally
- someone who puts others ahead of himself or herself
- someone who works hard and is responsible

---

[1]*It's a Lifestyle*, Nathaniel and Andrew Ryun, p. 81.

- someone whose father and mother I like and admire
- someone who displays no angry temper
- someone who is not preoccupied with himself or herself
- someone who is not a flirt
- someone who is not determined always to have his own way
- someone with high moral and ethical standards
- someone who values truth and would never tell a lie
- someone who listens and is not always talking about himself
- someone who is able to apologize
- someone with worthy goals and aspirations in life
- someone who is modest, not self-promoting.

Of course, you and your parents will have different priorities than ours, so your list may look much different. Some of the points you will write down you will consider essential, others may be optional. Obviously all are not of equal value.

Nor will *anyone* ever measure up perfectly. You are not looking for perfection in your friends, but *tendencies* and *directionality* of growth. You're looking for glimpses into what kind of person someone *wants* to be.

Obviously *no one* puts others first all the time. But does someone *try* to put others first? Is that his or her *motive*, even if he or she misses the mark and sometimes acts selfishly? If so, you've discovered something about the direction that individual is moving and what will likely become more and more evident in his or her life as the years go by.

Obviously we *all* become preoccupied with ourselves at times. But does a young man or young woman enjoy worshiping himself or herself, or is he or she *trying* (even in the midst of occasional failure) to be more humble?

It's the *trying* that makes the difference. It's what kind of person someone *wants* to be that reveals the momentum and growth toward the life priorities and values you share and that are important to you in a future husband or wife. Perhaps some of the points listed should say: "Someone who is *trying* to put others first," and so on.

Whatever your particular family's standards, however you have been raised, you need to choose friends so that they and you and your family will all be comfortable together.

You may see some of the things on our list and say they would not matter to you. We know a young man for whom it is very important that his future wife be a runner. And not merely a runner but a fast and competitive runner. His list will obviously contain that point. Music and books have always been important in our family, as our list indicates. Yours will have similar uniqueness.

It is vital to know what you expect and what you like in your friendships, because from your friends you will one day select your future husband or wife. Think about your list, spend some time with it. Ask your parents what they have found to be worthy qualities in their friends and in each other. Look for some of these things as you cultivate your relationships and friendships. Every one of them offers a tiny window into someone's character.

Hard work . . . the ability to listen or apologize . . . a sympathetic spirit . . . lack of temper . . . disinterest in being popular . . . truthful . . . these and a host of other tendencies and priorities give you glimpses into the direction a young man or young woman is moving and what kind of potential future husband or wife they will one day be.

Discerning maturity and quality of character in the people you meet is a *learned* skill.

THERE IS A COST TO UNWISE ASSOCIATIONS

We had a young acquaintance who did *not* choose her friends with care. Her parents warned her that the people she hung around with were really not friends at all, but she would not listen. Like many young people, she gave no thought to issues of character in the people she chose to be with.

This girl was from a normal and even spiritually minded family. Her father and mother loved her. She had been taught good values. They were involved in 4-H and other family activities. This was a young teen whose mistakes were only two: she did not choose her friends wisely, and she did not trust her parents.

Her "friends" led her further and further from her family, until she came to view both her parents as enemies to her freedom. Trust broke down completely. She began sneaking out at night. Her parents pled with her to listen to their warnings and to remain at home. But her "friends" continued to encourage her in wilder and wilder escapades. One night they came to her house, and she climbed out the bathroom window to go with them. Then her *friends* took her out to a lonely stretch of beach and put a bullet through her head. She was fourteen.

There is a heavy price to be paid for unwise friendships, and *you* may be the one to pay the price later in your life if you do not learn to discern character now.

Do you know a young woman who is up on every fashion and has to dress in the latest style? Stop to consider the implications of what such behavior implies. This is someone who is working vigorously to conform to the world. This one seemingly trivial fact opens a window into her character, revealing that the world and its value system is important to her—a clear danger sign to a future husband.

Going along with the world's value system at the age of fifteen may be expressed in how one dresses. But the character weakness at fifteen may lead to the breakdown of a marriage at thirty-five. If you marry without heeding what the windows of character early in life reveal, when marriage becomes difficult you may find your husband or wife going along with the world's value system and becoming involved in an affair. The character trait leading to it was there all the time, but you didn't heed it, and now you may pay a price for only letting yourself see what you wanted to see.

Does a young woman or young man do all he or she can to appear attractive to their friends—flirting and beguiling and trying to impress? Stop to consider the implications of what that behavior means. Those same character weaknesses will persist and may influence how the person carries himself or herself toward the opposite sex for the rest of their life. Marriage does not necessarily put an end to such behavior.

To look for good character traits is not judging, but is a sign of wisdom . . . as long as you are most attentive of all to the development of that character over which you have complete control—*your own!*

That's where your eyes ought to be most prayerfully focused. How can you choose friendships according to the character traits you admire if you are not seeking to grow toward those same qualities in your *own* life?

Who around you is trying to walk a different road than the world's, even at fifteen or twenty? What you see may tell a great deal about what sort of individual he or she will be in twenty years. People can change and grow, but many tendencies and priorities of character remain.

How do your friends dress? What kind of music do they listen to? What kind of movies do they watch?

Ask these questions! Then decide what answers you will accept. Because by your answers, you will determine your friendships. And from your friendships, ultimately you will choose your future husband or wife.

Going Too Far

Hal still wasn't convinced that courtship made sense.

When he shared with his own parents the plan Laurel's father had laid out, they thought the whole thing sounded ridiculous. What difference did it make how the young couple went about it? And living four hundred miles away, they were hardly in a position to have as much influence on the young couple as the Willards.

Now that he had Mr. Willard's permission, Hal called at the house as often as he could, spending whatever evenings he and Laurel both had free. Actually, Hal did have to admit that not being able to date was saving him a lot of money. Movies and restaurants were expensive!

Hal and Laurel's relationship began to deepen. Within a few months, they became officially engaged and a potential wedding date, approximately a year away, began to be discussed with the Willards.

It was not until about four months later that things began to sour in Hal's relationship with Laurel's parents. He thought he began detecting a certain coolness toward him. His suspicions were confirmed when Mr. Willard asked to see him one day.

"Hal," he said, "I would like you and Laurel to postpone the wedding."

"But why?" asked Hal, instantly irritated but doing his best to remain calm.

"I don't know exactly," replied Laurel's father. "I'm simply growing uncomfortable with the timetable."

"But it's been almost a year!" Hal said, a little warmly.

In truth, the months had accomplished one of the objectives of courtship— it had given Laurel's father time to observe and interact with Hal in their home sufficiently to know him much better. Mr. Willard had come to realize that Hal's level of spirituality as a Christian was more shallow than he had first assumed. He still thought a great deal of Hal as a man of integrity. And he continued to feel good about him as a future spouse for Laurel. But he realized that he would feel even **better** about the marriage if Hal could be encouraged toward a deeper commitment in his faith.

"I'd like you both to go through a premarital counseling program," said Mr.

Willard. *"That is also one of the key aspects of courtship, that a young man is disipled by an older and more experienced man."*

Later, as Hal drove home, his annoyance slowly turned to anger. The months of courtship had done nothing to alter his first impression of the Willards as old-fashioned and controlling. He had been willing to go along for the sake of the chance to be with Laurel. He had done everything Mr. Willard had requested. He had jumped through every hoop.

And now this!

Next thing he knew, he thought, he would probably be told they had decided he wasn't suitable and that the marriage was off altogether! Laurel's parents were taking this old-fashioned method of courting too far. He could see it clearly—all the talk of counseling was just a ploy. Mr. Willard was trying to bust them up!

Well, he wasn't about to let that happen. He would talk to Laurel. She loved him. Her loyalty was to him now, not her father. It was time he took matters into his own hands.

7 | DEVELOPING MIXED FRIENDSHIPS—A GRADUAL PROCESS

Words cannot express the joy that a friend imparts.

—St. John Chrysostom

As much as we have discussed various kinds of relationships and interaction between young people, it is not so much a matter of finding the right *method* for choosing a husband or a wife so much as the right *environment* for healthy social interaction between young men and women. In the right *atmosphere* any number of "methods" are workable.

Certain environments encourage healthy friendships while others *inhibit* them by moving relationships too quickly in the direction of romance. All the methods we will discuss in this book—dating, courtship, betrothal—*can* work toward a terrific marriage if carried out in a healthy friendship-before-romance environment. On the other hand, any method can also fail if friendship principles break down and romance takes a premature front seat.

WHAT'S WRONG WITH DATING?

If character is the most important ingredient in developing wise friendships, how *does* one discover that character and thus establish deeper friendships with members of the opposite sex?

In our society, dating is the customary method by which young people between the ages of sixteen and twenty get to know one another—the years immediately preparatory to marriage. The question becomes: Is dating a good means to establish relationships whose foundation is friendship and the development of character?

As commonly practiced, dating in fact represents one of the *worst* means. To repeat the point made earlier, this is not to say that great marriages cannot result through dating, only that it is not the best or most scriptural approach to forming a relationship.

We are not implying that for a young man and young woman to go somewhere together is wrong in itself. It is the dating *environment* today that is unhealthy. There are four important reasons:

One, the motive of dating, as Bill Gothard points out, opposes *genuine* love. The motive of a date is personal pleasure, fun, a "good time." *True* love, on the other hand, is born of sacrifice, not personal gain.

Two, dating tends to *hide* true character rather than reveal it. If you are looking for windows of character that will help you get to know another individual, a date is almost the *worst* place to find them. The windows are shut tight! Everyone is on his or her best behavior. The atmosphere is entirely artificial—real life does not function like two people on a date.

If a boy has a temper, he will certainly never let it show on a date. More than ever, in these days when abuse is such an escalating problem, whether or not he has a temper is an enormously useful fact for a young woman to know about a young man.

If a girl does not value servanthood, she will never let it show on a date. Whether or not she possesses a heart of service so intrinsic to the role of motherhood, however, is a useful fact for a young man to know about a young woman.

But neither of these traits is likely to show itself in the artificiality of a date. In other words, dating works to prevent the very thing that is supposed to be its purpose—that young people get to know one another. Among all the possible results of dating, this is one thing it surely does *not* accomplish in the early stages—it does not reveal true character. If you want to get to know someone, there are hundreds of ways to go about it, and dating must certainly occupy a position near the bottom of the list.

Three, dating feeds the romance mentality rather than friendship. If a young man and woman or their parents want to encourage premature romance and the expression of feelings of attraction toward the opposite sex, then dating offers the perfect atmosphere in which to do so. As we have already explained at length, however, it is our view that nothing could be more detrimental to future marriage.

Why does dating feed romance rather than friendship? The reasons seem too obvious to mention. Parents have no role in a date. No supervision exists, and the partnership we have spoken of vanishes immediately. The atmosphere of a date is clearly one of pairing off and of romance. It is the tone and undercurrent implied by the very word.

Dates by definition are private—only two people are involved. A date is in a sense the culmination of the misdirected youthful desire for privacy during the time when young people should be interacting in groups. And the problem with privacy is that it forms emotional and romantic attachments far too soon, and away from home.

Dates usually occur in the evening, increasing the flavor of "romance." Privacy makes physical contact easy, and the unsupervised atmosphere can too easily lead toward deeper and more destructive romantic involvement.

Four—and perhaps most detrimental of all—the dating game works against rather than establishes and builds commitment. With its process of forming emotional attachments that end in breaking up and then moving on to the next partner, dating prepares young people for the pattern of marriage, divorce, and remarriage.

MANY AGREE WITH OUR ASSESSMENT

We are not alone in our assessment that dating is not the best way. Josh Harris in *New Attitude* magazine says, "Dating has always been a way for young people to experience the exciting, romantic side of a relationship without commitment or responsibility. A boyfriend/girlfriend relationship provides the feelings of intimacy and creates emotional 'highs,' but it has nothing to hold it together. Because most teens who date are not in a position to marry, the relationship has nowhere to go."[1]

Jonathan Lindvall states in his brochure "Youthful Romance" that dating is a "relatively recent historical phenomenon. It arose out of the eighteenth-century philosophical movement we now call Romanticism, which emphasized among other things, passion rather than logic."

Lindvall further comments, "As a young, unmarried youth minister, I was challenged to develop a scriptural pattern for my own social life. I first accepted the principle that God wants young people to honor their parents by allowing them to give direction to their social life and by voluntarily submitting to their choice of a marital partner. . . .

"Secondly, I concluded that . . . dating is contrary to Scripture."[2]

Nathaniel and Andrew Ryun, like Josh Harris young men themselves, write: "One young gentleman recently wrote to us, 'To teenagers in the nineties, dating is a big part of our culture. As a seventeen-year-old male, dating is also important to me. Dating, to me, is the idea of getting to know the opposite sex, growing relationally with girls, and finding out what kind of characteristics or personalities really interest me.'

[1]Josh Harris, *New Attitude* magazine, Vol. 1, No. 2, 1993, Gresham, Ore.
[2]"The Teaching Home," (Dec. 1986/Jan. 1987).

"Dating is considered by many teenagers a given rite of passage to adulthood. This young man has perfectly expressed how we once reasoned.

"We viewed dating as the means to discover what we wanted in a future wife, giving little thought to the ramifications of dating. Christian leaders were approving it. Everyone was doing it, no questions asked. We assumed (wrongly) that it was God's way of finding a mate. . . .

"We cannot be Christians in name only . . . one of the affairs of this life [warned against in 2 Timothy 2:4] is the issue of dating. Distraction is one of Satan's tools in emasculating Christianity, and dating is one of his best tools in distracting Christian young people. A young person involved in a dating relationship is not so much concerned with pleasing God as he is in pleasing his girlfriend."[3]

Douglas Wilson unequivocally rejects dating as a viable practice for Christian young people in preparation for scriptural marriage. He writes, "The starting point for most of our relationships, the modern dating system, can be safely considered as bankrupt.

"Consider how our system works. A young man notices a girl who attracts him. He asks her out, and she agrees. They start going together, and one of two things happens. Either they like each other or they don't, and both possibilities bring problems in their train. . . .

"It is certain that everyone with a good will rejoices when a godly Christian couple date, behave themselves, and then marry. The success stories within the modern dating system, *which certainly exist*, are not the problem with it. But people survive plane crashes too, some of them without a scratch, and we are all happy about it. But this acknowledgment does not disqualify us from opposing the general habit of crashing airplanes.

" 'Success stories,' [however], are not as abundant as may be assumed through briefly glancing around at church. . . . Our dating system . . . does not biblically prepare young men and women for marriage . . . as God designed it. . . .

"The modern dating system does not train young people to form *a* relationship. It trains them to form a *series* of relationships, and further trains them to harden themselves to the break-up of all but the current one. At the very least, this system is as much a preparation for divorce as it is for marriage. Whenever the other person starts to wear a little thin, you just slip out the back, Jack.

"Further, the modern dating system encourages emotional attachments apart from the protections of a covenant fence. This has been accurately called emotional promiscuity. A man and woman cannot function within a romantic relationship without becoming emotionally vulnerable to one another. Nothing is

[3]*It's a Lifestyle*, Nathaniel and Andrew Ryun, pp. 20–23.

wrong with this vulnerability; it is just that we are delicate enough at this level to require protection, a protection which the Bible says is covenantal.

"The modern dating system also leaves the father of the young girl out of the loop. The father, who ought to be protecting his daughter's sexual purity, sends her off into the dark with some testosterone bundle, and does what he *thinks* is his job, which is to worry. 'Well, dear,' he says to his wife, 'we can only pray.' "[4]

A while back a friend asked if our sons were dating yet. We answered, "We don't allow dating." After a long silence, she asked, "But . . . how will they meet the girl they will marry?"

How unfortunate that even the Christian world largely assumes there is no other way of selecting husbands and wives than through the artificial setting of dating.

If young men and women truly want to get to know one another, want to discern character in the people they know, and want to establish healthy friendships with the opposite sex, then it is toward forms of social interaction other than dating they must look.

FRIENDSHIP DATING

Many will argue that they date for "friendship," just to have a good time. They insist that for them dating carries none of the romantic overtones we have been speaking of.

This is an easy response to make, but the reality is more difficult to back up. Most dates simply cannot escape the inherent foundation of romance on which they are based. Even if *you* may not think you place such a significance on it, society does. You cannot help but be subtly pulled into the romance mentality of dating simply because that is the intent as perceived by our entire culture. Even if *you* are only dating "for fun," the boy or girl you date may have entirely different intentions.

To say, "Oh, I date, but just for friendship—I have no romantic intent," is equivalent to saying, "Oh sure I drive, but it's only for fun—I never actually *go* anywhere."

The fact is, cars and roads and driver's licenses all point to one purpose, having a *destination* in mind toward which you are driving. Dating, too, has a single intent—to further romance. If friendship happens to result, that's a healthy side benefit. But it's not the foundational purpose of dating.

But, you ask further, if friendship *can* result from dating, why not date with mere friendship as the goal?

[4]"Credenda/Agenda," P.O. Box 8741, Moscow, ID 83843, Volume 7, Number 3.

Again—easier said than done. In our culture, romance is the implied destination toward which the dating car drives. That's simply a fact. Attempting to hitch a ride toward some other destination (friendship), though perhaps possible, is not the *best* way of getting there.

That's the point. Perhaps friendship *does* occasionally emerge out of the dating process unscathed, and not too much the worse for coming out of a romantic environment . . . but it's not the *best* way to discover friendship.

Why would you want to do *anything* by means of an inferior method? It is an open admission that you are willing to settle for mediocrity. Why not seek friendship in the *best* way possible? Why not develop friendships in an environment where friendship is the *primary* goal rather than a mere side benefit?

Best-friend marriages grow best out of the soil of *friendship*, not out of the soil of *romance*.

"There is a time for everything, and a season for every activity under heaven . . . a time to embrace and a time to refrain" (Ecclesiastes 3:1, 5).

HEALTHY ENVIRONMENTS FOR THE ESTABLISHMENT OF OPPOSITE-SEX FRIENDSHIPS

There are three necessary components of relationship between young men and young women that ultimately lead to marriage. These make up the friendship-soil that is best able to nurture best-friend marriages.

These three *environments* enable individuals to get to know each other, learn to interact, find out more about each other, learn to discern character, and eventually form the friendships out of which emerge best-friend marriages.

- Environment one—mixed group involvement
- Environment two—family involvement
- Environment three—private activities between young men and young women.

To continue the earthy analogy, these are three *soils* that mix together to provide the ingredients that nurture relationships in a healthy way so that deep and lasting friendship can form.

MIXED GROUP INVOLVEMENT

At the early ages of dawning opposite-sex awareness and attraction (generally ages twelve to fifteen), relationships between boys and girls should be limited to mixed group environments, where families are involved as much as possible.[5]

During these early years when opposite-sex awareness is beginning, to allow a relationship to grow in the soil of privacy and romance will only stunt the final human plant. There should be *no* pairing off between girls and boys at this stage, nor any expression of romantic thoughts or feelings. This is a time for "potty training" those very natural instincts (if we can make such a comparison!), and learning that their expression will come in time, but that time is not yet.

These are the years to *control* the teen-romance mentality, not express it, and to develop *non-romantic friendships* with both boys and girls. To develop friendships without the teen-romance mentality intruding requires mixed group and family involvement at all levels of interaction.

This is not to say that girls and boys should avoid one another or be afraid of accidentally crossing paths in a hallway and be too timid to greet one another or talk with each other. We're not talking about fearfulness, but modesty. Boys and girls can talk and laugh and have fun without being flirtatious or immodest. Learning to engage in and enjoy modest and appropriate social interaction should be one of the occupations of the teen years. Teens in partnership with their parents will be taught by their parents and then will practice it themselves.

How is the romance mentality kept out of relationships? By making sure friendships are not private, that girls and boys do not localize their attentions on a single person, that modesty is exalted as a preeminent virtue, and that flirting and immodesty are recognized by one and all as the cardinal sins against healthy interaction between men and women.

These priorities can best be achieved in group settings—clubs, 4-H, church groups, Bible studies, a church choir, sports teams, service opportunities, multi-family outings, and the like.

---

[5]Richard and Reneé Durfield offer this valuable insight about the pressures many young people face during the teen years: "Children tend to mature faster intellectually these days than in the past, and they certainly have access to more information about sex that can raise their curiosity. Yet despite rapid physical and intellectual growth, they seem to be maturing emotionally more slowly than their parents did—perhaps because of less contact with adults. Grown-ups in their extended families are absent; family schedules are busier than ever; latchkey kids spend most of their time with peers and the media; and more families than ever are headed by single parents. . . .

"The waiting period till marriage has gotten longer . . . with many people delaying that commitment until their mid- to late-twenties or early thirties. A hundred years ago, people typically had to wait a couple of years . . . between the time of sexual awakening and marriage. But now an interlude of ten to twenty years is not uncommon.

"Finally, our contemporary culture relentlessly preaches a message of sexual amorality, undermining the traditional conviction that sex should be reserved for marriage. Television, movies, magazines, and popular music today are reaching the saturation point with material that only a generation ago would almost universally have been labeled pornography. So adolescents daily hear countless seductive voices insisting that casual sex is normal and desirable, and that society has no firm moral standards by which to judge sexual behavior." *Raising Them Chaste*, Bethany House Publishers, pp. 17–18.

FAMILY INVOLVEMENT

During the years of heightening opposite-sex interest (ages fourteen to eighteen), when fascination and attraction is strong in some girls and emerging in boys and generally leads to the beginning of dating, interaction should still be mostly limited to groups that focus on friendship, and continue to involve families.

These are the years when we most earnestly recommend that dating as commonly understood be vigorously avoided. It remains far too early an age for pairing off into boy-girl "couples." For those who absolutely cannot go along with our view and who feel they *must* date, we earnestly recommend that it always be carried out in a family setting with supervision. Neither should there be pairing off in school, sports, or church settings, and parents, teachers, coaches, and youth leaders are wise to prevent it if they truly care about the best interests of the young people under their charge. Emphasizing modesty and preventing flirting, pairing off, and other expressions of immaturity is the greatest favor adults can do for young people during these ages.

This might be an appropriate time to explain why we continually stress "supervision." It is not primarily to make sure something doesn't "happen," and that a girl doesn't grant a kiss when no one is watching, or that a boy doesn't "try something." We're operating under the assumption that you young people reading this are supportive of these best-friend priorities. If you've read this far, you're probably not going to try any funny business the instant your mom or dad is not looking. Nor are we suspicious of every young person's intent. In fact, we trust you who care enough to read and consider these words. We respect your motives and your objectives.

The supervision we're talking about has two purposes.

First, nonsupervised settings tend toward premature pairing off. This leads to private rather than group and family relationships, and before long the romance environment cannot help but infiltrate.

Second, supervision reinforces the threefold cord of partnership that is intrinsic to this process. If a young man is developing a friendship with a young lady, his parents (and especially hers) need to be part of that friendship. It is a *three-way* or *four-way* friendship—a partnership-friendship—not a *private* boy-girl friendship. Thus parental involvement is vital to the process.

To keep this partnership strong and vigorous and full of benefit, you must work hard to tell your parents and family about friends you have made at school, at church, and at work. Talk openly about the people you know: good friends, irritating co-workers, ups and downs . . . everything. Bring your parents into the complete relational milieu in which you live. If you are uncomfortable talking with your parents about your friends, either there is something wrong with the friends you're choosing or there is something amiss in your partnership with your mom and dad.

More than just talking about relationships, bring your friends around. For the partnership to work, your parents need to be intimately involved in all your associations. They cannot be involved without your opening the doors. This aspect of the partnership rests largely upon *your* shoulders.

Involve your parents in your friendships by asking for their advice . . . then listen to it! Especially listen when they warn you about something you may not have picked up on. They will be *more* capable of seeing into the windows of character than *you* are, so trust their eyes even more than your own. This trust will be especially important when they detect character subtleties about a potential future husband or wife. You will be wise to listen even when your love-struck heart wants to tell you just the opposite of what your mother and father might be saying.

And, parents, this partnership is not *entirely* up to your son or daughter. You must contribute as well. Show a genuine interest in the lives of your young people. Attend events where they will cross paths with others their age so you are "in the loop" of their associations, not an outsider. More importantly invite your son's or daughter's friends over, get involved in their lives, be available to do things together. You have to make it easy and fun for their friends to be in your home.

All this develops a level of trust and communication on both sides of the fence that will be valuable later when more serious and lasting relationships form.

PRIVATE ACTIVITIES BETWEEN YOUNG MEN AND WOMEN

During the years specifically leading up to marriage (eighteen to twenty-five), all three of these elements will blend together in an expanding and broadening relational environment—mixed group settings and family involvement remaining foundational, but now with gradually more one-on-one interaction taking place between young men and women.

Obviously these age divisions we have noted are entirely fluid, subject to wide variation. Some young people will remain at home under what is referred to as the "parental umbrella" well into their twenties, others will be off and away to college at eighteen and effectively on their own in terms of daily decisions. In families where the latter situation is true, this whole process we are speaking of may need to be accelerated somewhat so that young men and women begin learning to responsibly conduct themselves in healthy private interaction while Mom and Dad's input is still nearby and available. And once such young people do find themselves living away from home, in a college dorm, for example, it becomes more vital than ever that they develop group and friendship relationships, and that they continue to discuss their new associations in partnership with their parents via letters and phone calls in a continuation of full trusting communication. Geographical distance does not in itself remove the parental umbrella.

The key element here is that this is a *process* that unfolds slowly, over *many* years. If this progression has been followed, and young men and women have learned to interact in healthy, fun yet non-romantic, non-flirtatious ways over the years, in group and family settings, then naturally as they get older, special friendships begin to form.

As long as modesty, purity, respect, and friendship-not-romance continue as unquestioned priorities, pairing off at eighteen or twenty is no longer so detrimental to friendship as it is at fourteen or sixteen. Adulthood and perhaps even marriage is now approaching, and it is natural and healthy for young men and women to feel special bonds of friendship more with some individuals than with others—and these deepening bonds include friends of the opposite sex. We urge you yet again, however, to be extremely unhurried and unanxious for privacy.

You see, contrary to popular belief, it *is* possible to get to know another individual well, to talk and interact and have fun together in a thousand ways, *without* hastening romance or adding a physical component to the relationship. As best-friend relationships do gradually begin to form—growing out of all three of these soils simultaneously—there remains no rush to turn the relationship into a romantic one.

Remember—feelings of romance are given to the human species for *marriage*, not the five or ten years leading up to it. They are given for the one person a young man or woman hopes to marry, not to be scattered among a variety of girlfriends and boyfriends.

Healthy environments for a best-friend relationship, therefore, can continue to avoid the pitfalls of dating. There are many opportunities for relational activity between maturing young men and young women that do not emphasize romantic relationships. Is there something you would do with your brother or sister? That is probably an activity that would promote friendship rather than romance.

Would you, young man, *not* do something with or for your sister (put on cologne, stay on your best behavior, give her a corsage, go dancing, take her on a moonlit drive)? These activities are probably not ones to engage in with your best friend either. (John Holzmann, in his *Dating With Integrity*, discusses brother-sister relationships, as well as the concept of "public" dating, at some length and we highly recommend it. *Dating With Integrity* and *Of Knights and Fair Maidens*, by Jeff and Danielle Myers, suggest many wholesome activities that young men and women can do together in a non-romantic setting. If you are looking for specific ideas for girl-guy friendship activities, both books are great.)

Even alone times don't have to be in a romantic setting. In fact, they will be far more beneficial to your developing friendship if they are not. Eventually you will have quality alone time with your future husband or wife, getting to know each other more deeply, sharing spiritual values and life's ambitions, praying together, serving together, taking classes together.

The two of us taught a Sunday school class, led a junior high Bible study, and participated in college campus activities together. We also attended various church functions, retreats, and conferences as part of the same group of students, went on outings as part of larger groups, talked and prayed and sang together, had lunch together on campus, and visited each other frequently in the presence of other roommates in a mix of diverse friendships. We "got to know each other" in brother-sister environments like these for almost a year.

When we started dating, the artificiality of it was so awful that it almost ruined our relationship! I (Judy) cried for most of the day following the first movie we went to together, and I (Mike) said I'd never do anything like *that* again!

Eventually, however, we were able to reestablish our best-friend relationship on a sound footing, continuing to grow more and more deeply as *friends*, until eventually we realized we truly did love each other and wanted to spend the rest of our lives together. We've always been so thankful to the Lord that he allowed us to know each other as friends first and lovers second. That simple fact has made all the difference in our marriage!

Be courteous to all, but intimate with few, and let those few be well tried before you give them your confidence. True friendship is a plant of slow growth, and must undergo and withstand the shocks of adversity before it is entitled to the appellation.

—George Washington

Courtship Cut Short

After discussing the matter with his father, Hal's mind was made up. The Gilberts had several years earlier given Hal's older sister a check for $2,000 and told her and her fiancé to elope. They did not want to be bothered with the fuss of a big wedding. If it had been good enough for his sister, Hal thought, why not for him and Laurel?

He would talk to Laurel that afternoon. Of course they would say nothing to her parents. The less they knew the better . . . until it was over and they couldn't interfere any more than they already had.

Hal wasn't the only one irritated with the courtship arrangement. Laurel was fed up with her father's rules too. He had always tried to dominate and control her life, watching her every move. She was anxious to be out from under his authority—the sooner the better—and saw Hal as her rescuer from a stifling situation.

However, when Hal suggested they leave and marry, against her father's will and without his permission, Laurel knew immediately it was wrong.

"I . . . I don't know, Hal," she hesitated. "My dad would hit the roof."

"Let him! I'm sick of his bossing us around and trying to tell us everything to do. I'm twenty-four."

"But my mother has had her heart set on a church wedding. It would hurt her so much if we took that away from her."

Hal was completely unmoved by any compassion for Laurel's mother. He had come to dislike her almost as much as he disliked Laurel's father. In fact, he and Mrs. Willard had exchanged heated words several days ago. Far from humbling him, the incident only increased his smoldering resentment at both Laurel's parents. He was certain they were trying to break them up.

"You're always thinking about what your folks want," rejoined Hal. *"What about what I want? Besides, my folks think it's okay for us to get married."*

"They do?" said Laurel. *"You told your folks?"*

"Yeah. I called my dad last night. Come on, what do you say? You're going to have to make up your mind. It's either me or your father. I've gone along with this courtship thing long enough. Make up your mind, Laurel. If you're not with me, I'm out of here."

Laurel was silent. This was a side of Hal she hadn't seen before. He was usually so quiet and polite. Now his face was red, and she could tell he was really angry.

"Do you want to marry me or not?" demanded Hal. It was not quite an ultimatum, but his tone was unmistakable.

"You know I do."

"Then tomorrow we'll go to the courthouse before work. We'll go separately, so if we see anyone from church, they won't suspect anything. We'll get the marriage license. Okay?"

"I . . . I guess so. But I don't like the idea of sneaking behind my parents' backs."

"There's no other way. They're trying to keep us apart."

"All right," Laurel agreed. She was nervous but afraid of losing Hal.

The next time they saw their daughter, Laurel's parents immediately knew something was wrong. Over the next few days she became more and more silent and withdrawn.

Hal planned their moves carefully, watching the work time notices at the store for the moment to take action. When the following week's schedule was posted, he saw his opportunity. He called Laurel on his first break.

"We're leaving tomorrow night," he said. *"You're off all day, and I'll see if I can get off about half an hour early."*

"Okay," agreed Laurel, still unsettled about Hal's plan.

"Good. And we're both off the next day. It'll work out fine. Now tomorrow, hang around home for the morning. Try to sneak a few things into your car without their seeing you. Then come over to the store in the afternoon and hang around until I get off."

"My dad's going to want me to stay at home all day. Mom's sick, and I've been taking care of her."

"I don't care what your dad wants. I'm sorry about your mom, but it's our life now. Find a way to get away, even if you have to walk out on them."

Laurel didn't like the sound of any of this. But her own frustration with her parents was enough to make her agree with almost anything Hal said.

"I'll be there," she said finally, without much enthusiasm.

"Come on, Laurel," said Hal, his tone softer now. "We're going to have a great life together."

"I know," she sighed. "But it's not right to do it like this."

"According to your father, maybe," Hal agreed. "But you know as well as I do that his view of what's right is out of step with the whole rest of the universe. He's never wanted you to grow up. You're nineteen, it's time you made your own decisions."

Laurel finally agreed. She felt the same way about her father as Hal did, but she couldn't get rid of the gnawing discomfort in the pit of her stomach. But she would do as Hal said. She had taken herself out from under her father's umbrella months ago.

The scene in the Willard home the following evening was somber. Mrs. Willard was feeling better and had prepared dinner. When her husband came home at five he noticed that Laurel's car was gone.

"Where's Laurel?" he asked, sensing something was amiss.

"She's gone, dear," replied his wife.

"Where?"

"I don't know. She said she was going out for a couple of hours."

"When was that?"

"About two-thirty."

Mr. Willard glanced at his watch. He immediately sensed the truth but said nothing to his wife.

He had spoken with Hal again yesterday, finally agreeing to let the two young people marry the following week. It was not what he thought best, but because they were determined to marry no matter what anyone said, he wanted to do what he could to keep the lines of communication open. The dream of a wonderful courtship and marriage for his daughter had broken down, and he was heartsick about it. But he loved them both and would continue to do what he could for them.

Hal had been unimpressed with Mr. Willard's offer. He remained belligerent throughout their conversation. That's when Mr. Willard discerned what Hal had already decided to do. He had prayed all day that he was wrong.

Dinner was quieter than usual. Laurel had a younger sister and two brothers, and they knew something serious was going on.

As the evening wore on, Laurel had been gone more than seven hours without a word.

A little after ten, the phone rang.

Mr. Willard glanced at his wife, then rose to answer it.

"Mr. Willard," said the familiar voice on the other end. "It's Hal. I just wanted to call to tell you not to worry about Laurel. She's with me. We're married."

After a brief interchange of unpleasant words, Mr. Willard hung up the phone. He walked over to the couch where his wife sat, a thousand thoughts flashing through his mind. He pictured Laurel as an infant when he first held her in his arms. He felt the love he had known for their firstborn. He thought of all they had done to discipline and train Laurel according to the Scriptures— the years of home schooling, trying to protect her from the influences of the world, teaching her about the importance of courtship and finding the right partner for marriage. It had seemed to be going so well. They loved Hal from the very first. They felt he was the right young man for Laurel. Now it had suddenly gone sour—their daughter had been snatched from them by a seemingly honorable young man. Where had they gone wrong?

He sat down, sighed deeply, and gently placed his arm around his wife's shoulders. When he told her what Hal had said, she laid her head on his chest and wept quietly.

8 | IT TAKES *TIME*

A friend loveth at all times.

—Solomon

In chapter 7 we spoke of a friendship pro-
gression that begins with mixed group settings and family involvement rather than
with dating. It progresses slowly, and not until much later does it lead to private
activities between a young man and a young woman.

One word describes more than any other what makes this progression work.
It . . . proceeds . . . *slowly*. It's the quality of relationships that leads to best-friend
marriages, and that takes time.

Young people, don't be in a hurry to rush this process!

Should we say it again? *Don't be in a hurry.*

And again? *D-o-n'-t b-e i-n a h-u-r-r-y!!*

Are you sick of it yet? Sorry, but we're going to *keep* saying it!

WAITING CAN ONLY BENEFIT A RELATIONSHIP

When you are young, time is your most valuable gift. Yet many are in a head-
long rush to grow up. You have all the time in the world, young people! There is
no need to hurry relationships or marriage decisions.

Do you think Hal would have dumped Laurel had she insisted on waiting, as
her parents suggested? If he had, he wouldn't be someone to depend on in a
crisis. If his loyalty had proved that fleeting, what kind of a husband will he be?
We don't think he would have dumped her, however, because he loved her.

And what would Laurel's decision have shown Hal if he had eyes to see it?
That under pressure Laurel was persuaded to step out from under the umbrella
of the person holding authority in her life. It was a sign how she is prone to handle
a difficult situation. Ten years from now, what will she likely do when she doesn't
like her *husband's* input in her life?

Do you get the picture? Character isn't revealed on a few dates or casual
encounters, but in adversity. When things don't go as we'd like, *then* we show

what we're made of. As it is, Laurel doesn't know what that little patience-window might have revealed about Hal's character. Nor the humility-window, nor the submission-to-authority-window.

Worst of all, Laurel doesn't *really* know how much Hal loves her. Did he love her *enough* to wait? Or would he have left, as he threatened? She can't know . . . because she was in a hurry too.

Hal missed a chance to see Laurel's true character as well. Was he worried that Laurel's parents might change her mind? Then did he really want to marry someone whose love for him was that fragile? He'll never know whether Laurel loved him enough to withstand the wait either.

Both Hal and Laurel lost a valuable opportunity to stand together in a difficult situation, to discover more about their strengths and weaknesses . . . all because they were in a hurry. They will have to forge that necessary part of their relationship later—alone, and probably under even *more* difficult circumstances.

If waiting destroys a relationship, then the relationship was likely doomed from the start anyway. Two people might as well find out *before marriage* what their love is made of—and if their commitment isn't what they think it is.

Waiting can only *benefit* relationships that are strong and are destined to work. God's best is never rushed. Hear it again: You can't go too slow.

WHAT WE DO CHANGES US

Delaying romantic attachments (as we advocate) or *hurrying* the expression of romantic inclinations (as society encourages) represent more than a mere philosophical difference between two points of view. It is an enormous distinction that determines the whole foundation upon which a marriage will be built.

To some, *when* or *how* two people come to marry may not seem like a significant issue, as long as they are in love and relatively mature, with their heads set squarely on their shoulders. At first glance, that is an appealing position. Unfortunately, it is not as easy as that. We believe *when* a couple marries is hugely vital to developing the character strengths upon which best-friend marriages are based.

There are enormous potential negative consequences to hurrying romance, which may not be immediately obvious, but which cause many couples to construct their marriages on shaky foundations. Certainly some youthful marriages survive very happily. But the statistics reveal that the older the couple at the time of marriage, the lower the divorce rate.

The longer a young man and woman wait, therefore, the better their chances of enjoying a good marriage. There is a clear reason why.

Time allows a couple to see the changes life's circumstances make on the other person—how his or her character develops and deepens. C. S. Lewis says in one of his most famous quotes that every action or decision makes a mark on the centralmost part of who we are, changing us either into more godly and unselfish people, or making us a bit more selfish and determined to have our way.

We are constantly setting behavioral trends in motion within us by what we think and do, and especially by the choices we make. Every time I behave kindly, it makes kindness *easier* the next time. Every time I am mean or get angry, it makes *meanness* and *anger* easier the next time.

It's a fairly obvious truth. We tend to continue past behavior. Habits form on the basis of repeated actions and choices.

HURRYING ROMANCE SETS HIDDEN MINEFIELDS OF CHARACTER IN PLACE

What does all this have to do with delaying the expression of romantic inclinations? Everything!

We have strongly emphasized the fact that *yielding* to natural instincts of romantic emotions and affections from an early age, instead of *controlling* and setting aside those impulses for a later time, tends to weaken relationships with the opposite sex and ultimately weakens a person's capacity for an enduring marriage.

Why? Because the character weaknesses revealed by immodesty and lack of self-control are symptoms of character that will *perpetuate* themselves. They are likely to persist into the marriage years.

If during the teen years those habits are never recognized as destructive and never brought under control, those *same* traits will become part of the marriage equation. They may disappear underground for a time. But when the going eventually gets rough they reappear with heart-wrenching consequences—all because the character windows were ignored *before* marriage.

In every marriage there are hidden explosive minefields left over from the teen years—covered over now and perhaps long forgotten. But if these dormant habit patterns are unrecognized as weaknesses, so that they are never faced and overcome, these "mines" remain armed and deadly, and can be triggered unexpectedly by difficult circumstances.

Why do we repeatedly stress the importance of *controlling* what some consider the "natural" romantic inclinations of the teen years?

- so that the character strength of *self-control* becomes dominant rather than self-indulgence. In this way, the potential mine of self-indulgence is disarmed.
- so that *modesty* emerges in one's character rather than immodesty. Thus the potential mine of immodesty is disarmed.

- so that the virtue of *patience* rather than the vice of impatience and haste grows and bears fruit. Thus the potential mines of impatience and haste are disarmed.
- so that what you *know* dictates your actions more than what you feel. Thus the potential mine of relying on fleeting emotions is disarmed.
- so that *friendship* becomes the foundation for relationship, keeping romance for God's time. Thus the potential mine of straying romantic affections is disarmed.

All these healthy traits become ingrained in the character by practice, by habit, by repeated choices. They are qualities of virtue only *time* can grow. And the years prior to marriage (the teens and twenties) are life's most important years to set these positive trends and habits in motion.

If the teen years are spent instead *indulging* immodesty and emotions of romantic attraction, then self-control isn't the habit that forms. Self-gratification grows instead.

It is easy to say, "Oh, but I'll change *after* I'm married. *Then* I'll do all these things you're talking about."

Good luck! Walking down the aisle doesn't reverse five- or ten- or fifteen-year habits.

If you've habitually allowed romantic emotions to have sway for ten years, are you going to be an altogether different person five years into your marriage, when your wife has put on some weight and is tired and noncommunicative after a day of chasing after two or three toddlers—and a ravishing new secretary suddenly shows up at work and starts hanging around your desk for long periods of time?

If you were in the habit of indulging your romantic fancies over and over for several years, doing all you could to attract the opposite sex, do you really think such ingrained patterns will suddenly disappear forever? What will happen when your husband's business trips grow more frequent—and an incredibly cute guy at the gym starts showing you more attention than your husband has since your honeymoon? Will you now have the strength of character to ignore this man's smiles and charm, even though you spent years of your youth thinking about what men thought of you and working at making them notice you? It's doubtful.

Character traits remain. That's why you must set habits of modesty in motion early and learn to *control* and *squelch* and *suppress* your natural romantic tendencies. (We used those words purposely. The psychologists can have a field day with us if they want!)

If all through your teen years you *gave in* to whatever you felt and pursued whatever you *wanted* to do, how equipped will you now be to do just the opposite? How will you ever be able to exercise *self-control*, not only in male-female relationships but also with food and drink and drugs and finance, and the thousands of areas where marriage demands prudence, sacrifice, servanthood, commitment—the denial of what your flesh and natural instincts may desire?

All marriages go through periods of adversity. *All* marriages occasionally grow cold. *All* marriages struggle over life's stresses. What are you going to do when those tough times hit *your* future marriage—flirt with someone else like you did in high school? If romance is rushed early in life, these hidden minefields of character will eventually be exposed during the marriage years . . . and one by one begin to explode.

Habits persist. It takes *time* to develop the selfless character traits so necessary to building solid best-friend marriages.

Clearly by now you know this is a book about preparation for marriage that is based on a solid friendship. In pointing out the potential minefields that husbands and wives face, we don't want to leave you thinking that *preparation* and *friendship* will *alone* prove sufficient to overcome every obstacle. There are dozens of elements that contribute to a lifelong marriage. Romance and sex are indeed aspects of the God-given glue that holds a marriage together. You'll need financial prudence as well as common courtesy and politeness, child-rearing skills, savvy in dealing with parents and in-laws, spiritual and relational maturity, and many other skills. Your work has just begun! But what you do now *greatly* impacts your life later. Every problem you foresee and work to solve now will be one less you carry into marriage.

MARRIAGE BRINGS CHANGE AND RESPONSIBILITY

In addition to the positive traits of character that time helps produce, there are compelling, practical reasons why waiting to marry later and giving yourself ample time helps establish stronger and more permanent marriages.

Young men, are you able to support a wife? How prepared are you to be a caring and compassionate husband? Are you *ready* for fatherhood? How much training and counsel have you had preparing to act sacrificially and responsibly? What about traveling, ministry, and higher education? Once you are married, everything changes. Marriage ends many opportunities that will never come again.

Young ladies, are you ready to begin the daily routine of being a wife? Are you prepared for how suddenly cut off from the excitement of the single life newlywed brides often feel? Are you ready to be a mother? This part of the marriage picture comes sooner than you think. Do you know how tired young mothers get? How confined they feel to the home when the children are young?

What goals and dreams do you have that will be impossible to fulfill later on?

Do you want to go to college or graduate school? Have you wanted to visit relatives living in other parts of the country, go on a mission trip, learn a life skill, or see the world?

It isn't that delaying marriage only gives you the chance to do what you usually cannot do after you are married. Time and experience prepare you to be a better husband or wife by rounding out your character and giving you opportunity for the habits of maturity and self-control to become deeply rooted. Such maturity increases your capacity to shoulder responsibility wisely.

AN APPROXIMATE TIMETABLE TOWARD BEST-FRIEND MARRIAGES

We hesitate to write the following section because of the enormity of variables that affect an individual's readiness for marriage. But we offer the following ideas in the hope that some concise practicality will prove beneficial. These steps are not legalistic constructions but rather signposts of progression as young people move through youth toward best-friend marriages.

Some of you will look at the ages toward the end of this list and wonder, for example, why we would advocate some young people live at home at twenty-one and be unconcerned if they haven't found a spouse or a prospective one by twenty-three. We don't apologize. Breaking away from the family at age eighteen is a cultural, not a scriptural, pattern. Noah's grown sons helped him build the ark. Jesus remained at home until he was thirty. God intended families to grow together longer than does our culture, and both parents and young people are responsible for this error.

Early Adolescence

Ten–thirteen (in girls) and twelve–fifteen (in boys) are the ages when youth experience the first hormonal stirrings that bring about physical and emotional changes and lead to an increased attentiveness toward the opposite sex. These are years for looking toward parents, teachers, and other adult mentors or guardians for help in learning what these changes mean and how to cope with them, gaining a healthy sense of worth and personhood in a suddenly changing world. These are years for learning "who I am" and what it means to "grow up," not for aiming all these new feelings of interest and attraction toward girls or guys. This is a time for self-control training, for practice resisting the messages with which society and the media continually bombard you.

It is vital during these years that modesty be ingrained as a foundation for healthy boy-girl interaction. Parents and adult leaders need to stress this from the start.

Girls especially must choose clothing with care and be taught principles of decorum (modest blouses, dresses to the knee or longer, loose-fitting pants, one-piece swimsuits, no makeup or heavy cologne) according to each family's particular standards. Boys should learn good grooming—keeping themselves clean, the benefits of deodorant, shaving when necessary, neatly dressing in clean, appropriate clothing.

Teen Years

The ages of thirteen–seventeen are the years when teenage boys and girls interact together in a variety of social situations, relating in their roles as young adults with new sexual awareness and discerning what comprises true *friendship*. Teen guys and girls need to interact comfortably together in well-supervised mixed settings (sports, music groups, clubs, church groups, community service groups, 4-H).

The goal of these years is to develop healthy respect and graciousness toward the opposite sex. Modesty and decorum must continue as fundamental if this learning process is to reap a harvest in character. Dating should not be a part of the relational equation. This is the stage when family involvement and activities are extremely vital, making home and family the nuclei for most friendships.

Parents and other adult leaders must teach boys during these years to recognize flirting and to flee it at all costs. They must likewise teach girls to recognize forwardness in boys and to avoid friendships with boys trying to be cool and to impress. At the same time parents need to teach their young people the positive character qualities to look for and appreciate in the opposite sex.

It is not necessary or wholesome during these years, as some may suggest, to allow young people to find out these things for themselves, unsupervised and unsheltered. Such real-life learning can better occur within the safe environment of the home and in parentally controlled settings. In our family, we purposefully chose movies and videos to watch together when our sons were these ages so that we could observe and discuss the characters' traits of duplicity, coyness, and selfish motivation, while at the same time teach them to spot integrity, honesty, and selflessness.

Boys and girls must learn during these years to pick their friends not based on beauty, personality, and popularity but on character.

Late Teen Years

Ages eighteen–twenty bring a significant transition out of youth and into young adulthood. Friendships deepen and young men and women begin considering more carefully and thoughtfully what sort of lifetime partner-friend they are truly looking for. These remain years to be careful about pairing off or allowing too much interest in any single individual. It's a season for observation and reflection, not haste, for slowly refining the ability to recognize character in friends of both sexes. It is a time when personal spirituality often becomes a greater concern, when spiritual growth should be your aim.

These are years to pursue higher education without the burden of serious relationships. Involvement in a variety of groups opens doors to new friendships—through church, sports, music, family ministry. Families should continue to help provide settings for such interaction.

Don't be too anxious to move out from under the parental covering, because it is as important during these years as ever. Keep the partnership strong! Your relationship with your parents now becomes more and more *your* responsibility. *You* have to initiate the daily interaction.

Young Adults

At the ages of twenty-one–twenty-three, young adults begin to develop significant opposite-sex friendships in casual environments. Establish and develop family associations with friends of the opposite sex. Learn to interact in a variety of group and small-group situations. These can be special and exciting years of developing your faith in newly personal and independent ways along with other young Christians. Out of these activities will now begin to emerge some potential best-friend relationships.

By this stage, marriage will become a strong concern for some, yet remain a long way off for others. Continue to take relationships slowly. Focus in yet deeper ways on what kind of husband or wife you are looking for.

The partnership between young people and parents needs to remain strong. Spiritual priorities deepen. These can be wonderful years to develop rich grown-up relationships with parents—an opportunity that will soon be gone and will never come again in the same way. Make the most of it!

As lifetime best-friend relationships begin to develop, at some point, clearly, romance begins to bloom. We don't intend to convey an either-or sort of thing, as if *friendship* and *romance* were mutually exclusive. But because of the alarming trends in our society, we feel it is crucial to heavily emphasize the friendship part of the relationship, which is clearly our purpose. However, young people should not fear romance when God blesses their *best-friend friendship* with it. Romance *does* evolve in the friendships between men and women destined for a lifetime together, and romance will be all the deeper and more meaningful when it has grown and blossomed in the soil of friendship.

When does romance begin . . . when *should* it begin? It will be different for every couple. We do not suggest that true God-given affection and romantic emotions toward the one you will marry should be held in check until the day of marriage, when everything changes suddenly. (Obviously, the sexual component of the relationship is reserved for marriage alone.) The day will come when best friends contemplating a lifetime union will write letters to each other (we have a scrapbook full of them) and daydream about their beloved and want to share every moment with him or her. Being "in love" is not a sin—just be sure you reserve your true and deepest expressions of affection for the one God intends for you to marry.

Twenties

If you are in your twenties or even reached thirty and have not found a best friend with whom you want to spend the rest of your life, it still is worthwhile to go slowly, to postpone romance, continuing to establish friendships within groups, at school, or in family settings, and allow such relationships to flourish and deepen. This is a time to refine your long-range interests and life priorities, to take advantage of opportunities open to you because you are not yet completely on your own. These may include travel, service, missions, additional schooling.

The twenties are a time when faith grapples with weighty real-world, long-term decisions. Spiritual and vocational directions begin to clarify themselves. During these years relationships deepen and, for many, lead to marriage. In preparation, develop rich opposite-sex friendships, out of which eventually will come the one true friend who will become your best friend for life.

Thirties and Forties

Are you unmarried at thirty or forty, filled with that sinking feeling that perhaps you never will find a mate? Don't be dismayed or despair. God's *best* gifts are never rushed. Perhaps his best for you is to remain single. Perhaps you will marry when you are fifty.

We knew a wonderful Christian woman who remained single until the age of fifty. She met and married a widower who had grown children. We first met her after she and her husband had celebrated their silver wedding anniversary. Theirs was a very happy marriage.

Do not waste your single years pining after what *is not*. Rejoice for what *is*. Use these years to do what you could never do if you were married. Then prayerfully learn not merely to accept singleness as your "fate," but to give thanks to God for such an opportunity, deepening your relationship with him.

Is your life in his hands? Rejoice! He is in control.

PART III

DISCOVERING A BEST FRIEND WITH WHOM YOU WANT TO SHARE YOUR LIFE

Being with you is like walking on a very clear morning—definitely the sensation of belonging there.

—E. B. White

Jerry and Michelle

Jerry Smith was in his fifth year at the university when he met Michelle Jones, a junior music major. Because he had transferred schools and had changed his major, Jerry would not graduate until the end of the current year.

Jerry and Michelle first met at a beach picnic sponsored by an evangelical campus group in which Jerry was recognized as one of the leaders. Both were committed Christians and mature enough—Jerry twenty-three, Michelle twenty-one—to know what they wanted in a permanent relationship with someone of the opposite sex.

At the time, neither was looking for anything serious, however. Each had dated another individual for several years, and both had recently experienced emotional pain as a result. Neither Jerry nor Michelle, therefore, was interested in resuming a romantic entanglement.

Michelle played guitar and was strumming softly in the beachhouse when Jerry joined others in listening to her sing a ballad to her own accompaniment. Her voice and quiet countenance drew him.

An hour later the two found themselves strolling along the water's edge, chatting informally. By the end of the afternoon they each had discovered in the other a kindred spirit. Their conversation ranged from books and favorite authors to observations in other areas—music, politics, scriptures, goals, hobbies— with even a little theology thrown in.

They saw each other again the next week at the campus meeting and visited for a while afterward.

"You going to the breakfast Bible study tomorrow?" Jerry asked as they parted.

"I think so," replied Michelle. "Do you know where it is?"

"Yes. Would you like a ride? I'm taking several people out."

"Sure. I'm in the dorms."

"We'll be at the bottom of the hill at quarter till eight."

"See you then!"

They did see each other then, and the next day at church, and several times throughout the following week. Never had either of them hit it off so quickly with anyone. There seemed to be so much to talk about.

Days, weeks, then two months had passed. Visits on campus and at Bible study continued, as well as phone conversations. Both found their relationship an exciting breath of fresh air in the midst of their demanding school schedules.

One Saturday morning, after they'd been good friends about four months, Jerry tracked Michelle down at a Laundromat where she was catching up on studies and taking care of her wash.

"Hey, I've been looking all over for you!" he exclaimed. "My family's going to our lake cabin. My mom has already left, but my dad's about ready to leave. How about it?"

"I . . . I don't know, Jerry."

"Come on, we're going water-skiing. It'll be lots of fun!"

"But my wash isn't done."

"When could you be ready?"

"Well, not less than half an hour."

"My dad will wait."

"Better make that forty-five minutes."

"Great. We'll pick you up at the bottom of the hill."

"What do I need to bring?"

"A sleeping bag, a pillow, a swimsuit . . ." Jerry called back.

There were lots of people at the cabin. Several families and young people had come for the weekend to build a chimney for the new fireplace. The experience gave Michelle the chance to get to know Jerry's family better in a relaxed setting.

Neither Jerry nor Michelle considered the deepening of their friendship a romantic thing. Not only were both shy about physical display, they had high standards of modesty. Neither had been heavily involved physically in any other relationship.

The thought of being a "couple" hadn't really occurred to them. They were **friends** *. . . very good friends, who talked and shared about everything.*

Their friendship deepened after the weekend at the cabin. They visited churches together, went on long drives, continued to be active in many campus Bible studies and other Christian events, read the same books, and began to share their lives more and more completely.

Because Jerry and Michelle and their roommates were all Christians and involved in the same campus group, their get-togethers usually included six or eight or a dozen people. The group setting allowed a variety of relationships to develop, without romantic pairing off.

After six months of seeing each other every day or two, Jerry and Michelle were practically inseparable.

9 CHASTITY IS GOOD ... BUT IS IT ENOUGH?

Marriage is not just a "happily ever after" ending ... but a lifetime of "I choose to love you" beginnings.

—Matt Anderson

A great and devastating moral plague of sexual immorality and impurity has engulfed our society. Yet in the same way that red spots on the body are not measles—only its symptoms—neither are AIDS and other diseases and dysfunctions the plague. They are rather the result of homosexuality, drug use, and extramarital sex—of all kinds of immorality and sexual impurity. These are blotches on a generation's skin—shouting that an invisible disease has taken over and is gradually destroying us.

Christians and a few allies in society are attempting to rise up and save our culture and our nation. But because they largely are addressing symptoms rather than the disease itself, little is being accomplished toward a cure.

Good comes through these efforts. We thank God for victories large and small. Yet our culture, meanwhile, continues to succumb to the ravages of the disease.

It is time to ask if these efforts are sufficient.

THE PROBLEM IS GRAVE—INDIVIDUALLY AND CULTURALLY

During the previous two generations, promiscuity and its medical consequences were hushed subjects. There was little need to talk about the life and ·

death issues of today. Moreover, as we have said, a basic moral standard was in place that most people recognized. This standard did not necessarily make people any more moral, but most everyone recognized the standard. Right and wrong existed, and everyone knew what comprised each. People still *did* wrong, but at least they *knew* it was wrong. They realized they had chosen to break the rules. If a girl got pregnant in high school thirty years ago, everyone was shocked. Wrong—true moral *wrong*—had been done.

It is fundamentally different now. Society has crossed a moral chasm into a land where right and wrong no longer exist. Of course, right and wrong *do* still exist, but most people do not recognize them in any absolute way. If a young person today experiments with sex, few consider it a big deal.

It isn't that lines of morality have merely been blurred. In a sense, morality has always had its blurry edges. But now the lines have been erased altogether. And grievously, many Christian young people scarcely recognize to what extent their thinking has been influenced by this change.

Today if a girl gets pregnant in high school, she simply signs up for the home skills class, and then is provided free daycare for her child while she learns to be a mother and puts in her time at school so she can graduate with her friends. Oh yes, the government also gives her money. But the A-student who doesn't "fool around" gets no such handout.

A full-page feature story on high-school pregnancy recently appeared in our local newspaper. While it didn't exactly extol the virtues of out-of-wedlock pregnancy, it explained how teen mothers overcome their difficulties and keep up with their studies. Thirty years ago, no girl would have *dreamed* of letting the whole county know her disgrace. Now there are pictures and dozens of interviews and the whole thing is viewed as an experience for a young person to take a kind of hardworking pride in. No hint exists of *wrong* having been done.

Sexual promiscuity is not only no longer viewed as a sin, it is *rewarded*. Our nation's topsy-turvy social environment rewards irresponsibility, carelessness, and immorality. Hard work and success are penalized by the tax code. Financial irresponsibility is excused through bankruptcy laws. Family values are eroded by the welfare system. We only make these statements to illustrate how thoroughly the standards that for two centuries held our nation together have evaporated.

Many recognize the problem. But it is necessary to remind ourselves how upside down our cultural standards have become. We must not lose sight of how greatly these subtle and devastating trends of thinking influence us. Francis Schaeffer said that the shifts in outlook of recent years are not the changes of merely two, three, or four decades, but rather of *centuries*.

The greatest shifts in our culture, of course, exist in the areas of ethics and morality. Sadly, though we cling to the mists of their memory, they no longer exist with any effectiveness in the Church either. This heartbreaking truth reveals exactly why there is so much moral confusion among Christian young people. Parents, youth leaders, and pastors have allowed the tides of secularism to float beneath their feet undetected, replacing the rock of absolutes with the shifting sands of permissiveness.

The Church won't call anything *wrong* today any more than will the world. Homosexuality used to be wrong. Not anymore. Divorce used to be considered wrong, or at least unfortunate, in the rare instances when it occurred. Now divorce is so common that half the members of some congregations are divorced. Divorce is seen merely as an unpleasant option everyone must be prepared for. We have dear friends and relatives who are divorced. We love them and value them as individuals and friends. So we say the above implying no judgment, only to illustrate what a tremendous change has occurred.

Marriage vows have been modified in many churches. Rather than counter the permissive tide that has crept in, we accommodate ourselves to it. *Till death us do part* is now a bit tricky to include in the ceremony because people don't want to break the vows they say before God if they happen to want a divorce later. Two of our acquaintances were married with the words, "We promise to love, honor, and obey until further notice." No kidding!

The utter breakdown of moral standards in our society *and* in the Church, to the extent that a majority of people no longer consider extramarital sex and homosexuality sin, has resulted in the symptoms of plague we see all around us. People are sick and dying. A dreadful curse has invaded our society because of its disobedience.

THE WORLD'S UNBELIEVABLY RIDICULOUS RESPONSE

For years, though we all saw such trends, we weren't doing much about them. Society sat like a proverbial frog in the frying pan. Now, at last, a great deal *is* being done in a belated attempt to stem the epidemic of permissiveness and immorality. But the attempt is largely in vain.

The non-Christian world addresses the problem in the most idiotic of ways—handing out devices and free needles to slow the spread of disease, and investing millions in so-called "educational" (has ever a word been so misused as in this absurd context?) programs to inform the public how to have "safe" sex. That otherwise intelligent men and women can be so blind to this symptom-treating folly is almost beyond belief. "Try to rub off the splotches on your face," they say, "though we will do nothing to treat the disease itself."

Such lethal foolishness is all the worse when we *have* the cure before our very eyes! It is no farther away than 1 Corinthians 6:13: "The body is not meant for sexual immorality." Or Hebrews 12:16: "See that no one is sexually immoral." It's a pretty straightforward solution. Yet the world would rather rub away at the red spots and continue to let the plague engulf more and more of our culture, all the while elevating so-called "victims" of AIDS almost into martyrs! Truly, AIDS is not the sickness. And we recognize that some cases of AIDS are unrelated to immorality. The real disease is our society's perverse outlook.

Yet can we really expect a world consumed with its own permissive self-worship to do otherwise? Paul said that truth would seem as foolishness to ungodly minds, and this is a principle that does not change. As disturbing, therefore, as is the world's hapless response, we find ourselves even *more* concerned at the incomplete response of those who *should* be able to apprehend the true depths of the disease.

MERE "WAITING" STILL ONLY TREATS THE SYMPTOM

Campaigns across the country attempt to bring reason to the battle by calling for abstinence rather than protected promiscuity. We applaud these efforts in the right direction, for surely reserving sexual activity for marriage is indeed a scriptural remedy. Promise Keepers exhorts men to promise fidelity. A variety of groups promote premarital purity with covenant rings and necklaces. The "True Love Waits" campaign encourages young people to wait until marriage for sex.

Much of the impetus for these programs, however, has been the medical consequences of sexual promiscuity rather than discernment of the true and deeper problem of outlook. Now that the HIV virus and AIDS have become such terrors, people are starting to think more seriously about their actions . . . but with mere stopgap measures.

Is making a commitment to premarital purity and marital faithfulness a complete solution? Will this alone address the crying need for sound marriage foundations? We endorse the beginnings offered by these wonderful programs, but we encourage Christian leaders to go even further—to help young people build *strong* marriages, not merely avoid bad ones.

These attempts in the right direction in a sense still only rub at the spots—more effectively, perhaps, than the world's inane methods, but in their own way they continue to address only the symptoms. Even with greater attention paid to sexual purity, marriages will continue to crumble and the divorce rate will continue to climb.

Roots must be examined. Divorce is not *caused* by unchastity. Immorality is a symptom of a deeper problem. Divorce stems from a misunderstanding of what comprises love and commitment in the first place, a misunderstanding fed by an emphasis on romance above friendship in the years leading up to marriage.

What good will it do in the long run to say to our youth, "Reserve sex for marriage, but in the meantime go ahead and order your life according to society's 'romance mentality' "? What good will it do to save sex for marriage if we don't recognize the destructive trends dating sets in place for a permanent relationship?

We're communicating opposite messages. We're saying, "Express your youthful appetites—just don't do anything to satisfy them."

"We may encourage your romantic inclinations in youth group, but you have to promise not to let those inclinations go too far."

"Dress as you wish, flirt and flaunt, have your teen-romance fling . . . but 'save yourself' for marriage."

It's a sexually schizophrenic response. We're implying that it's perfectly okay to yield to all manner of lesser romantic impulses, just not *the big one*.

Purity before marriage is of course a good and healthy thing to emphasize. We must stress it for it is imperative. Chastity isn't only good, it is a fundamental *requirement* for a lasting marriage.

But it isn't enough. It won't stop the plague. It won't in itself create strong marriages. The tendencies of heart that lead to unchastity and impurity remain.

If the teen-romance mentality has never been curbed inwardly by maturing modesty of character—even by those young men and women who *do* keep their promise to stay sexually pure until marriage—we seriously doubt all these efforts will achieve much in the long run to slow the divorce rate. Even sexually pure marriages can be wrongly founded on romantic feelings, and many will wither as a result.

A SOLUTION REQUIRES A NEW FOUNDATION FOR MARRIAGE—FRIENDSHIP, NOT SEX

A preoccupation with sex, and all these problems that accompany it, stem from the teen years, when *control* of romantic interest is rarely emphasized. Is it any wonder that later in life *control* of sexual appetites is not perceived as a virtue or a necessity?

What's the solution?

Friendship rather than romance between future lovers. *Friendship* is the solution to the plague by the lifelong commitment that best friends make to each other. Purity is an obvious result of a commitment to a best-friend marriage. Without commitment, purity *alone* is not enough on which to build a lifetime marriage.

Do best friends need artificial means to remember to remain loyal to their friend? Does a best friend need to wear a ring to remember to be faithful and not to lie to his or her best friend? Does a best friend need to be daily reminded not to steal from or hurt his or her best friend?

Of course not. A best friend would not *think* of doing such hurtful things to his or her friend—would *never* consider being untrue. Our friends are that important to us!

When *causes* are addressed, most symptoms take care of themselves. When friendship is elevated as the first priority in a relationship, and romance is relegated to a secondary (and subsequent) role, the promise of fidelity and the pledge to purity become expected fruits of a strong relational foundation. We do not mean that promises and pledges and covenant talks should not be continued. We support them wholeheartedly.

Here's our point: When friendship is elevated above romance (not to the exclusion of romance, but laying the foundation for it, thus leading *to* romance at the proper time), then all these other healthy benefits of commitment and relationship will of themselves fall into place.

Chastity is good, but a godly heart and the devoted loyalty of a true friend are best of all. Being chaste alone, if one remains consumed with romantic interest, won't necessarily produce a well-founded relationship.

Being good is a good thing, but it isn't enough.

We are not writing this book merely to get young men and women to the altar in one piece, so they can proceed to self-destruct after that. It's not only watching people marry with purity we care about. If they have arrived at their wedding day down the road of romance, how can we ignore the fact that a young man and woman may *continue* to be consumed by society's diseased perspective?

We call for an end to the plague by establishing principles for building great and enduring and happy and wonderful marriages—best-friend marriages!

When the cause of the disease is addressed and eliminated (an unbalanced emphasis on the role of romance in relationship), and the heart is filled with healthy relationship instead (friendship, commitment, and selflessness), the red spots (impurity, immorality, and promiscuity) will disappear.

Then and only then will lifelong marriages result.

"Dear friends, I urge you, as aliens and strangers in the world, to abstain from sinful desires, which war against your soul. Live such good lives among the pagans that, though they accuse you of doing wrong, they may see your good deeds and glorify God . . ." (1 Peter 2:11–12).

Nothing else can quite compare
to the happiness we find,
In the comfort of a friendship
that's the warm and lasting kind.

—Emily Matthews

Best Friends

After knowing each other for eight months, Jerry and Michelle were often together several times a day. They had never been on what would pass for an official date, and about the most romantic thing Jerry ever did was open a door for Michelle occasionally—even then not every time.

Never had Michelle known a guy who made less an effort to impress young women. Jerry said he was shy and that he had never taken a girl out on a dinner-and-movie date all through high school. Not until he was a junior in college, in fact. Michelle could hardly believe him, because he was so much fun to be around—real and down-to-earth. And she certainly did not think of herself as a romantic. She had only dated one guy in her life. She was not the kind of girl that guys naturally thought about dating. She was always thought of more as "a friend." Being overweight hadn't helped, and she had reconciled herself to the fact that "just friends" was probably all she could ever expect in a relationship with a guy.

Yet Michelle had never felt close to anyone like she did Jerry. Both continued to be active in the leadership of their campus Christian student group. They taught a children's Sunday school class together and co-led a junior high school Bible study. Not a day went by that they didn't do something together, even if it was nothing more than walking to the library and sitting for a couple of hours in silence, studying at the same table. It just felt good to be together, even if they were doing nothing special.

One evening they found themselves walking alone through the streets of the coastal college town before parting for the night. It was dark. A thick fog descended and seemed to bring a greater quiet than usual.

Side by side they made their way through the residential district near the university campus, both realizing that something was gradually changing between them. Their usual nonstop conversation fell silent. Block after block scarcely a word was spoken.

Their hearts were full. They hardly knew what it was. It was Jerry who broke the silence.

"You know, these last few months have been just about the happiest of my life," he said softly. "I really thank God for bringing you along when he did."

The truth had begun to dawn on Michelle long before this moment that something was growing in **her** heart more than mere friendship, although it could not be separated from the fact that Jerry had become the best friend she had ever had. As a result, Jerry's words, when they came, caused her heart to leap into her throat.

She was also shy and had tried to reconcile herself to the possibility of not marrying. And Jerry was good looking and one of the school's top track stars, dynamic and outgoing. Whatever he said about being shy, Michelle thought couldn't be true. He was one of the most popular guys in the whole group. She had overheard other girls talking about him.

What would **he** ever see in someone like **her**? He could have any of a half-dozen girls in the group by just speaking to them.

So when Jerry said what he did, Michelle could no more have found her voice than jump over the moon.

They walked on a little farther in silence.

"I, uh . . . I don't really know what I'm trying to say," Jerry went on after a minute or two, beginning to fumble over his words. "I just want you to know . . . how, uh—well, how special this time has been, and . . . well, how special I think you are."

Michelle's heart was pounding. If only she could say something. But she couldn't!

"You've been . . . such a good friend—**more** than a friend. Well, no . . . I mean a really good friend. . . ." He paused momentarily.

"I guess what I've been trying to say is that you've been like a **best** friend to me and it's . . . it's just been great."

Michelle could scarcely contain the explosions going off in her brain.

Suddenly a horrible new thought collided with her bliss. All this might have a far different purpose than she'd imagined! What if he was getting ready to tell *her that he was going back to his old girlfriend . . . or that he'd found someone else!*

The silence this time lasted longer. Michelle's heart was now pounding for a different reason. She was afraid to utter a sound. They were walking alongside the deserted elementary school now. The fog continued to give an eerie quiet to their surroundings.

Jerry let out a deep sigh.

"This is really hard," he said at length. "I'm trying to tell you something, but I'm not sure what it is, really."

"Just . . . just tell me," Michelle said softly. She was ready for the worst.

"Okay, I'll try." Jerry sighed again. "Like I said, you've become my best friend. And I . . . well, I know we've never really talked much about the future—I mean you and me, and . . . you know, that's just not really been the kind of relationship we've had. We've been, you know . . . friends."

Michelle nodded in the darkness but again couldn't speak.

"I guess what I'm trying to say is that—well, I don't know what's in the future. I'm graduating this year. I'll have my teaching credential. I've been looking around wondering where I ought to apply for a job. But even with all that going on, and as many uncertainties as there are about those kinds of things, and not really knowing yet what I want to do with my life . . . well, even with all that, I just can't think of anything about the future without thinking of you as a part of it. I can't envision you ever not being part of my life."

Jerry stopped and exhaled from the effort of getting the words out.

Michelle's heart began to pound again.

"There, I've said it," he said. "That's what I wanted to say."

*The explosions in Michelle's brain gradually gave way to a deeper sense of happy contentment than she had ever known. It wasn't very clear exactly what Jerry **had** said. But for now it was enough that he wanted to be with her. He didn't want to be with anyone else.*

*He had called her his **best friend**!*

It was more than she'd allowed herself to dream possible.

Yes, for this one evening, it was enough!

Slowly Michelle slipped her hand through Jerry's arm, and they walked the rest of the way back to Michelle's apartment in silence. Now both their hearts were full to overflowing.

And at last they both knew with what.

10 COURTSHIP–AN OLD-FASHIONED IDEA WHOSE TIME MAY HAVE COME

*It's wonderful remembering the happiness
we've shared . . . and it's even more
wonderful looking forward to the
future with you.*

—*Sangamon*

Alarmed by the plague of immorality infecting our society, and recognizing that dating as commonly practiced is one of the worst ways to prepare young people for marriage, many families today are returning to a custom whose very name may sound old-fashioned to you—*courtship*.

What comes to mind when you hear this term? Two young people dressed in their Sunday-best sitting on stiff chairs in a farmhouse parlor in 1880? "Courtship" takes one's mind back about a hundred years.

You may be in for a surprise. Courtship actually is not old-fashioned at all. In fact, it's a hot new trend among Christian young people preparing for marriage. *Courtship* is a word rapidly finding its way back into the common vocabulary of the evangelical community.

Courtship offers many advantages over traditional dating. Families are much more involved in the process. Many safety features exist to make sound marriages more likely to occur. And we happen to think the whole idea pretty exciting. We've found ourselves wishing courtship had been in vogue back when *we* were getting to know each other!

COURTSHIP—AN OVERVIEW

In a nutshell, courtship refers to an official preengagement period during which a young man and woman get to know each other in a parentally supervised and family involved setting.

But courtship signifies far more than formal visitation. It truly represents a major step toward marriage, because the goal of courtship is engagement. That objective is the underlying and specific purpose of the relationship. True courtship is the period of time two young people spend getting to know each other well, not merely as a substitute for dating, as was the case with Hal and Laurel, but when two young people are seriously ready to think about marriage.

Josh Harris comments: "Courtship . . . has a definite planning destination: lifelong marriage. A person is ready to begin the process of courtship when he or she is ready to marry in the very near future. While you might date someone you have no long-term interest in, you only court a person who has shown promise of possessing character qualities you and your parents have established as important."[1]

By allowing for a preengagement "trial period" of visiting, talking, discussing, going on outings, and deepening friendship, courtship also allows for circumstances to arise that make it clear that marriage between the two young people is *not* God's will. A courtship period gives time for couples and families to know one another with deepening intimacy as both parents and young people think and pray about marriage, seeking God's will for all the relationships a potential marriage would solidify between the two families.

Obviously, there will be a thousand specific applications that vary from situation to situation. In general, however, the courtship process moves somewhat according to the following progression.[2]

After two young people have become acquainted—through whatever means—or, as we shall see, even *before* they are acquainted, and a young man finds himself prayerfully considering a certain young lady as the one he would like to make his wife (and certainly one component of this feeling may be a romantic attraction, though it also may not be), he calls on her father, or the

---

[1] *New Attitude* magazine. Vol. 1, No. 2, 1993, Gresham, Ore.

[2] What follows is not an overarching definition recognized historically as *the* universal pattern for courtship. As we shall see, there really is no such precise pattern. Every set of individuals will apply these broad principles differently, and teachers and scholars all no doubt emphasize particular aspects of the process. What we attempt here is to set down what seems a general consensus. We have harmonized approaches to courtship from three sources—biblical, historical/cultural, and contemporary practice. In other words, we have blended what we find done in the Bible (which usually was called "betrothal"), what was and is still being done in Amish communities, and the modern interpretation and practice of courtship as it is now being advocated by many within the Christian home school movement and the evangelical church.

individual responsible for that level of authority in her life. He asks permission to visit the young lady with potential engagement in mind, to get to know her better and thus to establish a deeper and potentially lifetime relationship—in other words, he asks to "court" his daughter. It's different from asking a man to marry his daughter, though it represents a major step exactly in that direction.

If a young lady's father is favorably disposed toward the young man, and no doubt in most cases they will already be friends, he will give his answer.

This is no time for hasty response. A wise father will reply, "I will pray earnestly about your request and let you know what I feel is the Lord's answer." After all, his daughter's future rests in the wisdom of his fatherly counsel. In the days (and perhaps weeks) to follow, the young lady's father must determine whether he considers the young man a responsible, mature, and spiritually worthy potential son-in-law and suitor to his daughter. Again, he is not granting permission to marry, but his answer certainly admits to that possibility in the future.

If a girl's parents do indeed feel that a certain young man would potentially make a worthy suitor for their daughter, they find out how she feels about him. If she is interested (and here again, romantic feelings may or may not be part of her response), then the young couple will begin officially courting under the oversight of the parents.

The whole process provides a protection for the young lady that is not available in the "dating game." This original discussion between the young man and the young woman's father (which hopefully will not be the first time they meet, but after relationship between them has had a chance to develop) becomes the critical "partnership" that enables courtship to work. If agreement is given in time, the young man's parents and both entire families become involved in the dynamics of the process. But it is the understanding, communication, trust, and respect that develop between a young man and the father of his potential bride that becomes the key element in all prayers and decisions concerning the couple's future.

A young lady's parents now assume a vigorous role in the courtship period, inviting the young man to their home for meals and other family activities. The two young people will not spend time alone to begin with. At the same time the partnership widens to encompass both families, with the young lady and her family invited to spend time with the young man's family.

Throughout the courtship period both families will provide settings for deepening relationship between the two young people. Shared outings, short trips, conferences, church meetings, spending time at each other's home—helping with yard work, watching sporting events, playing games, watching videos, washing the car. There are a thousand family-related activities that will make this a fun and rich time for all. The role of the parents is not as mere "chaperones," though that is involved, but of true marriage-mentors. It is their role to "disciple" the young people into preparation and readiness for marriage—spiritually, financially, relationally, etc. This discipling role will hopefully involve both sets of parents. In some cases it might be the father of the young man who takes the more active role, perhaps in conjunction with the young woman's parents. A girl's father may not be interested in mentoring the two young people, in which case they could agree to go to the young man's father for more specific discipleship. Situations will vary tremendously.

The courtship can be broken off at any time if either of the two young people strongly come to sense discomfort or certainty that the other isn't the one they want to make their husband or wife. Likewise, either set of parents may for whatever reason come to feel the courtship should end. Communication and mutual respect between everyone concerned will make these decisions easier. Prayer, time, and trust are key elements in the courtship period.

How long a courtship lasts is entirely an individual matter subject to the Lord's leading. Some advocate a short courtship period. As you will see when you get to our proposal in Part 4 of this book, we think a courtship of a year or more is best.

In time there should begin to exist a unanimity and consensus among those involved that the proposed marriage *is* indeed the Lord's will . . . or it is *not*. If the latter, the courtship will graciously be brought to an end. If the former, at some point the young man will go to the girl's father once again to formally ask for his daughter's hand, requesting permission to ask her to marry him. If permission is given, the young man finds an opportunity to propose to the young lady herself. If she is hesitant or feels that this is not the man she wants to marry, then of course the courtship will be discontinued.

If she is happy about the offer and accepts it, the couple thereby becomes engaged and begins making serious plans for the wedding and their life together. By this point, the best-friend relationship will no doubt have blossomed into a rich and biblically based best-friend romance.

One of the great benefits of courtship is that it minimizes as much as is humanly possible the broken-heart syndrome so many young people experience. A couple in this environment is able to have fun and get to know each other in a comfortable family setting without either the pain often associated with the unsteadiness of "going together" or the uncertainty of flitting from one relationship to another without parental guidance. This isn't a frivolous dating time, but an honest search to know if this is the person God has chosen for you.

Paul Jehle comments: "Dating concentrates on nonserious, passionate involvement, often ending in separation, rejection, and heartache; only to be repeated again and again. Courtship is the stage when God is really drawing a man and a woman together seriously. Thus, to test, prove, and confirm their feelings they bring it to court—they court—in order to fully establish the truth of God's call. The court is where at least two or three witnesses will confirm that indeed God is calling them or is not calling them to be married for life. Since both are serious, the witnesses can never injure them, only help them."[3]

Three biblical examples come to mind, each different from the others: Isaac and Rebekah, Jacob and Rachel, and Joseph and Mary.

Paul Jehle makes the story of Isaac and Rebekah the cornerstone for his particular perspective on the courtship process, in which ministry and service play a key role in the pre-courtship stages. The courtship itself originates not (as we have suggested) with the young man and the father of the bride, but rather with the father of the *groom* (Abraham) seeking a wife for his son (Isaac). This difference points out the great variation of interpretation and practice. Jehle sees in this story a playing out of the larger relationship between man and God—Abraham representing God the Father, Isaac as Christ the Son, and Rebekah the bride or the Church—and his account is well worth reading.[4] Clearly, both fathers can and, if possible, *should* be involved in the courtship discipling process.

In Jacob and Rachel's case the courtship again was initiated by the father of the *young man*. Isaac told Jacob exactly what to do, leaving the specific choice to him. And because Jacob *obeyed his father* in this marriage command, God blessed him. "So Isaac called for Jacob and blessed him and commanded him: 'Do not marry a Canaanite woman. Go at once to Paddan Aram, to the house of your mother's father Bethuel. Take a wife for yourself there, from among the daughters of Laban, your mother's brother. May God Almighty bless you and make you fruitful . . .'" (Genesis 28:1–3).

In the case of Mary and Joseph we know nothing about how the betrothal came to be, because we are told nothing about the parents or prior relationships that brought the father and mother of Jesus together. Clearly, where parental involvement is foundational courtship can be made to work, whether it initiates with a parent or one of the young people.

Many families have committed themselves to the practice of courtship. Especially common among home school families, this new (or is it old!) approach to marriage is an effort to ensure lifelong, fulfilling marriages.

COURTSHIP—A TRUE-LIFE STORY

We quote the following story about the courtship process.

This is a true-life account still in progress. There have been questions and

---

[3]*Dating vs. Courtship*, p. 85. Plymouth Rock Foundation, Fisk Mill, Marlborough, N.H.
[4]*Dating vs. Courtship*, chapter 7.

uncertainties, even heartaches. A previous marriage is part of the scenario. They have had to work hard to prayerfully adapt the principles to fit their own particular situation—as will each of you reading this. But because the young people trusted the young lady's parents and desired full parental involvement, they have made it work.

We now introduce you to Howard Grant, who will tell you how he and his family implemented these principles.

> My wife of thirty-one years, Elizabeth, and I have five children, and have home schooled them all. We have generally followed Bill Gothard's ATIA program. Our oldest two, Jennifer, twenty-eight, and Elaine, twenty-seven, are unmarried as of this writing. Both, however, are presently involved in courtship. We have had *two* courtships in progress during the past year, which has made life interesting, to say the least!
>
> This has obviously been from my perspective, as a father presiding over two courtships that turned out very differently. I had the hard job. A father carries the tough part of any courtship. He has to bear the brunt of the difficult decisions.
>
> We have attended Basic Youth Conflicts many times and began thinking of courtship because it was originally Jennifer's desire to prepare for marriage in this manner, with me as her father very much involved. When the girls were eighteen, each of them signed Bill Gothard's Courtship Covenant between father and daughter, making the commitment to us as their parents: "I will keep myself pure for my husband. I will obtain your blessing on my courtship. I will wait for your full release before entering into marriage." On my part, I also signed the covenant, in which I made the following commitment: "I will protect you from unqualified men. I will teach you God's principles of life. I will pray for you and for God's choice of your life partner."[5]
>
> Let me say briefly that my belief in a father's authority is not because I have any desire to be a tyrant or to control anyone else's life. I am not my family's umbrella of protection because I choose to be, but because God asked me to be. I am the leader of my home because God asked me to be. My wife is in submission to me because God asked her to be. She is spiritually equal with me, but she is not to be the leader. God designated that I should do that. That being the case, I have tried to

---

[5]Such a covenant agreement exists between fathers and sons as well, in which the father makes this commitment: "I will protect you from strange women. I will teach you God's principles of life. I will pray for you and for God's choice for your life partner." The son reciprocates by promising his father: "I will keep myself pure for my wife. I will obtain your blessing on my courtship. I will wait for your full release before entering into marriage." *Sons* need to be as equally attentive to their father's leadership as daughters.

occupy that role diligently and responsibly.

Jennifer and Elaine were behind us 100 percent in the decision to keep any and all marriage decisions under the umbrella of my authority as their father. That was their *choice*. As the years went by, however, both began gradually to assume they probably would not marry. They never had a date, never had a boyfriend. As all the youth group experiences we have been part of were horrible—priorities and relationships promoted between young people that we felt were unhealthy—neither girl was involved in social settings where they met very many young men.

Obediently the girls waited, but nothing happened. It was very natural for them eventually to think it probably never would. They are intelligent, capable young women. By their mid-twenties they were carrying out a high level of responsibility in our family business. Jennifer, in fact, started her own business. But not being part of the dating scene, there just weren't opportunities for friendships with young men coming their way. They had saved dishes and linens in hope chests, but eventually began to say to themselves, "I don't need marriage. It's never going to happen anyway."

When I say they both began to despair of marrying, it wasn't that there was a desire on their parts to go back on their pledges. They still believed wholeheartedly in courtship. They did not want to become engaged any other way. They trusted Elizabeth and me completely and left matters in our hands. They just assumed it would never happen. In the meantime, therefore, they began to travel and take their jobs more seriously, and otherwise to move forward in life without moping about wishing a husband would come along.

Elaine was the first to become involved with a potential suitor.

A young man named Doug, whom she had met some months before at a college Bible study, asked her out for a date.

Elaine's response was, "You'll have to talk to my father."

So Doug and I went out to breakfast together. I explained our family's commitment to the idea of courtship. He didn't seem overly shocked by the idea, though I don't know how familiar he was with the specifics of how courtship worked. We got together a couple more times, then had him over for dinner. I interviewed him about his spiritual background, and everything seemed pretty much all right.

Finally I gave him my permission to court Elaine, though now I see I really didn't know him well enough at that point to make such a decision. I should have known a lot more about him before allowing the courtship to begin. But for as many years as we'd been planning on courtship, in a sense when we began with Doug, it was courtship by the seat of our pants. I hadn't really thought specifically about what I would *do* when the time actually came. When it did come, I allowed it to move too quickly and automatically to the courtship level.

Doug was a likable young man of thirty-three. You couldn't meet him without being drawn to him right off. He possessed what appeared to be deep spiritual convictions. He had been to Bible college and was a recognized leader in the local college-age Bible study group. He had dated other girls in the past, but even at his age had never kissed a girl. That spoke to me about how seriously he took the idea of marriage and his desire to fully reserve his romantic affections for his future wife. Both Elizabeth and I were favorably impressed. We felt Doug to be a young man we could envision as a son-in-law. Therefore, he began to call at the house and come over regularly for dinner as his and Elaine's courtship got underway.

Elaine's experience suddenly opened her sister Jennifer's eyes anew to the possibility that there *were* young men out there who were open to courtship after all. All at once marriage reentered her mind as a possibility.

In a talk with her around this same time, I took the opportunity to bluntly say some hard things about certain areas of her personal and spiritual life that needed to come into line before God could bless her.

"Jennifer," I said, "there are some areas in your life where you are not in submission to me as your father. If you want God to bring a husband into your life, you're going to have to learn to submit to *me* in a greater way first. I feel one of the primary reasons the Lord has not brought a young man into your life is that you simply are not ready for marriage. You are still resisting my authority as your father. If you'll humble yourself before the Lord, and submit to your father in these areas we have been talking about, and call on the Lord and ask him to bring the man into your life that he wants you to marry, he'll do it. It's time for you to do this."

Jennifer was twenty-seven then, and no doubt many people would think me out of line for being so bold and authoritative. After all, wasn't she a grown woman? What right did I have to speak so to her? That is the world's view. But as her father, I still took my role as her head seriously and prayerfully. Saying such things didn't make me a dictator, it only meant that was the role I was supposed to occupy in her life.

Rather than resisting my words, Jennifer acknowledged that I was right. She immediately began prayerfully to make a change in her attitude. She started praying and fasting, got back into God's Word, and began attending a Precepts Bible Study. There was a real shift in her attitude toward everyone in the family.

I believe it is no accident that only about a month later, things began to happen for her, just as they had a short time earlier for her sister.

By this time Doug had been courting Elaine several months. I was beginning to see a few things that concerned me. Not deep character problems, for as I said he was a man of virtue and spiritual integrity. But though he had a good paying job, there were too many loose financial ends in his life—mortgages and loans and unfinished projects. Something was amiss. These observations made me realize I had perhaps been a little hasty in giving permission for him to court Elaine. So when Marc came along and expressed an interest in Jennifer, I responded much differently and really put him through the third degree before giving my permission!

None of us knew Marc, though he had started coming to our church a month earlier. He was a young widower with a three-year-old son. One of his Christian friends at work told him, "I know the most perfect Christian young lady. In fact, it has always troubled me that she isn't married, because she would make the most wonderful wife. She's the Sunday school superintendent at our church, and I've worked with her." The friend gave him Jennifer's name.

Marc called and asked Jennifer if she would like to go to lunch. As I was out of town at the time, Jennifer said she would call him back. I had the chance to meet Marc personally at church the following Sunday, and the following day he called and asked my permission to take Jennifer out. I told him I would like to talk with him first. We agreed to go to breakfast together. I basically explained our position and gave him one of Bill Gothard's booklets on courtship. Being a quiet sort of young man, though he knew nothing about courtship and had no idea what he was getting himself into, Marc took everything I said in stride.

After perhaps being too lax with Doug, when Marc and I began to get together I suppose I overreacted in the opposite direction. I got right in his face and bombarded him with questions! I'm actually a little surprised he didn't just get up and leave right then! He didn't know Jennifer yet. And if she had such a firebrand for a father with such crazy ideas about marriage, maybe he didn't *want* to know her!

But he didn't leave. Marc stuck it out, quietly answered my questions, and we agreed to meet again. He went home and called the friend he'd been praying with and told him what had happened. His friend, unknown to Marc, was very familiar with courtship and reacted to the news with enthusiasm.

"You're going to have a great time," he said. "This is going to be an adventure!"

At the same time, Marc's former parents-in-law, who were also home educators, encouraged him, helping him to understand what he might expect if he got involved in a courtship.

Marc came over to the house the following week and met Elizabeth for the first time. It so happened that Jennifer was out of town for the next four weekends, during which time he came over every Saturday for dinner. Thus Elizabeth and I had the opportunity to become fairly well acquainted with Marc before he and Jennifer even met.

I think this is one of the key distinctions between the two courtships—in the one case Elaine knew Doug and had already, in a sense, "fallen for him" before we entered the picture. In the other case, Elizabeth and I had a deepening relationship with Marc *before* Jennifer entered the picture. I think this is a significant difference. The order of parental involvement right from the beginning was in place with Marc, and not with Doug. This would have consequences in both courtships.

Elizabeth and I talked with Marc and questioned him, as I said, pretty strongly. I wanted to know what kind of a person he was, how much money he made, where he was spiritually, and what he was doing with his life.

Marc was certainly not the sort of potential groom we had ever expected!

He had been married for eleven years and had a three-year-old son, Kevin. His wife had recently committed suicide due to lifelong medical and depression problems, combined with a dreadful mismedication at the hospital. So I felt there was a great deal about this young man of thirty-two that I needed to find out. Suicide and depression of a spouse usually have causes that involve the other partner, and I really got into his face about it. If a wife commits suicide, to some degree it seemed to me there must have been some kind of marital problem. If I was going to consider giving my daughter's hand in marriage, I had to find out all I could. Marc's parents were also divorced and remarried, making his family background obviously much different than Jennifer's. So there were *many* questions, and as I said, I was pretty blunt. But it was my daughter's future, and I wasn't about to take any chances.

At first, given Marc's background, we weren't sure whether to allow a relationship to develop. It wasn't what we had envisioned. Jennifer had never so much as been on a date, and now suddenly we had to think through the ramifications of her becoming an instant stepmother to a little boy!

I interviewed Marc's boss and some pastors and youth pastors who knew him well. I talked to the parents of his previous wife. I wanted to know if this man had done *everything* possible for his wife.

I left no stone unturned to see if I could find signs of a lack of commitment. I investigated Marc *far* more thoroughly than I had Doug.

But Marc received glowing recommendations from almost every individual I talked to. Everyone spoke highly of him. And the fact that he was in close spiritual counsel with the parents of his deceased wife said a great deal about that relationship and their love for him.

In the end, after seeing that Jennifer was interested, I gave Marc my permission to court Jennifer. And he bought into the whole idea of courtship all the way.

Thus we found ourselves suddenly involved in two courtships at the same time!

Marc and Doug could not have been more opposite. Doug was outgoing, full of spunk and fun, and liked to be the center of attention. Marc was quiet and reserved and was content to sit back and listen. In both instances, the girls were very involved at every step. We talked about everything. I asked, "Do you like this young man . . . what do you think . . . do you want to continue with it?"

There were two primary areas in which I established various rules for both courtships.

Elizabeth and I set certain behavioral guidelines:

The young people were not permitted to be alone together. Later on, if they were going someplace less than fifteen minutes away, they were permitted to drive to and from supervised activities alone.

At first the only "get-togethers" involved Marc or Doug coming to our house for dinner, or church activities.

There were to be no letters or phone calls, which we considered the same as a "date" according to common custom—exchanges that build a private relationship. All aspects of the relationship were to include Elizabeth and me. In a sense, the whole courtship hinged on this principle—a full agreement that there must not be a "private" relationship built up. Without such an understanding, it's not a true courtship. That's why an understanding about letters and phone calls is so important, because for most people these things become key building blocks toward privacy.

We observed a nine-thirty curfew, ten on weekends. Of course in time they would occasionally stay up later, but only when they were properly chaperoned. There were no visits Sunday evening after church, a time reserved for our family alone.

All activities were chaperoned, by one of us, one of the other parents, by one of the other children, by a friend, or involved some church or group activity. This was not a matter of my not trusting them, but of guarding and maintaining my two daughters' good names. I could have trusted Jennifer and Marc in particular almost immediately.

Finally, there was to be no physical contact whatever. When we told Marc about this, he found it a great relief. It took a lot of pressure off, he said. He found the guidelines of courtship to be wise rather than constricting and went along with our every wish graciously.

You must understand that I imposed none of these rules by my iron will, so to speak. All along I said to both Jennifer and Elaine that I would go along with *their* wishes. At any time, they could bolt from under my authority. Either of the two couples could have gone off and gotten married any time they wanted to. They were all adults. But this was something my daughters *wanted* to do, and thus willingly submitted to . . . for *their* best, not mine. Some of what I've said makes it sound as though I forced the rules and regulations and guidelines upon them. But at every step, it was *their* choice. As long as it was their wish to court, I would exercise my role in it to the best of my ability. I therefore tried faithfully to carry out my function as the father and authority in the situation—by providing wise and protective oversight.

They were the ones to actually carry the courtship. If either of them had at some point decided they wanted to date in an unsupervised setting, for example, or bring a physical component into the relationship, I would not have "forbid" it and chained them down. I would have simply said, "This violates your agreement. By so doing you will be taking yourself out from under the umbrella of my fatherhood. I cannot cover you spiritually if you do this. But you are certainly free to do whatever you want. It may be contrary to my will. But you are free to do what you want to do."

In addition to the "rules" of the courtship, so to speak, I established certain discipleship requirements for both young men in which they would be responsible to me. When a young man enters into a courtship relationship with the father of a young woman, the relationship they are entering into is really one of discipleship. A father is *discipling* a young man in the ways of God. He has an obligation to counsel and disciple the young man through the experience and wisdom he has gained in life. This does not necessarily make him better or more "spiritual"—though age does tend toward wisdom in the same way that youth tends toward folly—it just indicates the respective roles in which they stand to one another.

Even if a man is not a Christian, this sort of mentoring can still take place. I believe young people can apply the principles of courtship to their lives even when a father doesn't know any of this. That's not a prerequisite. Even if a father isn't a Christian, he still has a love for his son or daughter. There is still a level of honor and respect the young people can demonstrate by saying, "What guidelines will you set up for us toward a successful marriage?"

When such a request and responsibility are placed on a father—once he has to *do* something, and once that level of honor is extended toward him—most fathers will rise to the occasion. Such oversight is part of the God-given fatherly role, and I believe is as natural, though subverted by our society, as is the motherly role of women.

Courtship in our view was more than an alternative to dating. We truly saw it as a time for these young men to submit to me as their head, to learn from me, to be discipled in spiritual principles in preparation for marriage. Their willingness and responsiveness would reveal a great deal about their character, and about the future husbands they would make. Before giving my daughters' hands in marriage, I wanted to make sure these young men were mature, humble, financially responsible, and well-grounded in the spiritual principles of wisdom that would make them wise and loving fathers and husbands.

I would never imply that what we did represents some standard for courtship. Every father will have certain things he will emphasize more or less than other men. For me, financial freedom is an extremely important principle. Therefore, any son-in-law of mine will be a man who agrees with me in this area and has undergone financial discipleship. I do not say all men will place the same value on that. Other fathers will bring principles and truths into the courtships of *their* sons and daughters that probably never entered my mind. God's leading in every family and for every young couple will be distinctive.

I called my particular assignments for Doug and Marc their "projects." In both young men I saw things that concerned me about the future marriage. I was concerned particularly about Doug's finances and his ability to carry work through to the end. He had a good paying job, yet financially his life seemed a mess. I was also concerned about his relationship with his own parents. These things would affect what sort of husband he would be. I needed to make sure of his maturity in these areas before I gave him Elaine's hand.

Marc was in the middle of remodeling his house, and of course was still suffering from the death of his first wife, Kate. These were factors, too, which would affect Jennifer if they were to marry. I had to guard and protect my daughter emotionally, as well as make sure Marc was ready for such a major change.

As I've already explained, since I was pretty lax at the beginning, Doug really came in for an easier time of it to begin with. His only projects were to attend the Basic Life Principles seminar and to go through the twenty-week Financial Freedom Seminar under my leadership, and then work toward becoming financially free.

Marc's projects, on the other hand, were more extensive: Attend the Basic Life Principles seminar, go through the Financial Freedom Seminar with Elizabeth and me, work toward becoming financially free, write out the roles of husband and wife and discuss it in depth with us, write out his philosophy of child-rearing, and complete the remodeling of his house and prepare the home for a new wife.

The first time Marc came over for dinner when Jennifer was there, neither said more than a word or two to each other. Marc's three-year-old son, Kevin, sat and stared at Jennifer until it totally unnerved her!

The next time he came they began to talk a little more. Very soon we began the Financial Freedom course. They both had a workbook and were curious about what were each other's responses. They discovered that many of their answers were similar, and as that happened a chemistry began to develop between them.

Actually it didn't take long at all before they began to like each other a lot. A friendship developed quickly, and a oneness of spirit was not far behind. Marc and Jennifer's friendship grew over the months through such activities as walking together in the rain, on the beach, or in the park. There were bicycle rides, carriage rides, carnivals, family camping trips, and many other family activities, all chaperoned, a fact for which they were grateful, not resentful.

They were behind the courtship program 100 percent. Thus they did not chafe under the supervision rule, but thrived and rejoiced in it. Within a few months Marc was sending Jennifer chocolates and flowers, and leaving little notes at the house for her. As the weeks passed, they genuinely fell in love, and as a parent, it was a wonderful thing to watch unfold.

As time went on, the two guys spent a great deal of time at our home on weekends, especially on Sunday afternoons. And we began to work on the Financial Freedom Seminar with our whole family, including both sets of young people. In terms of discipling Marc and Doug, I never wanted to push. I established the guidelines, but in a sense left it to the guys to initiate meetings with me. I wasn't going to force my ideas or my mentoring upon them. They had to want it enough to seek it. In a sense, *they* each established the tone and schedule for their *own* discipleship.

Marc took to both the Basic Life and the Financial Freedom seminars like a duck to water. He worked hard at them, saw the wisdom and truth in them, and immediately began taking steps to implement them in his life the minute his eyes were opened to them. The minute he was finished with anything we had been working on, he called or came over to see me and said, "Okay, Howard, I'm done with that—

what's next!" I was pleased to see that he had a heart that was open to the Lord. When he saw a truth in God's Word, he was immediately willing to walk in it. Doug, on the other hand, though at first agreeable to the idea of being discipled, rarely sought me out with that same energetic enthusiasm.

After Jennifer and Marc had been courting about two months, we took a week trip, our whole family, both girls, and Doug and Marc, to attend the Basic Life Institutes seminar. Being in such a close-packed situation like that cannot help but reveal character in a deeper way than in the artificial setting of coming over for dinner.

Elizabeth and I continued to get to know the two young men better and better. We saw Marc, for instance, sitting attentively and quietly through the sessions making an effort to absorb as much as he could. Though he was a grown man, on his own, with a good job, and who well knew the responsibilities of marriage and fatherhood, he took no offense at being in a subordinate, learner's role. He eagerly entered into the process of being discipled. Doug, on the other hand, though he talked a lot about the seminar, did not seem to take it as seriously. He went so far as to poke fun at Marc's being so serious all the time, saying such things as, "I'm getting so much out of this, but I don't think Marc's getting anything out of it." In reality, I suspect just the opposite was the case.

This and another family trip opened our eyes to the fact that earlier we hadn't seen all there was to Doug. At first he seemed very spiritually mature. He knew all the principles. There was a lot of spiritual talk. But after a while we didn't see much to back up the words. He bickered with our seven-year-old, getting down on his level and that of the other children, relating to them not as an adult but as a child himself. By the end of these two trips, though he had previously been Mr. Personality, all the children but Elaine were sick of him.

After about six months we gradually began to have reservations whether he was mature enough to handle the rigors of marriage.

I happen to believe when a man says he wants to court a young lady, it implies that he has the financial wherewithal to support not only a wife, but a family as well. I place great emphasis on financial stability. Not wealth, but the wherewithal to put food on the table, clothes on the back, and a roof over the head. If a young man doesn't have this, he has no business asking a man to court his daughter.

I didn't ask Doug enough questions. Despite a good job, I learned that without taking renters into his house, he couldn't meet his payments. That didn't speak well to me of the financial ordering of his life. His house was mortgaged, he had a loan out to his folks, loans on credit cards, then a second mortgage on the house. All this time he was trying to work on his house, he had unfinished projects at his father's house. He was deeply in debt and behind in all these projects. It just gradually became apparent that something was missing with respect to financial responsibility.

About the time we were realizing some of these things, Doug confided in Elizabeth and me that he wasn't sure he was ready for marriage, but was reluctant to break Elaine's heart. He seemed unsure of himself, unsure of his readiness for such a commitment, unsure whether he even wanted to get married at all. That's when we realized he didn't have a clue what we were about, what we were trying to do. Yet Elaine remained obviously in love with him.

In addition to these warning signals, Elaine gradually began to change as a result of Doug's influence . . . and not for the better. People at church were saying, "What's wrong with Elaine?" when at the same time they were watching Jennifer and Marc grow more radiantly in love.

It is obvious from what I am saying that Elizabeth and I were having major second thoughts about Doug. Eventually Elizabeth felt it was time to put the cards on the table.

"Elaine," she said, "I've got to tell you what I see. If you insist on marrying this man, you're going to become a nag, because he never finishes anything. You're going to be after him all the time. He sleeps through church, for heaven's sake! You don't need me to tell you that—you sit right next to him. Doesn't that tell you anything? Do you want to marry a man who's going to come home every night and fall asleep on the couch? You're never going to get to do anything. It would be embarrassing to me if my husband slept through church. If a man in his early thirties, with no wife and no children, can't stay awake for a sermon, what's he going to be like ten years from now? Elaine, don't you see—Doug is undependable, has financial problems, and is a bore."

But nothing we said caused her to see it any more clearly. We said, "Elaine, make a list of all Doug's good qualities and his negative ones."

She agreed and actually was very honest in her assessment. Then we asked her to write down for us how she intended to deal with these things as Doug's wife. We tried to make her aware of these character qualities, which by now were obvious to everyone but her. By this time, Doug had pretty much ceased to communicate with me at all.

Still there had been no progress on Doug's house, no progress at becoming financially free. He was not doing a number of the things I'd asked him to do, nor was he coming to talk with me about them. Gradually the thing was breaking down as subtly he tried to separate Elaine from the rest of the family, communicating with everyone but me, and trying to talk to Elaine privately if he could manage it. He had an excuse for everything. He couldn't do this because . . . he couldn't do that because. . . . He was feeding Elaine his various lines of defense, gaining her support, and in a sense making Elaine his advocate with us.

According to the rules of courtship, however, he should have been communicating with us, which he was not. A division had clearly set in, with Elaine right in the middle of it. These kinds of discussions were not supposed to be taking place between them. What it boiled down to is that he was going behind my back to gain my daughter's sympathy, and thus win her as his wife in a way that squeezed me out of the central role.

I do not say it was his *intent* to deceive me. I believe Doug's motives were true. I don't doubt that he loved Elaine. But once we got into the real nitty-gritty of having to make *changes* in his life and do things *differently* than he'd been accustomed to, I don't think he took the courtship seriously, or at least as seriously as the rest of us did.

Subconsciously, perhaps he thought he could slide by without our discerning these weaknesses of character, and without having to really face them and deal with them. I'm not sure he knew they existed himself. When I did begin to discern them and began pointing them out, he reacted in self-defense rather than humility. The more seriously I took my mentoring role, the more his weaknesses became exposed. He quit talking to me at all. Elaine defended him, telling us everything he was doing, bewildered that we couldn't see his good intentions. She simply never saw, nor wanted to see, Doug's character deficiencies.

All this time . . . there was Marc, doing everything properly, graciously, and *grateful* to us for our role in his life.

Much more had been required of him. Yet he was growing cheerfully through it and did everything gladly. He sold an expensive sports car, sold some property, did all kinds of things to enable himself finally to pay off the mortgage on his house, and became financially free.

But I never got that far with Doug. It broke down. He quit seeing me, quit calling me to report on his progress. He never got past the first things, while all the time Marc was moving steadily and persistently through a much larger list of requirements.

Elizabeth told Elaine, "Doug is getting far too comfortable here. He comes over every weekend and eats and sleeps on the couch, and quite truthfully, I'm getting tired of it. He's not instituting activities. He just comes to eat and sleep. He's not making progress, not doing the projects your father has set up for him, still doing very little on his house."

At last Doug came to me and said he wanted to take steps to move toward engagement. I said there was still a long way to go, and that he hadn't yet done most of the things I'd asked of him.

He agreed to make more of an effort. We talked and I listed some things he needed to start doing, especially in the way of his finances and building back his relationship with his parents. I also told him I wanted him to start keeping a spiritual journal and to write up a thorough plan of how he intended to get his finances in line.

"Howard," he replied, "how many hoops do you want me to jump through before you let me marry Elaine!"

The courtship had been going nearly a year, and by this point I did not see a willing heart. So finally we told Elaine we felt we needed to bring the courtship to an end. She pled with us to give Doug a few more months. We agreed.

Meanwhile, after seven or eight months, Marc came to me and asked me for Jennifer's hand in marriage. I said, "No, it's not time yet."

A month or two later, however, I felt it was time. The next time he asked, I said yes.

Marc planned an outing to the Sea Scape Restaurant. The day was warm and sunny. After lunch, they went on a short walk on the beach to a secluded alcove, while their chaperones and friends who had accompanied them on the dinner watched from the pier. Jennifer was seated on a rock and Marc disappeared behind it and reappeared with a bouquet of four roses. He then explained the meaning of the roses, got down on one knee, and asked Jennifer to marry him. Of course she said, "Yes." Then he placed a beautiful diamond ring on her finger.

Once they were engaged a great deal changed in terms of the level of their friendship. We then encouraged Jennifer to begin asking Marc questions and talking about anything she wanted to, even intimate things. There was no change in terms of the chaperoning of their time together, but Jennifer asked if they could begin holding hands and we agreed that that would now be appropriate.

Finally we realized we could not keep postponing a decision about Doug forever, but had to nail it down. We told Elaine there had to be a resolution.

I got together with Doug—this was just two weeks ago—and asked to see his journal and his financial plan. He very openly told me that he hadn't done a thing.

"You didn't even open the journal?" I said. "You've made no entries at all?"

"No," he replied, just a hint of defiance in his tone.

I went home and sat Elizabeth and Elaine down.

"Look," I said, "I've been willing to work with Doug. I've bent over backward to accommodate all his excuses and delays. But when I gave him step by step instructions, and he said, *No, I won't do it*, then it is time to break off the courtship."

"I'm sorry, Elaine," Elizabeth said, "but this has gone on long enough. I'm behind your father 100 percent. We have to break it off."

Tearfully Elaine agreed. There was great sorrow. She loved Doug. But she backed us all the way through this difficult decision. I think gradually she had at last begun to see a few of the things we had been aware of. Therefore the decision to break it off was equally hers.

"If you really want to marry him," I told her, "I'll go get the preacher. I don't want you running off behind my back. If you want to get married right now, let's get it going. Obviously it will not be with our approval or blessing. But I'm not going to fight you over this guy. If you want him, you're going to get him. I'd rather it was out in the open. We're not going to split our family over Doug. So if you want him, say the word."

"No, I'm in agreement," she said, though as I said, with tears. "You can tell Doug the courtship is over."

I met with Doug. I told him we were discontinuing the courtship. I said he could continue to be Elaine's friend, though he could not see her privately, and any further communication with her would be through us. I said that we were not closing the door permanently, but that if anything further developed it would have to be according to the terms I had established all along.

A few days ago I received a lengthy letter from Doug that really revealed where he had been the whole time.

We saw that he'd been hiding a side of himself. I hesitate to say that it had been a con game, just to get my daughter. I am sure such was not intentional from the beginning. But gradually it worked its way in that direction. Doug stopped trusting me, and once trust breaks down, things rapidly fall apart. From the letter it was obvious that he had been sitting listening for a year, disagreeing with much of what we stood for, but not speaking up, just in the attempt to win Elaine. He wanted to marry her, without submitting to me as her father . . . even though he had agreed to do just that.

We had assumed that we were all functioning on a certain spiritual level and that we were walking in agreement with the courtship plan. Doug's letter revealed how far from us he had been all along. And the fact that he felt himself spiritually superior to me such that I stood in need of *his* wisdom and counsel effectively eliminated any basis for courtship at all. His responsibility in courtship was to honor me as his spiritual elder. I do not say that to exalt myself, but only in such a manner could he come to properly understand God's order in the world, and thus come to properly understand *his* role as husband and father.

Doug wrote: "I am a strong-willed and independent character. I think for myself, I choose for myself, and I form my own opinions about what is right and what is wrong. I will not believe anything that I am told until I see it with my own two eyes. . . . In other words, you have met your equal! We are men of strong character. That is a good thing but it is a dangerous thing as well. We have a choice to make. We can set our wills in opposition to each other and I will not bend and you will not bend. . . .

"I have no desire to fight with you. My one desire has always been . . . that you and I seek the Lord together in one accord. It is extremely hard for you to bend your will in deference to the Lord, let alone to another man. Believe me, I know. I am cut from the same stone. The day I met you the hair on the back of my neck stood up, and I know that yours did the same. . . .

"Now, I also have some areas of great strength. I have perceptions and understanding far beyond my years in the areas of relationships. I have great insights into people's hearts and minds. . . . And I submit to you, Mr. Grant, with no malice or disrespect, that just as you in your strength see my weakness and cringe at the thought of your daughter marrying into this financial mess, I in my strength see a great weakness in you. It is time for me to speak. . . .

"I see that the Lord has been gracious to you in spite of your failings . . . I do not say these things in spite or anger or rebellion. Humbly I speak the truth in love . . . I want above all else to see the Lord break through your spirit and heal you with his power and love . . . lean on my strengths and trust me just as I am trusting you and leaning on you . . . I beg you, stop defending yourself with the devil's weapons. Humble yourself before the Lord and allow us to love you. You are breaking our hearts. . . ."

Well, there is little point in continuing. Doug is certainly correct in that I am a man still struggling and growing in grace. The Lord knows and my pastor well knows the weaknesses against which I struggle in my life. But Doug's counsel is out of order, and the prideful tone reveals more about him than it does about me.

You see, I may be with the apostle Paul the very "chief of sinners," and for all I know the Lord may have in his plan for Doug to become the next Billy Graham. It's the spiritual *order* that such a response on Doug's part violates. There are so many glaring areas of weakness in me that it would take far more pages than these I've written to discuss them. I never set myself over Doug, or Marc for that matter, as a flawless man, but a father attempting faithfully to carry out the role the Lord placed upon my shoulders.

It is in God's order that youth learn from and be discipled by those older in the Lord than they. That is a scriptural principle. But it takes a humility many young people do not possess to appreciate that truth. And usually it is difficult circumstances and relationships that peel off the skin and expose that lack of humility.

I think Doug's letter finally opened Elaine's eyes to what kind of a husband he would be—one who does not fully grasp these important principles of spiritual order, and a husband who has difficulty taking account for the areas of weakness in his own life.

My response was a simple seven sentences. I left the door open to future relationship, both with our family and with Elaine, according to the same commitments I had previously asked for. Only time will tell what will come of it.

Elaine too wrote a response to Doug. She said, "I do not want to be courted by you anymore. Please do not call or write me. Anything you would like to say should be directed to my father. I do not want to court you anymore because I do not feel that you truly love me. Your pride and unwillingness to submit to my father are greater than your love for me."

Within just a week, Elaine has begun to come back to herself. There are many tears still being shed, but she is finally seeing Doug for what he really was—not a bad guy, just not yet mature enough to marry. At the same time as she is undergoing this change and grieving for the loss of a young man to whom she had given her heart, Elizabeth and I have asked Elaine to forgive *us* for not being a better protection for her. I failed to be attentive enough at the beginning. The failure was primarily *ours*, not hers.

Just a few days ago, Elaine said to us, "If there's another courtship somewhere in my future, I don't even want to hear the guy's name until you've thoroughly checked him out, and you say he's acceptable for marriage. Until that time, don't you dare bring someone around! That's the condition by which I continue to submit my future to you, Daddy, that you do your job, and you do it well."

What can a parent say to that? We *have* to be faithful to our calling and our parental oversight.

So the long and the short of it is, two weeks ago we ended one courtship . . . and next week, as of this writing, Jennifer and Marc will be married.

The testimony of Marc and Jennifer's courtship has really been marvelous, though a lot of the guys in church say that if they'd have had to do half the things I required of Marc, they don't know if they'd ever have gotten married! At Jennifer's shower they called it the wedding of the century.

Reactions

Well, what do you think?

You parents may be saying your kids would never go for this. They'd flip if you brought home an idea like that! And you young people are saying that your parents will never pull something like this off on you.

Let us ask a serious question of all of you: In your heart of hearts do you want to do what is right? Do you want the best marriage possible, either for yourself or for your son or daughter? Do you want God's will as you prepare for marriage? Do you want God's will for your young people?

Then don't you want to look at all the possibilities . . . including courtship?

Jeff and Danielle Myers, in their book *Of Knights and Fair Maidens*, explain: "Courtship . . . is a guy/girl relationship that leads to marriage. It focuses on three primary things: accountability to parents and other trusted adults, building each other's character rather than focusing on physical attraction, and waiting to develop serious relationships until you are really ready to get married. . . . The important thing is that courtship recognizes that the purpose of guy/girl relationships is to prepare for marriage, so you treat it seriously right from the start. You don't look for excuses to go off by yourselves, and you bring other people, such as moms and dads, into the decisions you make."[6]

How many fathers really get to know the future husband of their daughter? Would marriages be as tenuous today if parents had more input into the process ahead of time? Courtship provides an opportunity for parents to become involved. It allows a partnership between parents and young people to take place.

Reality Check

Let's pause for a reality check. Idealism can paint any picture a bit too rosy. We have said that courtship can allow relationships to develop without the pain that often accompanies dating through frequent breakups. True enough. But hearts can also be broken by courtships that don't work out, as in Elaine's case. The very process of courtship raises expectations, hopes, and dreams that may be dashed when the courtship does not culminate in engagement, perhaps in some cases deeper and more heartfelt hopes and dreams than those created by dating.

Neither can we overlook the possibility, even *with* parental involvement, that parents may make mistakes in judgment. Granted, they are older and wiser, but their discernment and impartiality is not without its blind spots.

When Paul Jehle says that the parental witness cannot *hurt* but only *help*, his comment assumes that the "witness" is speaking as an agent of God's wisdom.

---

[6]*Of Knights and Fair Maidens*, pp. 11–12.

When parents respond out of motives generated by self-will rather than the divine will, then hurt may well result. Parents must commit themselves to careful, serious prayer if and when their sons and daughters bring them into the process, so that they respond by truly seeking to discover *God's* will in the matter, not their own. They must be careful not to live out their *own* desires through their children, or they will seriously jeopardize the process of courtship.

Jonathan Lindvall looks back from the perspective of twenty years—in which he heeded his father's counsel rather than making a lifelong decision based on his *own* youthful emotions:

"I wanted to marry a wonderful Christian young lady whom my parents liked but didn't feel was God's choice for me. Thankfully I purposed not to even discuss marriage with her without their full blessing, although they insisted that they would not hinder me if I proceeded. After repeated unsuccessful attempts to persuade my parents that I knew God's will, I finally committed myself to die to the vision I was sure was of God. I was certain God would work miraculously in revealing His will to my parents. My father [however] hinted that I should pray [instead] about marrying [another girl] Connie. After initially resisting the suggestion I agreed to pray about it. In time the Lord showed me I was to marry Connie.

"Although I was not yet 'in love' with her (regrettably I had allowed my emotions to focus on the first girl), with my parents' encouragement I sought and acquired Connie's parents' blessing to marry her. All this took place before I had much emotional attachment to Connie, and certainly before she was at all interested in me. When I proposed to her, she had absolutely no idea I was even interested in her. Neither of us was 'in love' with the other. In time Connie concluded that I was God's will for her. It was during our engagement period that we actually 'fell in love' with each other."[7]

Now, after more than twenty years of marriage, Lindvall never speaks, in public or private, without reemphasizing his gratitude for his father's wisdom in discerning the Lord's choice of a lifetime partner and best friend more shrewdly than *he* was able to, and without expressing thankfulness for a long and joyous marriage to his wife, Connie, who is indeed the "love of his life."

HIDDEN DANGER IN COURTSHIP

As we saw in the case of Hal and Laurel and Doug and Elaine, a happy conclusion for all involved does not always result—even when everyone shares a basic Christian belief system.

---

[7]Pamphlet *Youthful Romance: Scriptural Pattern*, 1992.

As wonderful an opportunity as courtship presents, it has a hidden danger as well. Under the surface of courtship's seemingly placid waters lies a submerged rock, not always detected by many who assume that the courtship process will be a magical guarantee against marital error.

There are no such guarantees. As much care is required in courtship as in dating, for it too is fraught with opportunity for haste and mistake.

Any teaching that comes into the Church, after which large numbers of men and women run without adequate understanding and wisdom, provides the enemy huge opportunity for mischief and division. By shallow and hasty responses of immature individuals he invalidates many important truths and robs them of the power to advance the kingdom of God.

Satan will do all he can to exploit the subtle dangers existing within these truths, because courtship represents a godly attempt to return marriage to scriptural foundations. If these principles of courtship are unwisely implemented, we could actually witness over the next five to ten years many ill-advised courtship marriages, which were never God's will at all.

To isolate this serious hidden danger, let's return briefly to the subject of dating and reverse the coin for a moment.

What is a potential *benefit* of dating? Wouldn't you say it is the opportunity to know a wide variety of individuals before deciding on *one* person? If this knowing means romancing around with several people in order to have fun, it carries a terribly destructive side. "Playing the field" could not be a more detrimental practice for marital preparation. On the face of it, however, it is not a bad thing to know lots of people.

At the same time, one of the potential drawbacks of courtship is that young men and women *don't* have the opportunity to know a wide variety of potential mates. Thus the danger exists of rushing the process, entering into courtship *before* either a young man or a young woman is really in a position to take that giant step forward in the direction of engagement.

And enthusiastic as we are about courtship, it must be admitted that many of the foundational elements of the courtship process are out of sync with today's society. In a sense, courtship was not designed for our modern era. The reality is that it will be much more difficult to make courtship work today than a hundred years ago.

The reason is simply this: At root, courtship functions most smoothly and most easily brings to fruition its objectives in a close-knit rural community where families already know one another. The image of courtship in an Amish community or in a farming region around the turn of the century, for example, depicts an ideal environment in which courtship could flourish, as it has for generations. Families are intimately acquainted. Children grow up knowing one another, playing and working and attending church together. By the time they reach the teen years they have already been acquainted with most of the young people of their approximate age for years, with yet more years of maturing social interaction to follow. Children, boys and girls, parents, teenagers, and families all interact in a variety of settings over the years, sharing work and adversity and common values in the family-church-community fabric that weaves the society together.

By the time a young man of eighteen or twenty or twenty-two goes to a girl's father to request permission to court his daughter, it is likely that the principle players have known each other all their lives. She is a young lady he has been acquainted with since before he can remember. He really *knows* her. In no sense is he choosing blind, nor is she. He is aware at a reasonably astute level of *all* the young ladies of the community, and though he perhaps has not dated them, there have been a wide range of opportunities for getting to know them through the years.

Such a young man is therefore well equipped to say, "I am acquainted with this young lady's character, her strengths, her weaknesses, her family. . . . I know a great deal about her. I have known her for years. I admire and respect her. I have watched her conduct herself. I have heard her pray. I have listened as she has expressed herself and talked about her goals and ambitions. And as we have grown into young adulthood, feelings of genuine love have blossomed in my heart toward her. And I am ready to say that I want her for my wife."

Likewise, these same factors are all present on the young lady's part.

In such an environment, courtship really *works*. It culminates years of "getting to know" a person.

In our fragmented, urbanized world, however, it's not so easy. The closest parallel might be two church families who have known each other for several years. But how can young men and women who have known each other just a short time—and never dated others—wisely pick a spouse? If they met only a few months prior—and their families have met only briefly—how can they *know*, "I want to court this young lady and make her my wife," or, "I want to allow this young man to court me so that he can become my husband."

As much as two young people *think* they know each other, it's nothing like the courtship normally practiced in former times or today in rural communities. It is this "choosing blind" that is the danger in implementing courtship today. Families and young people often do not know one another as intimately as is necessary to a successful and well-ordered courtship.

Certainly, foundational to courtship is the conviction that God's will guides the process. Everyone involved *must* believe and work toward that central truth. Then God is able to (and we know he *does*) use courtship in wonderful ways, despite the limitations of our fragmented, urbanized world. But the watchword is: Proceed with caution.

So as we have seen, both dating *and* courtship can rush the process. In Hal and Laurel's case they *might* have been better off to have dated than to have rushed into a courtship marriage. This is why we placed Hal and Laurel's story early in the book. Even though we advocate courtship, we wanted you to come to understand it with sober judgment, to dispel the myth that courtship in itself is sufficient to make a strong marriage.

If not properly practiced, courtship causes young couples to *think too soon about marriage*. Hal and Laurel did not allow themselves sufficient time to become good friends. They were simply too young for romance, and it was too soon for marriage. As our three sons watched this true scenario play itself out, they all determined that if this was courtship, it wasn't for them! They watched Hal get in *deeper* than he'd planned, *faster* than he'd planned. Mr. Willard did exactly the right thing by stepping in to slow the pace and delay the wedding, and by suggesting that a new level of discipling and counseling enter the courtship picture. However, at that point rebellion on the part of the two young people took over, and there was little more he could do.

Because of our serious concern over this danger inherent in courtship, we will recommend (in the final chapters of this book) that couples take a dramatic step to slow the process. Indeed, there are strengths and weaknesses in all methods, which is why we have come up with what we believe is an "insurance policy" that brings a cautious pace to any and all marriage preparations. We call it a preengagement apprenticeship, and we recommend it be incorporated *into* the courtship process.

THE IDEAL . . . THE REALITY

Again we stress that although courtship can be made to sound like a cure-all, *reality* must be considered. The pros and cons must be recognized with sober judgment.

We can already see the following scenario lurking, waiting to happen.

A young man who is not so young anymore has a few undesirable habits and traits. He hasn't managed to favorably impress any of the girls he has dated, so he decides to try a new approach. He's a shrewd fellow in that he knows there are people who will believe anything you say if you use the right jargon.

Knowing that the Jacksons have home schooled their children and believe strongly in courtship, he puts on his best behavior and slowly turns on the charm toward twenty-year-old Loretta Jackson. He also makes it a point to begin attending every church meeting where Mr. and Mrs. Jackson will be present and to behave like a model Christian young man. He makes every attempt to humbly ingratiate himself to both parents until he is sure they like him. When the time is right, he goes to Mr. Jackson and says in flawless spiritual lingo, "I have been praying and seeking the Lord about my life, and I believe he has shown me that it is his will that I court your daughter. I am of course submitting this matter into your hands for prayer and counsel, because I know you to be a wise man of God."

What father wouldn't be impressed? Mr. Jackson believes in courtship, and now he sees it working in textbook fashion! What should he say?

The only proper response at this point is "I will pray and seek God's guidance in the matter."

In reality, Mr. Jackson knows nothing about this young man. He's new to the church. No one knows his family. No one has an accurate picture of his background. How long has he been walking with the Lord? What do the "windows of character" reveal about him? What are his habits? What are his father and mother like?

A close friend of ours fell victim to what we can only call a con game similar to what we just described, though not strictly involving courtship. Home schooled, sweet, and of godly character, she met a young man at church who turned on the charm and knew all the right spiritual phrases. Within a year she had been raped, was pregnant, the man was gone, and her life was in shambles.

There are many young men out there (and doubtless young women too) who will use the courtship angle to their advantage. Fathers, don't be in a hurry to say, "Yes, you may court my daughter." Before that time comes, *know* the young man, realizing that if the relationship continues to move forward, the young man will become your son-in-law and your daughter's husband.

It's a major decision! Take your time.

To respond, "No, I *don't* think it would be appropriate for you to court my daughter at this time," is an equally valid answer to give. You might also add, "If it truly is God's will, come and see me in a year. By then the Lord will have had ample opportunity to get through to me and let me in on it too." In the ways of God, going slow in this way nearly always ensures that God's will becomes *more* clear, not less.

Obviously, making courtship work requires that both families work *together*. And this can begin prior to the courtship. I think if I (Mike) found myself in Mr. Jackson's shoes, my response to the young man might be, "I haven't met your father and mother yet. I'd like to talk this over with them before going further."

What if one set of parents thinks the whole idea of courtship is nonsense? What if a girl's father has no interest in a close relationship with her young man and doesn't want to be involved in such an in-depth process? What if his answer is "I don't care who she marries. Just leave me out of it"? What can a young man do who really believes that courtship is the path he wants to follow?

These and other practical difficulties will make an ideal courtship next to impossible for many young people. Courtship will not work in every case. Moreover, though many might feel courtship has much to recommend, these ideas require bringing together two generations (today's parents—who came of age in the '60s and '70s—and today's young people) known for their abhorrence of authority.

Carrying out these ideas will often go cross grain to our backgrounds, on *both* sides of the partnership. These days, even Christian young people aren't into being told what to do. So the reality is that for some people courtship is going to work wonderfully . . . but obviously not for everyone.

Grow old along with me.
The best is yet to be.

—Robert Browning

An Uncertain Parting

A year later, Michelle's graduation was approaching and she would return to her home in the southern part of the state.

*Jerry was torn. He didn't want to let her go. He knew she **had** to be an intrinsic part of his future. Yet he couldn't bring himself to the point where he felt ready to commit to marriage.*

He just wasn't sure.

*As their friendship gradually progressed into **more** than friendship, it was awkward at first. Recognizing the change, they agreed to go out on an official "date." Michelle wore her nicest dress, put on perfume and a little makeup. But the conversation was stilted. As they sat in the car outside Michelle's apartment, Jerry put his arm around her, and that made it worse.*

By the time the evening was over, Michelle was in tears and they were both too embarrassed to see each other the following day. Where had their friendship gone?

"Why did we have to spoil such a good thing?" they both said—once they were able to talk about it. Maybe they weren't cut out to be a "couple" and should remain "just friends."

*Gradually the awkwardness eased, and they became accustomed to each other on the new level to which their relationship had progressed, as "**romantic best friends.**"*

That they cared for each other there was no doubt in either of their minds. Whether they were "in love"—neither could be sure. It didn't feel like the Hollywood portrayal. Actually it seemed better—deeper, with a stronger foundation of communication and spiritual oneness than what the world called "love."

They loved each other, they wanted to be together, they prayed together, they wanted to spend their lives together. But "romance" didn't drive their relationship. Even now, after the change, it was still friendship that cemented their hearts—camaraderie, oneness, communication . . . their best-friendness.

After his graduation, no teaching positions came Jerry's way. He had started a little part-time bookstore, more for fun than to make a living, until something more permanent opened up. Michelle helped out whenever she could, and before long it was a joint effort. The fact that they operated it out of a spare room in Jerry's downtown apartment kept overhead to a minimum and allowed him to slowly increase the number of books on the shelves.

Gradually marriage couldn't help but come up between them, though vaguely at first. Michelle was reserved whenever the subject arose. She would have married Jerry in a minute, but she knew he was reticent. Jerry had to talk things through, she knew that, though sometimes his frankness about his doubts made it hard.

Jerry was polite and gracious and more loving toward her than anyone had ever been. Yet he could be even hurtfully open. He was the most honest communicator she had ever known, and even though it could be painful, it only made her love him more. They found their way through these times by prayer.

By Michelle's graduation day, Jerry still had made no commitment. Though they had spoken of marriage, he'd never actually proposed. Michelle didn't really know what her status in his mind was. Gradually the doubts about their future together returned. What if he was just waiting for her to go so he could avoid hurting her? What if—it was awful even to think it—what if she never saw him again?

She had no choice but to make plans to return to her parents' home. She couldn't just hang around and wait. If she and Jerry had no future together, she had to get on with her life. So Michelle applied to a graduate school near her home and bought a Greyhound bus ticket. Jerry's family threw a going away party for her.

The day of departure approached. Their last visits together grew quiet. Uncertainty filled the air.

Michelle packed her things from four years of college. Her portable sewing machine, however, was a problem. It was too big and awkward to take on the bus.

"I'll keep it for you," said Jerry. "You can get it next time we see each other."

Michelle looked at him with an odd expression, then nodded. What could next time mean?

Jerry drove her to the Greyhound station. There was a brief awkward hug, no kiss.

Michelle boarded the bus and took her seat. A few minutes later the Greyhound pulled away.

The moment the bus was out of the station, she began to cry. Again came the question she couldn't erase from her mind—what if she never saw Jerry again? She could never love anybody else.

Almost the instant Michelle was gone, Jerry realized she was indeed the young lady he wanted to marry. It was as though the parting had to come in order to cement the bond.

He hurried home from the bus station and immediately began writing a long letter. He spent the entire evening writing. It grew to eighteen pages!

Michelle began attending graduate school near her home, planning to work toward a teaching credential. Jerry bought a small bookstore in a nearby town and now, with two bookstores to run, settled into an everyday working routine quite different from the student life that had occupied him for the past five years.

Throughout the months of the summer, the correspondence between Jerry Smith and Michelle Jones rivaled the conversations that had characterized their face-to-face friendship. Letters crossed in the mail daily. If absence made the heart grow fonder, in Jerry's case it served to unleash many new feelings and to put an end to much of his reluctance. His heart seemed to open in new ways toward Michelle via written communication. More and more he realized how deeply he loved her.

Michelle was not only his best friend, he said. They were soul mates. If the romance between them was slow to flourish, all the other forms of their love were so much greater that it more than made up for it. Besides, the longer they were apart, the more Jerry realized his feelings were becoming very romantic.

Jerry now openly declared his love, and Michelle reciprocated in kind. Before long, it was truly a series of spiritual "love letters" flowing between them. Their communications contained less and less of what each was doing, for they discussed even more openly than before everything they thought, hoped, dreamed, and wanted to do and be in the Lord, and their plans to share life together. Their separation had truly caused them to know each other even more deeply, and they realized they possessed an exciting relationship that was worth preserving.

In July, just a month after she had left the university, Michelle received a letter from Jerry saying he would be coming down with some friends for a visit in August. He had to return her sewing machine, he said. Michelle dared not hope for what might be Jerry's purpose in coming.

One evening, about a week before Jerry was to arrive, Michelle and her father were sharing a rare moment alone together. Michelle told him that she suspected there might be something in the future with Jerry and wasn't sure what to do about her commitments to graduate school. She had only a half year left on her credential work, and she had also auditioned and been accepted to study with a prestigious music teacher.

"From everything you've said," replied Mr. Jones, "it sounds like Jerry might be the real thing."

Michelle nodded quietly.

"You know your mother made a lot of sacrifices in marrying me too. Sometimes those are the kinds of choices you have to make."

"What kind of sacrifices?" asked Michelle.

"We were both finishing up our Master's degrees and working on our theses. But when we got married, I had to work hard to support our little family. Your mother devoted her time to typing my thesis."

"What happened to hers?"

"I finished my Master's, but hers remained forever untyped and unsubmitted. She never did have the chance to finish it. But we built a wonderful life together. I've never forgotten the sacrifice she made."

Jerry arrived at the Joneses' home in the mountains with four others, also friends of Michelle. It was a joyous reunion.

That evening Jerry and Michelle slipped away and in the twilight walked down the road toward the creek. When they found a good spot to sit on the bank, Jerry took her hand and prayed aloud, thanking the Lord for Michelle, his best friend ever. It did not take Jerry long to tell her why he had come.

"I didn't bring your sewing machine, after all," he said.

Michelle laughed. "Why not?"

"I left it back at my place."

"But . . . but why?"

"I think I'm finally ready," said Jerry. "I'm sorry it's taken me so long and that it's been so awkward for you . . . but at last I'm ready to ask you if you'll spend the rest of your life with me. I'd like to ask you to marry me."

11 | MANY METHODS— WHAT IS GOD'S WILL FOR *YOU*?

Friendship improves happiness, and abates misery, by doubling our joy and dividing our grief.

—Joseph Addison

We've spoken in detail about dating and courtship as the two most prominent means in Western society of selecting husbands and wives. Two additional methods, arranged marriages and betrothal, have been used throughout history and are still found in many parts of the world.

Let's examine each briefly, and then put all four methods together to see if we can draw conclusions about what best fits you and your situation.

BETROTHAL

Betrothal is actually very similar to courtship, in that it is likewise founded on parental involvement. Betrothal, however, carries with it a much larger parental role, to the extent that in most cases a father actually makes the marriage choice for his daughter.

"Betrothal" is derived from the two words "be" and "truth" (or troth)—meaning to give truth, to pledge or promise to do as you have said, to contract or agree together in truth.

Historically, betrothal signified a contract between a young man and his future father-in-law whereby the terms of a proposed marriage (and a financial dowry paid to the bride's father by the groom) were agreed upon. An agreement was drawn up only between these two, usually not involving the groom's parents, and in most cases neither the bride nor her mother. Betrothal, therefore, was actually in early times an arranged marriage, though the groom exercised a role in the choice.

Once the contract between the two men was struck, however, the betrothal became much like courtship, in that the young man and young woman had a period of time to get to know each other before the time of their marriage.

This "knowing" (betrothal) period was not, as in courtship, an opportunity for the parties to *make sure* the union was the right thing. Betrothal was a much more serious matter and signified far more than engagement. Though it came prior to marriage, there was no "trial run" to it. Once the marriage pact had been sealed by betrothal, Jewish tradition held that a divorce was required to break it. For most practical purposes the couple was viewed *as* married, though they could not engage in physical intimacy and the young lady continued to live with her parents. Betrothal was so serious and binding, in fact, that if the groom died during the betrothal period, his betrothed bride was considered a widow, even though the marriage had not yet been consummated.

In most biblical cases, arrangement *and* betrothal were both involved. *The New Manners and Customs of Bible Times* explains:

> Young people did not normally decide whom they would marry. It was marriage first and love afterward. Although there was therefore a great deal more "will" than "romance," it tended to produce a stable pattern of marriages (Genesis 24:67). Esau was in trouble because he married contrary to the wishes of his parents (Genesis 26:34–35). The practice of arranging marriages did not mean that parents did not consider the feelings of their children (Genesis 24:58), or that love did not sometimes happen before marriage (Genesis 29:10–20). . . .
>
> Arrangements had to be made for work compensation (the mohar) to be paid to the woman's family, and a dowry had to be paid to the bride's father. He could use the interest from the dowry but could not spend it (see Genesis 31:15) because it was to be kept in trust for the wife in case she was ever widowed or divorced. Where such sums of money could not be paid because of the poverty of the suitor, other means were found instead, such as service. . . .
>
> Marriages were arranged, if possible, with members of one's own kin. . . . Marriages sometimes took place outside the clan . . . and this usually happened for political reasons. . . . It was never approved, however, because people from other clans worshiped different deities and this affected the whole religious life of the people. . . .
>
> Once the arrangement to marry was entered into, there was a betrothal that was more binding than the engagement in contemporary society. . . .

The formal words of the betrothal between David and Michal were probably those spoken by Saul to David: "Now you have . . . opportunity to become my son-in-law" (see 1 Samuel 18:20–22). The betrothal could be broken only by a legal transaction (in effect, a divorce), and the ground for such termination was adultery (see Deuteronomy 22:24). Betrothal lasted for about twelve months, during which time the home was to be prepared by the groom, and the wedding clothes would be prepared by the bride. The bride's family would prepare for the wedding festivities.

Mary and Joseph were betrothed when it was found that she was pregnant. Joseph did not want to expose her publicly, because, as a supposed adulteress, Mary would have been stoned to death. It must have taken a great deal of love for Mary, and a great deal of trust in God speaking through his dream that enabled Joseph to marry her.[1]

Of betrothal, Jonathan Lindvall says, "I submit the betrothal model as a more scriptural and much less hurtful pattern of youthful romance than the typical dating game. Just as we teach our young people to reserve themselves physically for marriage, I believe the Scriptures call us to train them to reserve their romantic emotions for the betrothal period immediately preceding marriage, having enjoyed the benefit of God-ordained protectors (parents) in helping them seek and find His will for their lifelong companion. In this area, as well as every other area of life, our obedience to scriptural patterns can demonstrate that God's design for us is far superior to anything the world has to offer."

ARRANGED MARRIAGES

As foreign as it probably sounds to you, arranged marriages are becoming more and more prominent these days. Practiced for millennia, we now see them closer to home, practiced by some Muslim and Asian cultures in North America.

Little explanation is needed—these are marriages *arranged* by two families for any of a multitude of reasons about which a young man and young woman may have little to say. In some cases a bride and groom do not even know each other until the moment they first set eyes on each other at the finalization of the wedding vows.

What is remarkable to our Western minds is how readily young people of other cultures welcome having marriage arranged on their behalf. They see it not as a hardship or a violation of their individuality and autonomy, but rather as a wholesome aspect of their faith, involving trust in parents and respect for the

[1]*The New Manners and Customs of Bible Times*, pp. 64–65.

sanctity of marriage. We must admit, whatever we think of the specifics, that many Muslims demonstrate more fervency and obedience to the creeds and principles of their religion than many Christians do to theirs. (We are also well aware, however, of the serious abuses within the Muslim tradition toward women in general, and we certainly do not endorse the overarching Muslim perspective on marriage.)

Just how close these once-distant customs now come to us is demonstrated by a recent article in a local magazine, in which several Muslims living in our area were interviewed concerning their marriage practices. One young man who was soon to be married to a woman living on the opposite end of the country whom he has never met commented, "Muslim practice discourages unchaperoned meetings before marriage. I am happy to be spared the hypocrisies of Christianity, which blinks at permissive sexual behavior and ordains admitted homosexuals."

Another Muslim interviewed in the article said, "In family counseling in the university here in the United States we study how to deal with teenage girls who are suffering bad self-images because they have no boyfriends. In Turkey we must deal with teenage girls who suffer bad self-image because they *do* have a boyfriend. Modern Islamic custom bans dating. Intimacy even after engagement is completely unacceptable. Only marriage validates sex."

The astounding fact is that many Muslim young people enthusiastically support the customs that have come down to them through their parents. They happily devote themselves to faithfulness through arranged marriage. Yet what would be the general response of Christian teens in America if parents, pastors, and youth leaders across the country began unanimously teaching that betrothal was the biblical pattern? Would *Christian* young people demonstrate the same level of trust and respect? We'd probably have World War III on our hands!

PRACTICALITY—A WORD TO PARENTS

So, what is the answer?

Is it betrothal or arranged marriages? That system may work for devout Muslims, but would it work for American teens?

Is dating the answer? Not if the current U.S. divorce rate means anything.

Is courtship the perfect solution? It got Hal and Laurel married, but the road was a bumpy one and the whole process did not go as planned.

Pros and cons exist everywhere! That is why parents and young people must form a plan and a partnership and talk together about every aspect of the process. Parents must think hard about these ideas—and consider whether betrothal, courtship, and arranged marriages are practical alternatives to our existing methods.

But are the potential advantages enough to make Christian parents in the United States say that they ought to arrange the marriages of their sons and daughters?

Practicality is perhaps the most important test of the plan. Can we actually make it *work*?

All of us must admit, parents and young people alike, that the independence that rules our society will generally make betrothal and arranged marriages very difficult for most families to carry out. We don't say this is bad or good. It is simply a fact. These are approaches to marriage that are not going to be practical for most people. Parents must subordinate raw idealism to practicality, recognizing that young men and women forced into marriages to which they did not give their consent will grow resentful.

Believe it or not (and you may find it difficult to believe) there are a growing number of Christian parents who genuinely believe that arranged marriages are best. But the question they must ask is this: Will it really work for *my* son or *my* daughter . . . or will it drive them from me? We must examine such questions prayerfully, not in the vacuum of unreality but in the practical settings of our own families. If a parentally imposed plan would plant seeds of anger and bitterness within the heart of a young person, no matter how valid the plan in the abstract and ideal, those parents would be wise to moderate their approach. Practicality must be incorporated into every stage of the partnership between parents and young people.

Believe it or not again, I (Mike) have already had two fathers ask *me* what I thought of arranged marriages. Knowing neither of these men's daughters, however, I did not pursue the subject further! But the dismal state of marriage among Christians today is causing many concerned parents to consider this huge step away from dating in an attempt to regain biblical foundations. Alternatives that might have seemed unthinkable a few years ago are now serious options.

It isn't that I believe the notion to be without merit, but I seriously question whether it is practical in our society in a widespread way.

On the other hand, let's say you are a young person thinking and praying through these ideas, and you are of the few who absolutely trust your parents. You may have read the above sections and liked the way they sound. You may want to go to your mother and father and say, "Mom, Dad . . . I trust you completely. I know you have nothing but my good in mind. I believe that you hear from God on my behalf. I believe you are more mature in your walk with God than I am. Therefore I would like *you* to decide for me whom you think God would have me marry. I want your help."

We hope many of you *will* say something similar to your parents. However, there is a sobering question for *you* to ask as well: Where are you likely to find a potential bride or groom who *also* believes in arranged marriage, who has *also* read this book, or whose parents *also* feel about it exactly as you do?

That may be needle in a haystack time! You young people will need to bring realism into your perspective too. These are still new ideas in the Christian community at large.

As important as our ideals are, they are not the only considerations. We must look to *do*-ability. In relationship, *trust* can be even more important than *truth*. We must not let stubborn idealism destroy the trust that holds the partnership between parents and their sons and daughters together.

THE SPECTRUM OF VARIOUS METHODS

Now, let's take stock of where we've come so far. Let's sum up.

We've discussed four chief methods for finding husbands and wives. These might be seen on a spectrum of increasing parental involvement in the process.

DATING	COURTSHIP	BETROTHAL	ARRANGED MARRIAGE

0 ———————————— parental involvement ——————————— 100%

Dating, on the one hand, generally assumes very little parental involvement, while arranged marriages assume near 100 percent parental involvement.

These percentages are flexible. Parents, of course, often *are* involved in the dating process to some degree, but not in the *decision* of whom to marry. Young people may ask advice, but they *decide* themselves. In each of the other three methods, the parents play a key role in the decision itself. There is also no doubt that consultation with the young people often takes place in many arranged marriages, though the *decision* rests primarily with the parents.

ADDING TO THE POSSIBILITIES

Are these the only possibilities for husband-wife selection?

Not at all!

Now it becomes interesting—mixing and blending these methods in infinite variety to prayerfully discover how exactly God wants your parents-and-young-people partnership to work.

This is the exciting part! Making it work in real-life situations.

Let's say that you and your parents or you and your son or daughter decide to pursue courtship as your method of choice. But then Mom pipes up, "I like most of what the Phillipses say about courtship, but I'm still not convinced dating is as bad as they say. Why couldn't we work through the method of courtship, but with some friendship dating thrown in too?"

The others around the table nod their heads.

"Yeah, that makes sense, Mom," says the daughter. "I like it. Can we do that, Dad?"

"I don't know why not," says Dad. "Didn't they say I was in charge of the courtship anyway? If I'm in charge, then I'll make our own rules about how we're going to do it!"

"Sounds good to us!"

"Okay, then," Dad goes on. "We'll utilize courtship, but allow you and the young man who is courting you to friendship date after some time has passed—maybe friendship public dating. Is that an agreeable progression?"

"Great, Dad. I appreciate your being so flexible. And I'll remember everything you said to me the night you took me out to dinner and gave me the covenant ring."

"Just as long as we know about the date ahead of time," Mom adds with a note of caution. "You'll still have to ask our permission."

"Of course—we'll still be *courting*, not exactly *dating*."

"And afterward, all four of us will talk about what you did," adds Dad, "so that we get the family benefit of courting, even though you've been out somewhere alone."

"We could call it *dateship!*"

And just like that, this partnership of daughter and mother and father has come up with an in-between method that brings friendship public dating into the courtship process. They've individualized it and come up with their *own* unique brand of courtship.

Their spectrum of options now includes a fifth possibility, which they made up. It sits somewhere in the middle . . . like this:

DATING	DATESHIP	COURTSHIP	BETROTHAL	ARRANGED MARRIAGE
	courtship with friendship public dating			

Do you understand why we say this is the exciting part?

These four primary methods are not meant as legalistic constrictions inhibiting the premarriage process, but rather as general guidelines to use in designing whatever particular method and process you feel God wants *you* to follow toward a best-friend marriage.

He has something absolutely unique in mind for you! He has some specific place on this dating-to-arranged-marriage spectrum where he wants *you* to blend together the principles into a practical plan that will work in *your* family. This will involve a mix of decision-making between parents and young people, where communication is the key to making it work.

May we emphasize again, especially to you young people: This is a *partnership*. But your mom and dad are the chief partners. There will surely be discussion and prayer, but coming up with the method that God wants for *your* family will be a decision that rests primarily on *their* shoulders. They will want your input, but in the end *they* will make the decision.

You might, for instance, want to date as a part of courtship. Your parents may pray about it, however, and say no. It is for you to abide happily and cheerfully by their decision. (That is, unless you are twenty-eight or thirty—by then you are probably old enough to make the decision on your own, even though you will still be wise to ask for their input.)

INFINITE VARIETY OF APPLICATION

There are a variety of ways God will lead families, because every young man and every young woman is different, and every marriage will be unique—especially best-friend marriages. Notwithstanding that we have spoken sternly against romance dating, there will continue to be those who date and find best-friend marriages as a result. We have pointed out the flaws of dating, because we think the teen-romance mentality has seriously corrupted a scriptural perspective on youthful relationships. But we're not so out of step with our society and so untrusting of God to say that there is *no* good that can be achieved through dating. We do not see it as the preferred method, but dating *can* certainly be used of God. If a godly best-friend marriage and purity before marriage are your unwavering goals, and trust, time, and prayer in partnership with your parents undergirds the process, you will be led into a wonderful marriage through distinctive means, which may include a godly form of dating.

There will be those who will decide that friendship and public dating are fine and healthy. Others may say they will permit dating only of Christian young people, or dating that involves Christian functions, or only daytime dating. Other forms of dating may enter the courtship scenario in the later stages of the relationship. Fathers and mothers will take more or less active roles depending on how they perceive the need for their individual input.

Even those families who choose courtship as we have outlined it will find ways to vary it as they go through the process. And as we have already shown, the principles of betrothal and courtship mix and blend as well. You may not actually conclude an "arranged" marriage is the way to go, but your father, or you as a father, may bring some element of betrothal or arranged marriage to play in your family's particular plan.

It is the *plan* that is the key—to plan ahead of time so you do not enter the premarriage years blind and without sufficient thought and prayer.

In *all* these cases, it is the *partnership* of parental involvement and the *planning* that make these principles work. They remain the key ingredients, regardless of the method used.

Let's take another look at our spectrum of methods.

We're not saying, "Take your pick," but rather, "Look at how great the options have become!" And remember—these are not all of them. God will reveal the perfect and unique method for you and your parents.

dating under parental supervision

courtship with dating reserved for later

dating only Christians

public dating   mingled courtship and betrothal

DATING   DATESHIP   COURTSHIP   BETROTHAL   ARRANGED MARRIAGE

friendship dating

courtship with dating

dating only at Christian activities   mingled betrothal and arranged marriage

courtship with friendship public dating

only daytime dates

Now . . . seek God's unique and wonderful best for your life and family situation!

*Friendship, of itself a holy tie, is made more
sacred by adversity.*

—John Dryden

Moving Ahead in Faith

*Jerry and Michelle's wedding was scheduled for the next day. All the plans
were set. Michelle's parents and relatives and friends had all come north for the
happy occasion.*

*The only trouble was, neither Jerry nor Michelle had counted on having an
argument. Now, as they sat in the front seat of Jerry's '64 Chevy, staring straight
ahead into the night, neither of them felt very romantic. Michelle was hugging
the passenger-side door, two feet of space between them.*

Never could any couple have appeared less in love.

It wasn't supposed to be like this!

*Tomorrow was supposed to be the happiest day of their lives. Instead, both
felt depressed. If there was any way to call off the wedding, either one of them
might have done it.*

"What are we going to do?" said Jerry at length.

"I don't know," shrugged Michelle.

"I'm really sorry. I didn't mean for this to happen."

"That's okay, it's not your fault."

*"It's more my fault than yours," rejoined Jerry. "I know I've gotten moody
and quiet this week. I've just . . . I don't know, I've been assaulted by all the old
doubts again."*

"Doubts . . . about me?"

*"No, no—not about you . . . doubts about me. I guess I'm still scared at the
whole prospect of marriage. It's a big commitment. I don't know, maybe it's not
that exactly."*

"What, then?"

"Well, you know—it's supposed to be all flashy and romantic and exciting, and here we are sitting together the night before our wedding like a couple of bumps on a log."

"It's always been different with us," said Michelle. *"That's one of the things that makes it special. There's more to it than romance. There always has been."*

Jerry sighed.

"Yeah . . . you're right."

"So what are we going to do?" asked Michelle. *"Are you really having second thoughts?"*

"No, not really—just jitters, and, I suppose, a few lingering doubts—like I said, not about you, just about the change . . . what it all will mean. I suppose we have to find out what the Lord wants us to do."

From their very first meeting, Jerry and Michelle had prayed together. To do so now was as natural as being together.

"Lord Jesus," began Jerry, *"we come to you now without a lot of feelings and emotions to guide us. We know you have led us to this moment. You brought us together for a reason. You have given us the most wonderful friendship. Now we ask you to guide us and help us know what you are trying to say to us."*

Michelle moved across the seat next to Jerry. *"Yes, Lord,"* she prayed, *"we do love each other, but if you have other plans, or if you want us to wait, help us to hear your voice clearly and to be willing to obey whatever you tell us."*

"We are willing," said Jerry, *"even to cancel the wedding, as hard as that would be, if that is the reason for what has happened this week, Lord. Please show us. Make your will clear."*

"Whatever happens, Lord, we commit ourselves again to you—each of us, as well as our relationship. We want to serve you, whatever that means and whatever future you have for us."

Both fell silent. They sat staring straight ahead for ten or fifteen minutes.

"You know what I'm sensing?" said Jerry at length.

Michelle turned toward him.

"I'm feeling that we're to go ahead. God didn't bring us together and establish this unique and special bond between us for no reason. He has something planned for us. But he wants our marriage to be based on him, not on our emotions."

"Are you saying that what has happened today could be his way of reminding us of that?"

"That's how the Lord works, isn't it? What better way than to allow something to come between us, temporarily stripping away our romantic enthusiasm and causing us to turn to him, putting us in the position of having to move

forward in trust and obedience instead of on the basis of our emotions."

"I'm sensing the same thing," said Michelle, "that we can trust God. He brought us here. He led us. We can go ahead *knowing* that he is in it."

"That's exactly it. He *is* in it. We can trust **him**—more than I can trust my unpredictable emotions."

"So . . . decided then?"

"Decided!" said Jerry. "I promise, no more cold feet."

Michelle smiled.

Jerry reached over and took her hand, then held it a moment.

"I do love you, Michelle," he said.

"Thank you. I love you too."

"Almost since that first day on the beach I knew you were the one I wanted to marry. It just took me a long time to be ready. I'm sorry I've been so slow."

"The best things are worth waiting for. Isn't that what they say?" smiled Michelle.

"I hope so!"

They got out of the car and slowly walked toward the building where Michelle was staying with friends.

"Get a good night's sleep," said Jerry. "We've got a wedding to go to tomorrow!"

"I'll try."

"Good night."

"Good night. See you in the morning!"

12 | IT TAKES *PRAYER*

Fame is the scentless sunflower,
With gaudy crown of gold;
But friendship is the breathing rose,
With sweets in every fold.

—Oliver Wendell Holmes

Much of the emphasis these days in books
for young people about developing relationships and planning for marriage is on
"getting" a husband or wife—even in books from Christian authors. Young people
learn how to "attract" the opposite sex, how to deal with their "sexuality," ideas
for "great dates," and what to do to make themselves appealing so that guys or
girls will like them. Is it any wonder that such a perspective offers an inadequate
spiritual base for marital preparation?

CONFORMING TO THE WORLD'S PREOCCUPATION WITH SEX AND ROMANCE

The entire foundation for much of what is presented to today's teens assumes
dating, romance, glamorous movie-style "love," and the expression of "natural"
teenage impulses to be part of youth's normal progress toward adulthood to which
we must allow full rein rather than curb in any way.

How can Christian youth leaders and authors not realize the quagmire into
which they are leading today's Christian young people? We look at this material
and are at once sickened and angry to see how far down the world's road they
have gone in order to make their counsel palatable. How can such blindness have
overtaken the Church?

The entire perspective represented by this outlook is not only backward and
destructive—it is wrong. Nowhere does Scripture tell us we are to try to make
others love *us*. What could be more antithetical to Jesus' teaching than purposefully trying to be sensually and physically appealing?

Me, me, me! It's me-first, me-above-all-others.

What do *I* want? What will satisfy *me* and *my* fleshly appetites? It is the cry of our self-indulgent culture. Never do we stop to think what someone *else* might want, what might be *right* above what I want, what might be the *best* thing rather than what seems the most fun to our lower natures.

We in the Christian church have systematically taught our young people to flagrantly *disobey* Romans 12:2—*training them precisely to conform to the pattern of this world rather than to stand against it.* What preparation are we giving for mature spiritual adulthood when the underlying teaching we give to teens is to *disobey* what could not be a more unambiguous command extending from Genesis to Revelation:

"Separate yourselves from the peoples around you" (Ezra 10:11).

"Do not conform any longer to the pattern of this world" (Romans 12:2).

"Come out from them and be separate, says the Lord" (2 Corinthians 6:17).

" . . . some people . . . think that we live by the standards of this world" (2 Corinthians 10:2).

Learning how to snag a husband or get a wife in the way the world does will never lead to great marriages. There is only one way that can happen—coming at marriage from an almost directly opposite angle.

Even an emphasis on "waiting," as much as we applaud programs that stress purity, carries but one underlying theme—sex.

Better to wait than not. It is imperative . . . it is *required* to wait! There is no choice, no option about it for Christian young people. But why must sex, even if the message is *"no* sex," be the sum total of our preparation of young people for marriage?

GOD, WHOM DO YOU WANT ME TO MARRY?

Isn't it time we asked God what *his* plans and methods might be rather than pursuing our own, according to the false and destructive value system of the world?

"God, whom is it *your* will for me to marry?"

That is the foundation, and the *only* appropriate thing to ask. The decision of whom to marry has far less to do with my will or my parents' will than with *God's* will. Prayer should be the underlying foundation for any and all decisions that are made.

Finding *God's* will is the overarching purpose of including parents in the decision of whom to marry. That is their function—not to approve or disapprove of a particular choice of potential husband or wife because of what *they* want, or to impose their *own* choice, but rather to help young people, by their wisdom and insight, to discern what *God* wants.

Parents and young people, are you able to pray together? Has this been a part of your relationship in the past? If not, what better time to develop this important aspect of communication with each other and with the Lord. Establishing a prayer life together will open new doors of guidance you may not have encountered before.

It isn't only between parents and sons and daughters that prayer needs to take place. Young people, do you pray with your friends about developing relationships and finding God's choice of your spouse-to-be?

Are you saying, "What, are you crazy . . . *pray* with my friends?"

If you can't pray with your friends, maybe you need to revise your list about how to choose a friend.

More importantly, you need to pray with your potential future husband or wife. Prayer ought to be a more vital component of your relationship than any physical expression of affection, or sweet talk about how much you love each other.

NOT MY WILL . . . BUT YOUR WILL FOR ME

The will of God is the mortar that holds best-friend marriages together. How can you know God's will unless you seek his heart together? How else will you learn to seek God's will for all your decisions unless you sit down together and ask God what he wants you to do, and then work out together how to be responsive to his voice?

Prayer was an important part of the lives of Jerry and Michelle even before they met each other. Both had committed every aspect of their lives to the Lord. So when they became friends, prayer continued as an integral part of their friendship. They prayed that very first day at the beach. One of their first activities as new friends was to join together in acknowledging God's sovereignty in their lives.

If only more young people would begin their relationships in such a way!

Jerry and Michelle not only believed that God answers prayer, they knew they could trust him. So when they sat in Jerry's car the night before the wedding, experiencing tension, frustration, and doubts, they knew to turn to God. Emotion did not regulate their decision that night . . . but prayer and trust in God.

"God, what do *you* want us to do?"

It is *this* question that will ultimately make all these principles work. Without it, what can we seek but to satisfy our own selves? And feeding *self* ruins marriage.

This heart-passion to know what *God* wants above what *I* want is the fuel with which best-friend marriages run. It is seeking God's will above my own that enables me to put my best friend ahead of myself when the going gets tough. And *that* is marriage!

Dear Father, I trust you for everything in my life, and especially my future. I know you see much that I cannot see. You know me better than I can ever know myself. You know my strengths, my weaknesses, you see into the hidden places where no one else knows what I feel. You know what makes me happy, you know the quiet hurts.

You alone know just the person I need to share my life with. I ask you now, Father, to lead me to that person, in your way and in your time. Help me not to be anxious nor hasty. Let me trust your method and your timing, and let me do nothing now that will detract from the closeness of that future relationship with my lifetime partner and friend.

Let me be pure in all my ways—in body and mind and affections. Keep me from being preoccupied with romantic fantasies, and help me focus my attention on developing good friendships with both young men and young women.

Mature me in friendship, Lord. Let me seek and recognize individuals of spiritual strength, moral fiber, and integrity of character. Make me such a person as well. Make me into a modest, gracious, kind, caring, Christlike person.

Thank you for my mother and father—for the fact that they love me and want only the best for me. Help me to look past the daily conflicts and see into their hearts. Help me to do the one thing that is sometimes harder for me than any other—to trust them! Help me believe that you give them wisdom on my behalf.

Help me to recognize the truth that Mom and Dad see things about me more exactly than I do myself. Help me to joyfully submit, and even eagerly seek their will for me, though everything around me and many of my friends tell me to fight for my own independence. Help me, Lord, to resist that inclination and to seek your order in my motives in all I do.

Bring good friends into my life. In your time and in your way, show me a best friend with whom I can share the rest of my days on earth.

Give my parents insight and wisdom into your will concerning my future husband or wife. Show them the method that is best for us in preparation for my marriage. Help me not to merely comply with their will, but to eagerly desire it, knowing it will be your will for me and will prove to be for my very best. Lead me into the best-friend marriage that you have for me.

Thank you, dear Father, that you desire only good for me, and that I may trust you in all things.

PART IV

BUILDING A SOLID MARRIAGE RELATIONSHIP— PREMARRIAGE APPRENTICESHIP

You can always tell a real friend: when you've made a fool of yourself he doesn't feel you've done a permanent job.

—Lawrence Peter

Jerome and Kirsten

When one of Kirsten McRae's friends became engaged she asked Kirsten to be her maid of honor.

They talked for months about the wedding—dress patterns, fabric, colors, flowers. It was almost as exciting for Kirsten as it was for her friend.

Kirsten was an attractive young lady. She would make a lovely bridal attendant.

The rehearsal was scheduled late in the afternoon the day before the wedding, leaving plenty of time for an elegant dinner that evening. The groom's mother put nearly as much time and energy into the rehearsal dinner party as the bride's mother had put into the wedding itself.

Only moments after Kirsten walked into the church that Friday afternoon, she found herself being introduced to the most charming, handsome southern gentleman she had ever met.

"Kirsten McRae . . . meet Jerome Berry, my best man," said the groom-to-be. "He just got into town."

"Charmed, Miss McRae," Jerome said in a smooth Georgian accent, taking her hand lightly.

As soon as Kirsten could get her friend alone she said, "Why didn't you tell me the best man was such a great-looking guy!"

"I didn't know, honest," she replied. "I never met him either until a few minutes ago."

*"I nearly died when he took my hand—and he called me **Miss** McRae! Have you heard him **talk**?"*

Jerome and Kirsten hit it off immediately. If there is such a thing as love at first sight, this was it.

How romantic to meet at a wedding! Kirsten could hardly keep her mind on the rehearsal. She kept sneaking glances at Jerome. He disguised his attention with a casual air, but his brain was as preoccupied as hers. During every little break in the rehearsal, they wound up side by side.

The best man and the maid of honor. Weren't they the second most important couple in the wedding party? Why shouldn't they stand together?

As if by unspoken design, they also sat beside each other later that evening. The candlelight dinner at a historic hotel offered the perfect setting. By the time the evening was over, the two felt as if they had known each other forever.

The following afternoon they talked all through the reception and into the evening. On Sunday they met at church and went to lunch together before Jerome had to start for home, a six-hour drive away.

They promised to write and exchanged phone numbers.

13 | THE INSURANCE POLICY TO MAKE ANY METHOD WORK

Two persons cannot long be friends if they cannot forgive each other's little failings.

—Jean de La Bruyère

You've reached a part of the book that could get controversial. You've come this far with us. You may have thought arranged marriages in this day and age sounds pretty wild, but at least you kept reading.

But now will you finally say, "This is the most impractical, ridiculous thing I've ever heard!"

We hope not. Because we think this is the most important idea we have to offer you. Everything we've written thus far has been preparatory to Part 4. The principles that follow will make all the rest come to life!

AN INSURANCE POLICY THAT WILL TAKE AN INVESTMENT OF TIME AND WORK

We know that there are scores of variations and personalized applications to all these premarriage principles we have been talking about. In your particular family you will no doubt devise a strategy unlike that of any other family.

Now we offer you a universal insurance policy that is *almost* guaranteed to make any method or combination of methods or application of principles work toward a best-friend marriage.

Almost . . . because there are no absolute guarantees. But this will significantly increase the likelihood of a successful marriage.

We call this insurance policy "Christopher's Plan," for reasons that will become clear when you get into the next chapter.

After you've read what follows, you may exclaim, "Do you *really* expect us to make such a huge investment and sacrifice, to devote so much time and work and bother . . . to prepare for marriage?"

We hope you will. Here's why.

Most of us prepare two, four, even six or eight years for our careers. We plan and scheme all our lives to attain financial security. Some plan their vacations a year or more in advance. Some of you will devote more time and preparation to taking your SAT exam or training a new employee on the job or getting ready to take your driver's test than you will for your own marriage or the marriage of your son or daughter.

Isn't a strong, sound, lifelong, fruitful best-friend marriage worth dedicating a year of your life to?

Isn't it worth a year of parents' time and energy to make sure your son or daughter marries the right person, the one God has in mind for their life partner?

We think a year is a *small* and ought to be a *joyous* price to pay for all concerned!

The reward of this year's investment is a lifetime marriage established on a sound scriptural base, with full parental involvement. What could be more wonderful? You'll look back and consider it among the greatest twelve months of your life!

THE PLAN IN BRIEF

Our plan goes like this:

Sometime during the courtship, preengagement, engagement period—once the preliminary decision has been made that two people will marry and believe it is God's will for them to do so—a year will be devoted for each to *live with and work alongside their future parents-in-law.*

We call this period a *premarriage apprenticeship.*

The primary goal of this time is to give the Lord further opportunity to confirm that the marriage plans have progressed according to his leading . . . or to clarify his will that plans for the marriage be discontinued.

These goals are achieved through the secondary objective of allowing all the relationships involved to deepen in the real-life practical settings of a shared home and strenuous daily work.

Toward this end, we recommend that a young woman's parents invite her potential husband to live with them for a year, at the same time as the young man's parents host their future daughter-in-law. It thus becomes a working apprenticeship, a time to learn new skills—perhaps to become acquainted with a family business—and to engage in spiritual, practical, and vocational mentoring.

MICHAEL & JUDY PHILLIPS

These take place in particular between the father and his future son-in-law and between the mother and her future daughter-in-law.

These are no mere visits, but provide occasion for a young man to serve in the full capacity of "apprentice" to his future father-in-law in whatever work the arrangement can accommodate—full-time with the girl's father, if possible, or in some other capacity if not. Mother and future daughter-in-law will establish a similar relationship.

Obviously if the girl's father is self-employed this will be easier. If not, arranging it may be more difficult. But anything is possible. Where hands are willing to work hard, work can always be found. Whether there should be payment for services or not is an individual matter. Each should come expecting no more than board and room.

If a man works in a capacity where he does not have the option or funds available to hire an apprentice, where legalities can be complied with, very few employers will turn down free and willing or minimum-wage labor. If a man is a teacher, for example, he could bring the young man into his classroom as an aide. A father with a factory job might be able to arrange a job for the young man elsewhere in the factory. Perhaps there are jobs at his future in-laws' home that the young man could do, such as painting or other maintenance work.

Circumstances will vary tremendously. The goal is for a young man to work, sweat, eat and sleep, study the Bible and go to church with, and fully interact in the daily grind of life with his future bride's family. They will thus get to know what he is made of, how capable he will be of supporting their daughter, and how he handles hard work, stress, and adversity. At the same time, he will get to know his potential bride's family and their occupation and see what awaits him in relationship with them in future years.

As all of this is going on, back at his home, the young woman will be apprenticing under her future husband's mother. Perhaps the mother will have the sort of job that can incorporate her future daughter-in-law. If not, perhaps the young lady will serve her "apprenticeship" in the home, keeping it clean for her prospective mother-in-law, doing housework, making meals, and so on. If the mother works at home, the two can work together, and the young lady can be incorporated into additional phases of her life—volunteer work, Bible study groups, and perhaps the care and training of younger children. If there is a family business, there are a multitude of ways the young lady might be brought into it.

We know that a year of learning and relationship-building such as this will disrupt life in a hundred ways for both families. There will be a financial cost involved to all concerned, though these would likely balance out in the long run. There may be pauses or breaks in educational programs. It will complicate the parents' lives in particular, because having an apprentice to account for always adds to one's own work.

It may not be an easy thing to pull off. In some cases, as in the true-life accounts of Marc and Doug—both in their thirties and holding responsible jobs—it will be impossible. We simply urge you to consider the enormous potential benefits in those situations where it can be done.

A Thousand Applications

If you've read this far you know that we do not advocate legalism in carrying out any of the many principles we have discussed. In none is individuality, prayer, flexibility, and personal application *more* required than in the premarriage apprenticeship.

Some of you will have serious objections to our plan. Loss of job, school opportunities, other considerations can be endless. There may be a thousand practical objections that spring immediately to your mind. We acknowledge these are real concerns that could make our plan extremely difficult. Before you throw out the possibility altogether, however, please devote some thought and prayer to asking yourself how you might modify the plan to fit your particular situation so that it *can* become practical and possible.

Bringing your daughter's young man into the lab where you work may simply be out of the question. But maybe your brother across town operates a little freight company and can always use another forklift driver, especially if you explain the situation.

Then again, maybe no such practical work situation presents itself. The young man is in the middle of his college education and you don't want to ask him to interrupt it. Might you look into the possibility of his transferring to the university in your area for a year? He could live with you but continue his studies in your city. On weekends you and he could work together, for example, clearing off that acre on your country property you've been wanting to get to.

Perhaps a year *cannot* work, for whatever reason. There are summers, weekends, and other vacation times in which to build a mini-apprenticeship program. Or perhaps it will prove best to postpone the whole program until after graduation. Remember the importance of going *slowly*?

We own a business and write. In our case, we have a dozen places where young people can plug into our lives. Have you grown up on a farm? Your family environment will likewise offer many opportunities. It's a perfect setting for an apprenticeship. This, however, isn't the case for everyone. We recognize the difficulty many of you will face in devising a workable strategy. Yet work can *always* be found. And work is the key here, because in *working* side by side people get

MICHAEL & JUDY PHILLIPS

to know one another in a singularly beneficial and non-artificial setting.
You have to devise *a unique apprenticeship plan* that will work for *your* situation and for *your* two young people. Every set of circumstances throws special challenges into the mix.

RELATIONSHIP AND CHARACTER TESTING

Anything of value is worth *fighting* for, worth *working* for, worth *sacrificing* for. Things of great value will not only withstand rigorous testing but will come out of the purifying fire shining all the more brilliantly.

Tested relationships are the strongest relationships. Why not allow potential marriage relationships to experience some of the testing that will come later? How strong are they? Are they gold or kindling? What will happen when the going gets rough? Will one of the young people bolt? Better to find out now than during the adversity of marriage.

If one is unwilling to subject the love he feels for a certain young lady or young man to the testing fires of sacrifice, hard work, and waiting—all in the interest of getting to know each other—how true is that love? Would *you* want to marry someone who is unwilling to give a year of his or her life for you? If he or she is unwilling to give *a year* now, do you really think he or she will give you the next *thirty or forty years* without wavering in that commitment?

What does it reveal of an individual to say, "I am ready to dedicate my entire life to you . . . but I am unwilling to take a year of my life to confirm and prove and validate my love."

This time of testing has the enormous benefit of strengthening and solidifying and confirming commitment and love that is simply not possible any other way, for the simple reason that work and life together can be *hard*. And only *difficult* tests reveal what is hidden deep inside—reliability, accountability, and maturity . . . or irresponsibility, selfishness, and lack of commitment.

DEEPENING OF THE FAMILY RELATIONSHIPS

There are four primary relationships the apprenticeship tests, strengthens, and deepens—or breaks: the relationship of the young man with his future father-in-law and with his future mother-in-law, the young lady with her future father-in-law and with her future mother-in-law, as well as the reverse of these relationships.

Apprenticeship moves all these relationships from the artificial, stuffy, best-behavior environment of dating and courtship—planned outings, get-togethers, and polite dinners—and forces them into the ups and downs of daily life where significant growth occurs, maturity develops, and true character is both revealed and produced.

When a young man and the father of his proposed future wife work alongside each other for a long period of time, in an environment sufficiently difficult to genuinely get to know each other well, they hopefully will bond together as father and son. This time gives a young lady's father the opportunity to know the character of the man to whom he plans to give his daughter. Either he will say, "This is a man of integrity and character—indeed a worthy groom and son-in-law," or, because he will see things that would never become apparent even in a traditional courtship setting, he may conclude, "There are hidden flaws in this young man that signal danger in the future. I'm not comfortable giving him my daughter's hand . . . at least not yet." Thus, he averts the future heartache of his daughter.

Apprenticeship isn't only for parents' peace of mind. The year also provides an insurance policy for the young people.

It is a well-known fact—though little heeded by starry-eyed lovers—that in general young men grow up to resemble their fathers and young women grow up to resemble their mothers. These are obvious generalizations, but they bear notice.

Apprenticeship may reveal to a young man that his future mother-in-law is crabby, overweight, undisciplined, a poor housekeeper, and a lousy cook. He would be wise to pause and consider his own marriage plans, recognizing the odds that these same characteristics might someday emerge in his own potential wife, as beautiful and selfless and wonderful as she *now* seems to his smitten heart!

This sobering realization may inject a dose of reality into his perspective. Does he really want to marry a young lady who may become like this woman he has come to know in the last seven months? His love is extraordinary if such a possibility does not dissuade him. And their potential marriage will be all the stronger, for his love is now founded less on romantic idealism and more on open-eyed commitment about what to expect.

Likewise, a young woman may come to realize that her future father-in-law is silent, moody, and unkempt. He doesn't shave on weekends, gripes about every meal, never picks up after himself, and rarely says a nice word to his wife. Does she want to marry a man who may turn out like *that* in twenty-five years? Does she love him enough to marry him knowing such to be a possibility? Can she accept these things about him? Can she love and be part of this family, knowing them as she does?

If the answers to such questions are *yes*, then the potential marriage will have been immeasurably benefited. The two young people have moved away from romantic naiveté and further toward friendship. If the answers to these questions are *no*, and the engagement ends, then a future divorce has been forestalled and much heartache avoided.

You see, it isn't only the young people who are in apprenticeship. It is the parents as well. Though there are four relationships to consider, there are *eight* testings in progress:

> *Young man*: "Do I want this man for my father-in-law?"
> *Father*: "Will this young man be a good husband and provider for my daughter?"
> *Young man*: "Do I want a wife that looks and acts like her mother?"
> *Mother*: "Will this young man protect and love my daughter?"
> *Young woman*: "Do I want this woman for my mother-in-law?"
> *Mother*: "Will this young woman be a good mother to my grand-children?"
> *Young woman*: "Do I want a husband that looks and acts like his father?"
> *Father*: "Will this young woman be a good wife for my son?"

Does it sound heartless to speak of testing one another and of so-called "trial" relationships, as if we aren't accepting one another or are expecting everyone to be perfect?

Not at all. Our goal is to prevent future divorce by injecting marital preparations with an opportunity to view potential lifetime relationships with realism.

Who would think of entering a business partnership blind, without knowing even obscure details about a potential partner? No one expects anyone to be perfect. We're trying to help parents and young people look realistically and practically at the question, "Do I want to spend the rest of my life with *this* person, with *this* family, in *this* environment?"

And the foundation of the entire apprenticeship is the fact that all individuals involved must continually ask the Lord to confirm or oppose the marriage through this time of waiting, working, and testing. Such is its purpose.

THE BIGGEST APPRENTICESHIP QUESTION OF ALL

Do a young man and young woman really love each other? Is their love truly sacrificial? Would they do anything for the other? Do they want the other's best above their own? Do they want the ultimate happiness of the other, no matter what it costs them?

If their love passes these tests, then the period of premarriage apprenticeship gives each the prayerful opportunity, while apart, seriously to ask the most important question of all: *What if God wills that my beloved marry someone else?*

This is the greatest expression of the deepest form of love: a willingness to lay that love on the altar—seeking not your *own* will, but the will of the Father, seeking not your *own* happiness, but the happiness and best of your beloved. Even if that best means your loved one marries someone else.

The world may scoff at such a foundation for marriage. We believe it represents God's way. What is *love* but wanting nothing but the highest good, the absolute best—not for yourself, but for your beloved? Can it truly be the sacrificial love that will sustain a marriage when one of the persons wants his *own* way above that highest good?

The apprenticeship is designed to bring young people to this point of willingness to give up their beloved, to create in them not only the love of romance but the love of sacrifice. Why shouldn't young people apply (as did Agnes in Dickens' *David Copperfield* and Aggie in MacDonald's *Castle Warlock*) this same principle, agonizing as it may be, to their future marriage plans? This is a testing fire out of which true love and a lifetime marriage will emerge radiant and pure, while love made of anything less than gold will be revealed for what it is.

Can a young man or a young woman say: "If there is the slightest possibility that marrying me is not the very best for you, then I love you enough to step aside. I want all the insight available to us to help us know that our being married is truly for the best. My love for you dictates that I lay aside my own will in the matter (of course I want to marry you with all my heart) and heed the wise counsel of our fathers and mothers. They may be able to see more clearly than we do what is best. If they feel I should not marry you, painful as it would be for me to hear it, I would not marry you. I love you too much to allow you to marry the wrong person . . . even if that wrong person is me."

In our age of seeking the best for "number one," these are factors usually left unconsidered, and to the world they are incomprehensible.

But God's way is not the same as the world's. We believe it is time Christians took drastic measures to found the marriages of future generations on *his* principles, and relinquishment and sacrifice are fundamental among them.

*Without a friend, thou mayest not long
endure.*

—Thomas à Kempis

Young and Competent

At twenty-two, Kirsten McRae was competent, efficient, and full of spunk—
a "together" young lady whose clothes never seemed to wrinkle and who had
the world by the tail. She had it together before she was a Christian, but when
she gave her heart to the Lord at seventeen, she gave the appearance of being
just about perfect.

She could cook and sew and handle almost any job that came her way.
Wherever she worked, she quickly rose to indispensable status. Whatever ill effects she may have suffered from a non-Christian broken home, you could not
discern it from looking at her. She did have a temper and an independent streak,
but in light of her many other shining qualities, these could be overlooked. She
had been on her own since the age of sixteen and certainly knew what she was
about.

Kirsten lived with several other single Christian women in the spacious
home of a Christian couple several years older than she and her friends. And
though it was a comfortable arrangement, since meeting Jerome, Kirsten had
grown discontent. She felt that none of her housemates understood her. The
pressure of her accounting job, along with that of college classes, had been
slowly getting to her. She felt she needed a change.

When a young couple in her church, the Raynolds, invited Kirsten to move
in with them in exchange for help with the housework and meals, she jumped
at the chance. It was just what she needed— a little more space and an environment where she could be more independent. It was a nice house and the
Raynolds were gone most of the day. She would have one end of the place practically to herself.

Kirsten had dated a lot when she was younger and really had no interest in dating for fun. Now that she was older and was a Christian, things were different, especially after meeting Jerome. All she wanted now, besides him, was to focus on establishing a career. She loved being in the middle of the active, exciting business world, and anyone could see that she was likely to go far.

Because her parents were divorced and were not Christians, Kirsten began to look to the Raynolds for spiritual leadership. She especially respected Mr. Raynold, a bright, mature man of God. She began to share problems regarding work or school with him. Usually he had some insightful word for her.

His wife, however, sometimes got on Kirsten's nerves. She was a schoolteacher and could be bossy about how she wanted things done in her home. She was also pregnant, and her moodiness made Kirsten irritable. Most of the time Kirsten did things her own way and didn't pay attention to Mrs. Raynold's requests.

Everything would have continued fine despite such annoyances if the Raynolds hadn't interfered when Kirsten wanted to buy a new car. She was astute in business and had been managing her own finances for years. This was one issue where she didn't need their advice.

"Kirsten," Mr. Raynold began one evening at dinner, "I'm afraid you're getting in a little over your head."

"I can swing the payments," she replied, already on the defensive.

"But why an Audi?" he asked. "There are many less expensive cars that would provide great transportation."

"I've always wanted an Audi."

"Do you think that's a good enough reason? It's an expensive car."

"It's a good enough reason for me," replied Kirsten.

"I'm not sure that's a sound basis for such a big decision. You've been planning to go to school full time next semester. It will be hard to keep up the car payments."

*Well, thought Kirsten, **nobody is going to tell me how to spend my own money!***

A week later she was driving a smart new yellow Audi.

14 | "Christopher's Plan"

Friends are necessary to a happy life. When friendship deserts us we are as lonely and helpless as a ship, left by the tide high upon the shore. When friendship returns to us, it is as though the tide came back, gave us buoyancy and freedom, and opened to us the wide places of the world.

—Harry Emerson Fosdick

In the Introduction we mentioned the book *A Home for the Heart*, book 8 in the series THE JOURNALS OF CORRIE BELLE HOLLISTER, out of which *Best Friends for Life* grew. *A Home for the Heart* tells the story of a young lady named Corrie Hollister and a young man named Christopher Braxton as they prepare for marriage. It is in this book that "Christopher's Plan" first appeared.

Early in his life Christopher was a pastor. At that time he devised a premarriage apprenticeship plan he hoped to put into practice in his own life should the chance to marry arise. Of course, meeting Corrie presents just that opportunity. In a lengthy letter to Corrie, Christopher explains how he came up with his plan and why he believes in it so strongly. Then he tells her what he would like for them to do regarding their own preparation for marriage.

We hope you read *A Home for the Heart*. Though it is fiction, we believe it will help you to envision and practically implement your own version of Christopher's Plan perhaps better than anything we might add here.

To allow those of you who have not read *A Home for the Heart* to more fully understand the premarriage apprenticeship we propose, we will quote here, with a few minor changes, from the book.

How Christopher Devised the Apprenticeship Scheme

When I was pastoring, the subject of marriage *was one about which my views differed widely from those held by most of my parishioners. The points of contention grew to encompass what many considered my radical notions on the subject—if taking the holiest and oldest human relationship seriously enough to desire that it be strong, well founded, and give God glory is "radical."*

I was often in the position of having to counsel young people—not much younger than myself, actually, and once or twice older—in preparation for marriage. Almost without exception I found myself discouraged and disheartened, saying to myself, "These two people do not know each other in any depth. Neither do their respective parents have the slightest idea what manner of individual will be joining their family. This young man and young woman are not ready to marry. They are not prepared for the stresses that being married will bring. They need to pass beyond their present superficial feelings in order to truly build this marriage on a solid foundation. They need time to prepare themselves—a great deal of time."

Some of them were so young. Many came wanting me to rush through a ceremony. They wanted me for no other reason than to perform the service. The last thing either they or their mothers and fathers wanted was an overzealous young pastor throwing a bucket of cold water over their euphoria. They did not want spiritual counsel. They did not want me to speak the truth. They did not want to be told that perhaps there was a better way to go about this, a way based on Scripture, a way based on God's intent for man and woman.

All they wanted from me was a blind acquiescence to their desires, so as to give the illusion of spiritual approval to their plans, about which the will of God could not have been further from their minds. That was not something I could in good conscience do. I did not enter the ministry to preside over a social club, but to confront people with the truths of God and his will for our lives.

In my mind I knew many of these ill-advised marriages could only lead to heartbreak. This is not to say that all such marriages ended in divorce. Some did. But mostly it was a matter of the marriages I performed being built on sand rather than stone. Almost invariably I saw futures constructed on hopes that could never sustain the giving and commitment and self-sacrifice so necessary between a husband and wife.

I saw marriages founded on mutual attraction, on financial considerations, on ties between families. And always, it seemed, ego, pride, desire, vanity, and self were ever-present ingredients in the mix of factors—in the parents as much as in the children, for whom making what is called a "good marriage" for their offspring in the eyes of society was of paramount importance. Unfortunately, that all-important guideline was almost always based on the worldly norms of a false set of societal standards.

Witnessing these tragic circumstances—and I do consider it tragic whenever the holy institution of marriage is undertaken with less seriousness than God intended it—repeatedly caused me to consider not performing marriages at all. Yet that did not seem to be the answer. I labored over it for some time before the Lord began to stimulate my thinking in a new direction.

As more couples and their parents from my congregation came to me for the purpose of being joined in matrimony, I began to encourage them to wait at least a year, and to put that twelve months to good use getting to know one another. I suggested that, if circumstances allowed, young men be invited to join the family of their fiancée, to live and work with the future bride's parents for a year, hopefully working with and alongside the future father-in-law in whatever activity the latter was engaged. At the same time I suggested that the young woman spend the same period of time with her fiancé's parents, living and working daily with her future husband's mother, in her fiancé's home.

What a wonderful setting, I thought, for the parents of both the young man and the young woman to get to know personally and in great depth the individual they would be welcoming into their family! And how eye-opening to the young persons, to find out what sort of a family they were contemplating joining.

It was such a brainstorm, such a revelation, that I was certain all to whom I told it would be eager to adopt my plan in an instant. Ah, but how wrong I was!

The first young couple to whom I proposed it turned and left my office on the spot, saying that they would find someone else to marry them. They were not interested in all my spiritual talk on the subject, they only wanted to get married . . . and soon.

I was visited the next day by one of my elders, a powerful man in the community with an attractive daughter of his own approaching marrying age. He had heard of my proposal from the father of the other young woman and had come to tell me what he thought of the nonsense, adding that he hoped I was rid of such a foolish notion by the time his daughter was ready for marriage, because he wanted her married in his own church. Furthermore, he added, he was uninterested in having any business dealings with whatever young man his daughter may decide to marry. If he was of a family of good standing and had means, that was what mattered. He saw no reason for two families to expose their personal lives to one another in such a ridiculous fashion.

He was not the only one to react so. In fact, my proposal fell on not a single receptive ear. But I was not dissuaded within myself. I continued to ponder the whole thing and to study what I could find from Scripture.

The story of Jacob, and Laban's two daughters in Genesis 29, spoke to me particularly. Jacob loved Rachel so much that he worked not one year, but seven years for her father—only to be deceived in the end and be given her sister Leah instead. But did Jacob despair? No. He served as a faithful husband to Leah, then willingly agreed to work another seven years for Rachel. Even though Laban had lied to him, Jacob submitted to him for fourteen long years.

After all that time, you can be sure they all knew one another very intimately. Jacob would have known his future father-in-law like a brother—they worked side by side for fourteen years! Jacob and Rachel, likewise, would have known each other like sister and brother. They surely would not have married on the basis of physical attraction or superficial acquaintance! Fourteen years had passed. They must have truly loved each other!

As I pondered the account, I saw that even though Laban played him false, Jacob proved his worth and integrity of character by being willing to work all those years. Both Rachel and Laban knew what manner of man they were getting in Jacob!

What a demonstration of a man's love!

I love the passage that reads, "And Jacob served seven years for Rachel, and they seemed unto him but a few days, for the love he had for her." Time is not so long for people who truly love.

No wonder God was able to bless Jacob so that in time he became more wealthy than Laban himself, and eventually fathered the twelve patriarchs of Israel!

In the end, though I cannot say I determined that such a premarriage apprenticeship with one's future parents-in-law was what could be termed a scriptural "standard," I did become persuaded that it was biblically sound and in line with God's intent. I was certainly convinced that God intends parents to play a more determinative and vigorous role in training their sons and daughters for marriage than is commonly accepted.

The conclusion of my reflection was that if I was unable as a pastor to effectively communicate the importance of such preparation, I determined that if I was ever blessed by God with a son or a daughter of my own, that I would place such an injunction upon them before giving my approval to a marriage that they might consider.

Some would consider it a hard thing to exercise such control over his sons and daughters.

A hard thing!

Is it not the most loving kind of fatherhood imaginable that would seek to protect his child and spare no effort to obtain the best of all possible future marriages for him or her? Is that not exactly what God is constantly doing for us, watching out for us, helping us, guiding us, instructing us— he the loving, protective father, we his obedient and submissive children?

Has he not arranged just such a marriage for us with his own dear Son? Is he not working day and night all our lives long to prepare us for that marriage? How can our earthly lives look anywhere but to that coming heavenly marriage as our example?

Some perhaps consider God's overlordship a severe thing. But I say they know not what manner of father their heavenly Father is! If they knew him, they would rejoice in his authority over every phase of their lives. But I was speaking as though I were myself a father facing the marriage of one of my own.

If a young man was to come to me and say, "I love your daughter and I want to marry her," I would measure his character and the depth of that love by his willingness to go along with my proposal.

"I would like nothing more, young man," I might say, "than to shake your hand as my son and to give you my daughter as your wife. But first I must know what manner of young man makes this request of me. So tell me, do you love my daughter sufficiently to give yourself to me for a year, to live under my roof, to work with me, to interact with me and talk with me and minister to people alongside me? Do you love her enough to make such a sacrifice? Do you love my daughter sufficiently to earn the right to ask for her hand? Do you love her sufficiently to allow me to test your faith, to allow me to get to know you perhaps better than my own daughter knows you, or than you even know yourself? Will you allow me to test your character as a man and as a Christian, to determine if I judge you right for my daughter?"

Such a one could well reply, "No, sir, I will be party to no such plan. It is not your right to decide whom your daughter will marry. That should be a decision between her and me alone. I am a free agent, an adult, capable of directing my own life, and I will offer to no other such a complete submission."

If this was his reply, then I would know that he did not understand the most fundamental of all human institutions—the role of fatherhood—as evidenced in every line of the Gospels by how Jesus ordered his life. I would know further that his resistance to my authority and my oversight over his and my daughter's future indicated a flaw in his relationship with his heavenly Father—a flaw that goes by the name independence. He has not apprehended his role as a child, in submission to God's authority, and therefore he takes umbrage at the thought of submission to me as the father of *the woman he would make his wife. Is not such submission to God's authority both the visible and invisible message inherent on every page of the Bible?*

I would therefore have no choice if I wanted the best for my daughter but to say, "I am sorry, my dear, but I cannot consent to give your hand to this young man. I know you love him a great deal. But believe me, in time the independence that is in his heart and his resistance to authority would inevitably cause you grief as his wife. He does not grasp the most fundamental truths of fatherhood or childship and therefore he is ill-equipped to be a loving and sacrificial husband. He is even more ill-equipped to step into the proper role as a wise father to your children, for he does not grasp the underlying, pulse-giving life to the scriptural story."

I imagine such a daughter might reply, "But, Papa, he is young. How can you expect him to share your perspectives when you have been walking with God so much longer than he? He may well grow into all that you say."

"Then he would have been willing," I would reply. "Willingness is the indication of growth to come. I do not say he has to see all I see. But trust is a significant window into character, and he professed himself unable to trust me as his spiritual elder. No, my dear, of course I would not expect him or you to see things altogether as I see them. I look not necessarily for a present level of maturity, but rather for willingness. A willing spirit is a spirit that will grow and will mature in time. Your young man was not willing, not even willing to inquire as to my reasons or into the biblical validity of my plan. He did not care to know my heart in the matter. If he does not love you to that extent now, to even display a willingness to investigate, how much will he love you when the great stresses of life come to your marriage fifteen years from now? I simply ask you, in love—if he does not love you enough to trust me, does he love you enough for you to commit yourself to him for life? I am sure he says he loves you. But love is more than what one says, it is what one does . . . and is willing to do."

During such a period of what I have, for lack of a better term, called premarriage apprenticeship, all the façades would in time be peeled away. Both parents would come to know deeply the quality of belief and the depth of character in the one their son or daughter wants to marry.

What father does not want his daughter well provided for by a husband with foresight, integrity, and common sense? How better to determine whether a young man is capable of sustained work and a healthy outlook than for a future father-in-law to work alongside him?

What mother does not want her son's home well ordered and his children well raised by a woman with homemaking intuition and skills, who loves children and understands how they are to be trained? What better way for a mother to determine such things than by bringing her future

daughter-in-law into her own home to work alongside her?
Perhaps such a plan would not work in every case. And how widely the
individual circumstances would vary in its application. But how many pre-
mature marriages between couples ill-suited for one another might be
avoided if parents shared more of the responsibility for a wise and well-
thought-out decision?

How wonderful if the young man and young woman could share time
under both parents' roofs, perhaps for even three of those twelve months,
in an atmosphere highly supervised by the parents. They too need to see
each other with their hair down, in a family environment where stresses
and strains reveal to the often cloudy eyes of love the stark realities of what
a beloved may really be like when not on his or her forced best behavior.
Perhaps just as many ill-fated marriages would be avoided by reconsider-
ation of one of the two young people as from counsel by either set of parents.

"I didn't know that's what you were like!" one might say. "I didn't know
you were so prone to anger . . . so self-centered . . . so irritable . . . so lazy
. . . such a poor cook . . . so moody."

Better these things be said and the stars removed from the eyes now,
while there is yet time, than after the marriage has been performed, and it
is too late.

Is the idea too radical?

I admit, it is a far-reaching proposal with astounding implications if
Christians practiced it in a widespread way.

I need not worry, for they will not. Alas, it is the grief of my adult life
to realize that most Christians do not take their faith seriously enough to
allow its light to penetrate into all the many and varied corners of their
existence. Marriage is a sad case in point.

ONE INDIVIDUAL WITH THE VISION CAN SET THIS IN MOTION

Christopher next outlines a proposal for Corrie and himself to follow as they anticipate marriage. As you will see, it is reminiscent of courtship, borrowing elements from many of the things we have discussed, yet it is wholly unique to Corrie and Christopher's situation.

Both Christopher's father and mother were dead, so there was only one family to consider. Corrie's mother was also dead. Corrie's family lived in a rural setting, operating both a business and a gold mine (the story takes place in the 1850s and 1860s in California), which clearly afforded ample opportunity for putting Christopher's ideas into practice. As with all these principles, Christopher's plan must be adopted to your individual circumstances. You may be in a separated, blended, or divorce-altered family. These factors and others will add complexity to your considerations. The plan may not be quite so easy. But if you are willing to creatively seek God's special plan for you, there is no end to the possibilities.

There is one further point to glean from Christopher's experience. Of the six principle players in any premarriage planning—the two young people and both sets of parents—any one of the six can be the impetus behind attempting something as bold and new as this. Neither Corrie nor her father nor her stepmother had ever heard of such a thing. It took Christopher's speaking of it to set the process in motion. You may be an engaged young woman or a parent or a young man contemplating marriage. *You*, and you alone, might be the one to implement some of these things, as Christopher did. Everything has to originate somewhere, and perhaps *you* are the one to originate the apprenticeship in your situation.

CHRISTOPHER'S PLAN FOR CORRIE AND HIMSELF

Let's turn again to Christopher's story and listen in as he introduces his scheme to Corrie. At this point, though they have spoken of marriage, Christopher has not yet asked Corrie's father for her hand.

I am one who takes his faith seriously. I want the light of God's truth to shine into every corner of my life that I can point it. I know you share that desire. It is one of the chief reasons I love you and why I want you to be my wife and hope to be your husband.

Here is my plan:

Your father does not know me. In one sense, Corrie, you do not know me that well either. You think you do, but the time together with which the Lord has blessed us has been relatively brief. There were many unusual circumstances that could have artificially drawn us together. I want both you and your father to know me—really know me in the intimate way in which family members come to know one another. For me to put to your father now the subject of marriage to his daughter would be to place him in a position in which he could not make a wise and prudent decision. How could he? He has no possible way to determine whether I will make a worthy husband.

Don't you see the wonderful protection there is in it! Both of us are protected from allowing our love for each other to blind us to practical realities that only one who is married is capable of seeing.

I have never been a husband or a father. I cannot say with certainty whether I am capable of carrying out the responsibilities of either with the wisdom and love and sacrificial Christlikeness that each requires. I love you too much not to want the very best for you.

What if that best is not me? How can I possibly know?

Because I am right in the middle, I am the least *equipped to be able to answer the question insofar as it concerns me. And, my dear one, as much as I respect your maturity and judgment, neither are you equipped to be able to answer the question as to what kind of husband and father I will make. You and I are both young, and your eyes too are clouded with love. If you will forgive my saying so, your judgment is no more to be depended upon than mine.*

Similarly, how can either you or I know whether you are ready for marriage? How can we know how prepared you are to be a wife and mother? Neither of us has spent years training and preparing ourselves for marriage. Is it wise for us to proceed?

But there is one whose eyes are not clouded, who is not young, who has been both a husband and a father for many years, a man who is a Christian and who has a wide background in making decisions for himself, for his family, for his town, and even for his state. What wisdom such diverse experience must have deepened in him. He is clearly in a much stronger position than either of us to evaluate the decision we face and to speak wisdom into our lives.

I am, of course, speaking of your father. If my father or mother were alive, they too would enter into this process. But as they are not, the decision must rest with your father and stepmother as well as with you and me.

I want, therefore, not merely to ask your father for your hand in marriage. I am going to ask him to allow me to submit to him in the ways of which I have spoken. I will tell him I do not want him to merely agree to what you and I would like to do, but that we desire to place the decision for what course we should follow into his hands. I will add that his decision must not be made until he knows me well enough and has seen me in sufficiently diverse circumstances as to make a wise judgment concerning me.

Without pushing myself upon him, I want to ask him if he would consider allowing me to work with him in whatever activities he is engaged. As long as I have a place to sleep—whether in a barn or with friends of your father's in town—and my daily sustenance, I will consider it ample.

In other words, with both your consent and his, my plan is to state our hopes of marriage, then to submit my way entirely to him for a year, at the end of which time he will be able to give us his decision and advise us in any way he chooses—counsel that you and I will gladly and eagerly welcome.

I want to love you with the love Jacob demonstrated. And I want to prove that faithfulness to both you and your father. I feel it is right and

proper and scriptural for me to earn the right to call myself your husband.
So that, my dear Corrie, is what I would like to do when I come to
Miracle Springs, which I hope will be soon, before the year is out.
What do you think?
Do you consider it altogether radical and ridiculous? I hope you do not.
But I have been so in the habit of my ideas being looked askance upon by
most with whom I share them that I find myself anxious about how you
will react. Forgive me. I should trust you more than that. I will learn!
I am of the strong conviction that a man and wife must move together
in all things, not separately. It seems that we must begin even at this stage
to function as one, and therefore, though I am convinced this is the proper
course to follow, I earnestly desire to know your heart on the matter. If it
should not be as mine, then I would rethink and repray the whole idea.
I will await your reply. Obviously I do not want to proceed if you have
objections, though I sincerely think such a course would ensure us a much
stronger marriage in the end.

HOW PA HOLLISTER RESPONDED TO CHRISTOPHER'S REQUEST

As you might expect, Corrie's father was nearly speechless when he heard
what Christopher wanted to do. You might find the same reaction when you share
your plan with your parents, or your son or daughter, or your special friend. We'll
quote once more from *A Home for the Heart*, with Corrie now narrating the story.

Dinner was much like the night before, though I kept feeling too self-
conscious with both Pa and Christopher there. Toward the end of the meal,
Christopher began to get a little quiet too, and I started getting nervous.
"Mr. Hollister," Christopher said, "I wonder if I might have a few words
with you?"
Oh no, I thought. Christopher—I didn't think you were going to do
it this soon! The two of you just met! But then Pa's answer made me die
another two or three deaths!
"Sure, Braxton," Pa said, easing into his favorite chair, "have a seat."
No, no . . . not here—not right in front of everybody!
Suddenly there was a crashing sound and everybody looked my way. A
plate had fallen from my hands onto the hard wooden floor.
My hands were shaking. I had to get out of there! If they were staying
inside, I was leaving!
As I stooped down to pick up the plate, I heard Christopher again.
"I mean in private, sir," he said.
"Oh . . . oh yes . . . why, of course," said Pa, still completely unaware

of Christopher's intentions. He stood up again. "How about we take a walk outside?"

Christopher nodded and they left the house.

I continued to help clean up, but I had never been so agitated or distracted in my life. Every little sound I heard startled me and I would jump and look toward the door.

Almeda knew, but she kept her peace. Every once in a while she would look at me with a tender, motherly smile, and I knew she understood. Oh, this was all too mortifying! I was simply going to die of embarrassment!

They were gone over an hour. When we had the kitchen cleaned up I made an escape to my room, lay down on my bed, and pulled my pillow over my head. I didn't want to see anyone!

A while later the outside door opened. I heard Pa say something to Almeda.

Oh, I would die if I had to go out there now! What could I do? I wondered if I could escape through the window and make a dash for the safety of the woods.

"Where's Corrie?" I heard Pa ask.

It was silent a moment. The door of my room opened. A moment later I felt someone sitting down on the side of my bed. A hand reached under the pillow and lay gently on my head.

"Corrie, dear," said Almeda, "I think I have some idea what you are going through, but your father wants you to come out and join the rest of us."

She stood up and I joined her, and we walked out into the family room where everyone else was gathered.

Pa's face had a big smile all over it. I knew in an instant that Christopher had asked him.

"Well, what is it, Drummond?" asked Almeda. "You look as if you know something and are dying to tell all the rest of us."

"I reckon I do at that!" said Pa.

"Then tell us, for heaven's sake!" laughed Almeda.

"Well it's just this, then," said Pa. "Blamed if this young Braxton fellow didn't just ask me if he could make my oldest daughter his wife!"

Almeda gasped.

"Corrie!" she exclaimed, bursting into tears. Pa and Christopher hung back, chuckling and smiling to themselves.

Christopher caught my eye and smiled. I returned it kind of sheepishly. Of course I was happy—wonderfully, deliriously happy—in spite of my embarrassment! Who wouldn't be happy? And I guess I felt relieved, too, that it was finally all out in the open and we could talk about it. How could I have ever thought that Christopher would change his mind! But I still felt red and hot and was perspiring all over.

"Well . . ." said Almeda impatiently, when the silence became complete and still Pa hadn't said anything.

"Well, what?" asked Pa.

"Well, what answer did you give the man, Drummond, for heaven's sake!" she said, nearly stamping her foot with laughing impatience.

"Didn't give him no answer at all."

"What!"

"He wouldn't let me answer. Before I could say a word," Pa went on, "Christopher here told me he didn't want my answer right yet. Matter of fact . . . he didn't want it for a year."

"A year!"

"That's right. Seems the young feller's got the notion that it ought to be my decision whether he and Corrie Belle are right for each other. And he doesn't figure I can say one way or the other till I know him a mite better than two men can who just met."

"But what will happen, then, for the whole year?" said Almeda, bewildered by the whole thing.

Pa shifted on his feet, then glanced over at Christopher.

"You wanna try and explain it to my wife, Braxton?" he said. "I ain't sure I more than half understand it myself."

Christopher laughed.

"I'll try, Mr. Hollister," he said as gradually we all took seats again.

Christopher began, speaking mostly to Almeda, but glancing now and then toward Pa or me. He told them what he had written me about his church and how he had arrived at the idea.

"I don't know if you'd call it an apprenticeship engagement," he said, "but something like that. During that time I would like to work for your husband, and you too, Mrs. Hollister, and submit myself to you in every way. If I'm wanting someday to be called your son-in-law, then I feel I have to earn that right in your eyes. I want the two of you to know me so well that you know whether you want me for a son or not and whether you feel I will make a worthy husband for your daughter. Maybe this is a way of taking the guesswork out of marriage. After a year, you'll probably know some things about me that I don't even know about myself. Corrie and I will know each other better too. I realize it's highly unusual, and probably most folks would consider it just about the craziest thing they'd ever heard. But I happen to think there's wisdom in it and some scriptural precedent as well. Marriage is too sacred an institution to take lightly, Mr. and Mrs. Hollister. I don't take it lightly myself, and I want to give the two of you and your daughter enough time to make a wise decision among yourselves regarding Corrie's future. I care too much about her to rush into it."

A long silence followed. Neither Pa nor Almeda had ever heard the like of it in their lives.

"Well, what do you think about all this, Corrie?" Pa said finally, turning toward me.

"He's a wise man, Pa," I answered softly. "I trust him."

Pa just nodded his head, then rubbed his chin thoughtfully.

"Yep," he said, halfway to himself, "I think I'm starting to see that already."

What happened with Corrie and Christopher?

We'll tell you this much—they *did* implement Christopher's plan, with results both expected and unexpected. Beyond that, you'll have to read the book!

Chance makes brothers—hearts make friends.

—Duane Booth

In Love and Headstrong

Letters flew back and forth. Kirsten's phone bill mounted. Not many months after their first meeting, Kirsten took a long weekend and drove south to visit Jerome.

She returned engaged. She and Jerome would be married at the end of the summer, just three months away.

It all happened with lightning speed. But they were in love!

Mr. and Mrs. Raynold spoke to Kirsten, as they had regarding the car, urging that the young couple slow the pace.

"You've only been together twice during two weekends," said Mrs. Raynold. "How well do you really know each other? It's a big step promising lifelong companionship."

"You really need to take more time," said Mr. Raynold. "I can't say that strongly enough. I'm not sure you know enough about Jerome yet, or that he knows you well enough."

"We know each other very well," answered Kirsten defensively.

"Don't get us wrong," Mr. Raynold went on. "We like Jerome. We like him a lot. We don't think you could do better. But there is so much involved in getting to know someone well enough to get married. That takes time."

"The two of you are jealous of how happy we are," replied Kirsten in a huff. They could see her anger rising.

"Kirsten, please—that's not it at all," said Mrs. Raynold.

"One of the things a marriage needs most," Mr. Raynold tried to explain, "is self-denial. Let's face it, Kirsten—that is not one of your strong points. I think more time would be to your advantage."

"You two think you know all about marriage!" said Kirsten, raising her voice.

"Well, I think Jerome and I will do better than you. From what I've seen, your marriage isn't all that great. What business do you have telling me anything?"

The Raynolds looked at each other and sighed as Kirsten rushed from the room. What could they say? She had shut them out. Kirsten was determined to have her way, and it didn't look like they were going to be able to stop her.

15 | RESPONSE TO CHRISTOPHER'S PLAN

*Time draweth wrinkles in a fair face, but
addeth fresh colors to a fast friend, which
neither heat, nor cold, nor misery, nor place,
nor destiny can alter or diminish.*

—John Lyly

As we have said, *Best Friends for Life* grew out of
letters we have received from readers in response to *A Home for the Heart*—from
young men, young women, mothers, fathers, aunts, uncles, grandparents. If you
are encountering these ideas on nontraditional marriage preparation for the first
time, you may think our suggestions outlandish and completely impractical.

Maybe you are saying, "No young person today would ever go along with anything like Christopher's plan!"

We've got news for you. Many committed Christian young people today are
hungry to build such practical and spiritual depth into their relationships. They
want strong marriages and are eager for adult leadership to help them prepare.

Young women *want* to find young men like Christopher who are committed
to sound marriage foundations.

Young men *want* to find young women like Corrie who desire God's will above
all else.

So to you young people we say, "Find best friends like Corrie and Christopher
with whom to share this adventure! Trust the wisdom of your mothers and fathers
to help you recognize them when you find them."

To you parents we say, "Support and encourage your sons and daughters, and
be willing to assume your rightful place in their marriage planning, even if it
means hard work, time, and extra energy on your part. What greater gift could
you give them?"

Several months after *A Home for the Heart* was released, we sent out the following letter to readers who had written to us.

To *all* of you who have written, I want to say a big *Thank you!* My wife, Judy—whom you probably know as well as me by now if you are reading either *The Journals of Corrie Belle Hollister* or *The Secret of the Rose*—usually answers most of my mail. There are several reasons for this. Mainly, if I spent half my days writing letters I'd only get *half* as many books written!

So as much as I'd *like* to correspond with each one of you and answer all your questions . . . alas, I have to try to focus my energies on the books themselves. In spite of this, I hope you know that I *do* read every letter—and appreciate them so much—and Judy and I talk about them. So her replies really are from both of us. We consider all you who write to us our friends, and we look forward to meeting you all one day— maybe here, maybe there . . . but we *will* meet sometime.

Almost the instant *A Home for the Heart* was released, we began receiving more letters from you dear readers than for any other book. Never has there been anything like the response to Corrie and Christopher's engagement and Christopher's marriage plan.

Because of this, I felt I had to write something more personal in reply. I am sorry this isn't completely personal—I mean *just* to you. There are too many letters to respond to! But . . . this letter really is just "personal," because as I write it, I *do* have your letter right in front of me—*your* letter (along with others, of course)—and I have read what you've written to me and thought about the questions you've asked, looked at the picture if you sent me one of yourself, and I've prayed briefly for you too—*just for you,* and asked the Lord to bless your life, to reveal himself more and more fully to you, to lead you and guide you into his perfect and complete will in your life, and asked him to accomplish his full and best purposes for you. I hope you can receive this letter as personally as possible, therefore, from my heart to yours, because that is sincerely how I write it.

I often tell people that their letters are a great encouragement to me. You cannot know how true that is! I was greatly discouraged over my writing just three days ago. Sometimes I honestly cannot help but feel I ought to quit entirely. I go through phases of great doubt as a writer, and every book has its periods of struggle and discouragement.

But so often through the years the Lord has prompted a stranger miles and miles away to write and express the very word of encouragement I needed to lift me up and keep me going. Some of the letters of those to whom I am writing right now helped me with the discouragement of a few days ago. So again I say—thank you! Your letter meant so much!

I am doubly appreciative of your responses to *Grayfox* and *A Home for the Heart*. To be very honest, I did not know what people would think of these two books. I was afraid readers might not like them for going a little too far with so-called "spiritual" content.

Your letters of encouragement have confirmed to both Judy and me that people *do* want to read stories about serious and deep commitment to Jesus. Therefore, I intend to keep writing them!

Many of you asked questions about "Christopher's Plan." They were good questions too! Judy and I have talked and laughed over and discussed a number of them and I'll try to answer a few here.

Several of you asked about specifics of the plan—how to do it if both sets of parents are alive, which was not the case with Corrie and Christopher, or how a young man and young woman get to know each other if they're each off with the other's parents, etc.

The most important ingredient to a successful premarriage period, I think, is applying prayerful wisdom, sensibility, and flexibility to the manner in which it is carried out. Obviously every set of circumstances will be utterly unique and therefore "the plan" must be incorporated into those circumstances in a way that works well for all six (young man, young woman, both sets of parents), or whatever number of people is involved.

Our situation in the Phillips family is a lot like that of the Hollisters. We have a business, a large home, my writing involves the whole family, and therefore some plan similar to Christopher's would be easily workable for us. Obviously it will not be easy, or perhaps even appropriate, for everyone. A home, for instance, where there is no room for another person, or where both parents work at jobs that would not be able to include other people . . . it would not work so smoothly for them to bring in a potential husband or wife for their son or daughter and "work with them." Likewise, multifamily situations from prior divorces will complicate these arrangements for many young people.

The key is God-led, prayerful flexibility. Every couple, every set of parents, every father/mother/son/daughter combination will have to seek the Lord and discuss with one another what is the best way for *them* in *their* circumstances to prepare a young couple for marriage. Every "plan" will be different. It may be a year, it may be fifteen months, it may be four months.

As I have said, someone asked that if the girl was at the man's parents' house, and the man at the girl's parents', how are they supposed to get to know *each other*? I would hope that a young man and young woman would know each other pretty well before their plans progressed to this stage. But then during the year, there would obviously be frequent visits and joint activities between the two households. The families need to become more intimately acquainted too. Such opportunities will enable both sets of parents not only to know the young people individually, but also to know them as a couple, to see how they interact together, and to help and advise and counsel them *as* a couple.

I could conceive of a situation in which each set of parents had the other young person, say, for a time, and then another part of it with *both* young people, because there is the need for them to see each other and work beside each other too. Of course, that becomes difficult as well in that an unmarried young couple should not live under the same roof together until marriage. This difficulty would be solved if another relative or grandparent were nearby with whom a young man or young woman could live while their potential spouse lived at home with the parents, similar to Christopher's staying in town and then later in the barn. Where such is not possible, creativity will have to be used to discover prudent ways to enable the plan to be carried out where propriety is not compromised.

These are not firm answers. I can give none. The parents of a young woman whom a young man wants to marry might not *want* him to come and be part of their family for a year. What will they do then? It may often be like this, where one set of parents will want to work together with the young people to a greater extent than the other. We do not live in an ideal world. Let's face it—many people will think a plan like this completely loony! We believe, however, that it will save much marital grief.

Well, that is an attempted answer to some of the questions you raised.

Now for a word of encouragement to you from *me*. . . .

Many of you are young, unmarried, and are wondering about your own futures. Everywhere, all about you—from society, from family, from TV, from advertisements, from friends, even from church relationships—will come pressure to conform, to be like everyone else, and to hurry the romance/dating/courtship/marriage process.

Don't listen . . . don't give in to the pressure . . . dare to take a stand and be different!

Here are three simple tips of advice that will help ensure a happy marriage:

Don't rush.

Wait! Don't rush dating . . . don't rush commitment . . . don't rush engagement!

Take everything slowly. Think in terms of the minimum marriage age being around 24–25, the ideal perhaps 27–30, and any time between

30 and 40 equally great. The older and wiser you are before you marry, the wiser will be your decision, and the more solid will be your marriage. Better a good marriage of 30 years than a miserable one of 45 . . . (or two or three miserable ones). You will only be young and single once. Enjoy it. I could tell you story after story of people we know who married too soon . . . and paid the price. You will hear stories, too, about people who married at 19 or 20 and who had a long and happy life together. But for every one such story there are a hundred that end in divorce.

Keep yourself pure.

Be pure in all your relationships with the opposite sex. Any compromise here will undercut your future marriage relationship. Be pure even with the person you intend to marry. Sex before marriage, in *all* cases, is wrong and will weaken marriage.

And finally,

Aim high in a mate.

Don't settle for second best. Wait for God's perfect choice for you. There *are* Corries and there *are* Christophers in the world for you to meet. This does not mean you should be so idealistic that no one will ever measure up to your standards, only that you determine to marry someone who is as committed to the Lord as you are, not someone who happens to be "cute."

You are not waiting for a perfect person, but for *God's perfect choice.* Wait until you meet *your* Corrie, *your* Christopher. Wait till you're 40 if need be . . . till 50. Don't let yourself marry someone who isn't God's choice for you . . . wait for your Christopher or your Corrie.

Well . . . this was longer than I intended it to be. I hope I may have said something helpful for you. It has been fun visiting with you. I hope to hear from you again!

God bless you!

Your friend and brother,
Michael Phillips

*A friend is one who incessantly pays us the
compliment of expecting from us all
the virtues.*

—Henry David Thoreau

Serious Counsel

Mr. and Mrs. Raynold continued to be concerned.

*Kirsten and Jerome's wedding was approaching rapidly, and they could not
help but be nervous.*

*"I don't want to interfere," said Mr. Raynold, "but Jerome has no idea what
he's getting into."*

*"Why don't we talk to him?" suggested his wife. "Kirsten wouldn't listen to
us, but maybe he will. Neither of them has parents nearby. You're the closest to
a spiritual advisor either of them has right now."*

*"Maybe we ought to. He seems like a level-headed guy, and I do think he
respects us."*

*"It's worth a try. Kirsten has lived with us for a while, and we've learned a
lot about her that we wouldn't have guessed when we first met her."*

*Jerome came for a long weekend during the summer a few months before
the wedding. While Kirsten was gone at work for the morning, the Raynolds
sat down and asked Jerome if they could talk seriously with him.*

"Sure," he said, "what's up?"

*"We feel we need to express some of the concerns we have about you and
Kirsten," began Mr. Raynold. "Kirsten's been with us over a year now, and we've
come to know her pretty well. And . . . well, frankly, Jerome, we just don't feel
you know her well enough yet to marry her."*

"I . . . I don't understand, what's your concern?"

"Please realize that we love Kirsten. She's like family to us, and we feel

terrible talking behind her back like this. But . . . well, she has a real temper—"
"Oh, I've seen it a time or two!" laughed Jerome. "Although it's never been directed at me."
"She's very self-centered as well," Mr. Raynold continued. "We're not sure she's ready for marriage. We think you both need to take a little more time."
"You don't have to worry," said Jerome in a serious tone, though obviously not feeling there was anything to be concerned about. "We know each other so well. We talk for hours on the phone, and in our letters we share like we never have before with anyone. Besides . . . we're in love! That counts more than all the rest!"
"Do you know that Kirsten is a fairly new Christian?"
Jerome nodded. "She's told me everything about herself."
"Are you aware that her mother has been married and divorced three times?"
"I, uh . . . I knew her mother was divorced—she's been married three times? Hmm, no I didn't know that. But," he added, brightening, "that's one of the things I want to do for Kirsten, give her a loving home where she can be herself and feel loved. She's had a rough life, too rough for someone her age. I plan to make all that change for her. Kirsten told me that when she became a Christian, God made all things new for her."
"I suppose you know what a strong will and stubborn spirit she has," said Mrs. Raynold.
"Oh, sure."
"And there's a harsh side to her personality that I doubt you've seen. These traits rise to the surface when the stresses of marriage—"
"I'm not going into this with my eyes closed," Jerome interrupted. "Hey, I appreciate what you two are trying to do. I know you care about Kirsten and me and want us to have our feet on the ground. But you really don't need to worry. We've both dated before. We know this is the real thing."
"Have you ever seen her lay down her own will for the sake of someone else . . . lay down what she wants?" asked Mr. Raynold seriously.
"She is loving to me in every way," replied Jerome with a smile.
"Because she wants to be. But have you seen her lay her own will down?"
"I don't know. What does all that matter—we are in love. Believe me, I am going into this with my eyes wide open. I appreciate your concern, but I love Kirsten and she loves me. That's the only important thing."
Mr. Raynold sighed. "Well, I would just ask one more favor of you," he said. "Please don't mention our talk to Kirsten. She really does have a temper."
Jerome laughed good-naturedly. "It's that spunk that makes me love her so much!" he replied.

16 | A PERSONAL ASSIGNMENT

The essence of true friendship is to make allowance for another's little lapses.

—David Storey

We now come to what we hope will be one of the most interesting, challenging, and thought-provoking sections of this book. Certainly it is one of the most important. We pray you will take it seriously and devote a little extra time to this chapter.

As we told you earlier, all four couples whose lives we've peered into—Bill and Candi, Hal and Laurel, Jerry and Michelle, and Jerome and Kirsten—as well as Jennifer and Marc's, are real people, all very close to us. The stories of their relationships, as we have presented them here, are mostly true (with names and places changed, of course, and with story details added and certain facts omitted to prevent recognition). We have been personally involved in these relationships and were participants in three of the four weddings.

These are not mere stories, then, but real lives and real marriages, each approached in an entirely different way. All the individuals involved are Christians. Most came from Christian homes. Most of the parents involved were Christians. All these young people were taught similar spiritual principles about fidelity and man-woman relationships and, except for Laurel Willard, given similar training (or no training) concerning marriage and preparation for it.

We explain this background simply to stress how distinct are the circumstances in which we, even as Christians, find ourselves and how infinitely varied are the pathways that lead to marriage.

SOME PROBING QUESTIONS FOR YOU TO INVESTIGATE

Most Christian parents counsel their sons and daughters, "Whatever else you do, *make sure* you marry a Christian." And then we quote the verse cautioning against being unequally yoked.

Yet *is* a strong Christian background a guarantee for marital success? Is finding a "Christian" life-partner enough? Does Christian commitment alone guarantee success? Apparently not. The divorce rate among Christians is rising even more rapidly than that of non-Christians. We have shared with you the lives of these four couples so you can begin to answer these questions for yourself and keep your marriage from adding to this alarming trend.

Those of you drawn to the courtship approach, will the process of courtship rather than dating *of itself* produce strong, well-founded marriages?

There are no simple answers. There are many factors to consider.

We would like you to try to answer these questions in the examples of these four true-life "case studies." We would like you to stop reading after you have finished this chapter and think about the four couples and how their relationships progressed. You may want to reread those portions relating their stories.

Then we suggest that you—young people *and* parents, together if possible—discuss each of the four processes for selecting a husband or a wife and determine how you think each of these four marriages will turn out.

To help you begin your discussion, photocopy the following pages for each individual, and then take some time to fill them out. When you are finished, compare notes. This isn't a school exam, with specific right and wrong answers. It only represents a starting place for your discussion.

We will tell you this: all four couples did certain things right . . . and certain things wrong. All four of the relationships contain strong points . . . and weak points.

Can you identify those strong and weak points in each relationship? What did each young person do right, and what did each do wrong? Parents, can you also try to identify what each set of parents—to whatever extent you have been introduced to them—did well, and in what ways they didn't?

Now let's throw Marc and Jennifer's courtship into the discussion too. If you are trying to guide your *own* son or daughter into a wise, sensible, and lasting marriage, you need to be able to spot strengths and weaknesses in a given parental approach.

The discussion sheets to copy follow.

BEST FRIENDS FOR LIFE DISCUSSION SHEET

Grade each couple on the following aspects of marriage and relationship preparation, and add whatever brief thoughts come to your mind for later discussion.

A—*Tops*. They did everything right. They have the process of preparing for marriage down cold.

B—*Better than average*. They handled it mostly okay. Room for improvement.

C—*Average job*. They did it no better or worse than 90 percent of the rest of Christian young people.

D—*Definite trouble ahead*. They did not prepare well for marriage in this area.

F—*They flunk*. They are utterly unprepared and trouble is guaranteed. This will be a bad area in their marriage.

Inc—Don't have enough information to say one way or the other.

1. Are these two young people well-prepared in their relationship with each other for marriage?
   - _____ Bill
   - _____ Hal
   - _____ Jerry
   - _____ Jerome
   - _____ Marc
   - _____ Candi
   - _____ Laurel
   - _____ Michelle
   - _____ Kirsten
   - _____ Jennifer

2. Are these two young people mature enough to be married?
   - _____ Bill
   - _____ Hal
   - _____ Jerry
   - _____ Jerome
   - _____ Marc
   - _____ Candi
   - _____ Laurel
   - _____ Michelle
   - _____ Kirsten
   - _____ Jennifer

3. Rate chances of their marriage lasting 5 years.
   - _____ Bill and Candi
   - _____ Jerry and Michelle
   - _____ Marc and Jennifer
   - _____ Hal and Laurel
   - _____ Jerome and Kirsten

4. Rate chances of their marriage lasting 10 years.
   - _____ Bill and Candi
   - _____ Jerry and Michelle
   - _____ Marc and Jennifer
   - _____ Hal and Laurel
   - _____ Jerome and Kirsten

5. Rate your projected happiness quotient of their marriage.
   - _____ Bill and Candi
   - _____ Jerry and Michelle
   - _____ Marc and Jennifer
   - _____ Hal and Laurel
   - _____ Jerome and Kirsten

6. Rate what you know of their relationship to future in-laws.
   _____ Bill   _____ Candi
   _____ Hal   _____ Laurel
   _____ Jerry   _____ Michelle
   _____ Jerome   _____ Kirsten
   _____ Marc   _____ Jennifer

7. Did this couple know each other long enough before their engagement?
   _____ Bill and Candi   _____ Hal and Laurel
   _____ Jerry and Michelle   _____ Jerome and Kirsten
   _____ Marc and Jennifer

8. Rate their capacity for handling the kind of adversity that comes in marriage with maturity, patience, and wisdom.
   _____ Bill   _____ Candi
   _____ Hal   _____ Laurel
   _____ Jerry   _____ Michelle
   _____ Jerome   _____ Kirsten
   _____ Marc   _____ Jennifer

9. How well were potential danger signals heeded?
   _____ Bill and Candi   _____ Hal and Laurel
   _____ Jerry and Michelle   _____ Jerome and Kirsten
   _____ Marc and Jennifer

10. This couple is a good match.
   _____ Bill and Candi   _____ Hal and Laurel
   _____ Jerry and Michelle   _____ Jerome and Kirsten
   _____ Marc and Jennifer

11. Rate the spiritual foundation of their relationship and marriage.
   _____ Bill and Candi   _____ Hal and Laurel
   _____ Jerry and Michelle   _____ Jerome and Kirsten
   _____ Marc and Jennifer

12. From what you know, is the love in their relationship *selfless* or *self-motivated?*
   _____ Bill   _____ Candi
   _____ Hal   _____ Laurel
   _____ Jerry   _____ Michelle
   _____ Jerome   _____ Kirsten
   _____ Marc   _____ Jennifer

Now for some essay questions (everyone's favorite). Write down your subjective thoughts about each relationship—things you thought they did well, or areas where you see some potential trouble spots. Some of these marriages worked, others didn't. Can you see the subtle signs that reveal how they turned out?

• Further thoughts about Bill and Candi:

• Further thoughts about Hal and Laurel:

• Further thoughts about Jerry and Michelle:

• Further thoughts about Jerome and Kirsten:

• Further thoughts about Marc and Jennifer:

TIME TO PUT YOUR PARTNERSHIP TO WORK

Now for some tougher questions.

What danger signals did you spot in the four relationships that should have indicated rough waters ahead, but which everyone ignored? Were there danger signals in the *method* of spouse selection and the process of *preparing* for marriage?

Who was too idealistic and naive? Who showed practicality and realism?

In three of the five cases there was little parental involvement in choosing a mate, but in Hal and Laurel's and Marc and Jennifer's there was a high degree of parental involvement. How do you think these differences will affect the relative strengths of the marriages over the years?

Perhaps the most important question is this: how well suited were each of the ten for their spouse?

Do you feel they discovered God's will for them in a husband or wife? Were any of these marriages ill-advised?

If you were a family counselor and had nothing to go on but what you have read here, how would you counsel these young people about their chances for a healthy marriage? What if you were a pastor who was asked to marry these five couples—how would you reply? Base your answers on the information you have.

We have not tried to trick you by withholding crucial information. We simply want you to think seriously about these five relationships, discuss them together, and then arrive at a few conclusions about what you think the future holds for each couple.

No one is going to grade you! But we honestly think this exercise will help you in your own relationships and preparation for marriage.

So give some thought to your predictions before continuing on. Pay attention to the strong points of the relationships and to the subtle danger signals that escaped notice.

When you have finished your evaluations you are ready for the next chapter, where you will learn more about Bill and Candi, Hal and Laurel, Jerry and Michelle, and Jerome and Kirsten. We don't know about Marc and Jennifer's future yet!

"Be very careful, then, how you live—not as unwise but as wise, making the most of every opportunity, because the days are evil. Therefore do not be foolish, but understand what the Lord's will is" (Ephesians 5:15–17).

PART V

WHAT HAPPENS WHEN THE GLITTER FADES?

What Happened to Bill and Candi?

Bill and Candi had two children, remained active in the Redsdale church, and became one of the church's most popular young couples, singing in the choir and working with youth.

When Candi became pregnant and the ladies in the church began to make a fuss over her, she thought she could never be happier. At her baby shower, her mother's friends commented that they'd never seen such a stylish mother-to-be.

Bill and Candi continued to be active in church functions, and for several years gave every appearance of being Mr. and Mrs. Model Christian. It was fun to receive all the oohs and aahs and be thought of as "such a beautiful family."

After giving birth to their second child, Candi took up jogging in order to get back in shape. Everyone marveled at what a good mother she was, pushing her jog-stroller with the baby while her four-year-old daughter was in preschool.

Still in her twenties, Candi's natural athleticism made it easy for her to get in shape. She began racing and soon became one of the best female road runners in the area.

She joined a running club and was involved in a race or activity almost every weekend. Bill and the children became her cheering section. Bill was proud of his attractive wife and glad Candi didn't let herself go like so many young mothers he'd seen.

Gradually, however, being around athletic men all the time made Candi disenchanted with married life. After a few years she couldn't keep her flirtatious personality in check. Her teen preoccupation with trying to be noticed by guys emerged again as a desire to be noticed by men. Bill's athleticism and youthful good looks proved unable to sustain her undivided interest forever, and as Bill gradually put on weight and showed signs of thinning hair, her eyes strayed. While he was at work she spent more and more time at the gym, and eventually one thing led to another.

Bill did his best to remain true, though eventually Candi's pretty face and radiant personality turned sour in his mind. He knew he was no longer the object of her affections. Seven years after their marriage, Bill and Candi were divorced. Candi quickly married a runner from the local club, and on most weekends they traveled out of town for races. Bill struggled to take care of the two children.

When Candi had a new baby by her second husband she decided she wanted the others with her. She sued for custody and Bill was cut out of the parenting picture altogether.

A number of years has passed. Both are now on their third "relationship," and neither is walking with the Lord. The two children bounce back and forth between them, sometimes in school, sometimes not. One of them, a teenager now, has been in trouble with the law. They now live with one of the two parents in a one-room apartment.

Years later, Mr. and Mrs. Pickering sat quietly at the kitchen table. Two of their grandchildren had just left with Candi's new boyfriend.

"What did we do wrong?" asked Mrs. Pickering after a long silence.

"If we had it to do over again," said Mr. Pickering, "I would have kept a closer watch on that girl."

"I said it years before, and I'll say it again—she was too pretty for her own good," sighed her mother. "At the time I thought how fortunate for her to be pretty and have friends and be so popular. Now I see what a handicap a pretty face is to building character."

"We should have seen it coming—she was a flirt before she was ten."

"It bothered me when she didn't want to be called Candace anymore. Such a simple thing as trying to spell her name in a more cute way revealed more than I wanted to admit."

"She wanted to be noticed by boys more than anything."

"Could we have done anything to prevent that?"

"I don't know, but the way things have turned out—we should have tried."

"Even as much as I liked Bill right from the start, their attraction wasn't as spiritual as we thought. From their first meeting, their relationship was based on looks and the physical attraction they felt for each other."

"And how well did we know Bill? We were so relieved that she was dating a Christian for a change that we didn't bother to ask any questions about his character, his past, his spiritual life."

"I feel so sorry for him."

"He was a pretty decent guy through all this, but Candi ran over him like a bulldozer."

"He didn't know what he was getting into. She was always so strong willed.

She was used to having things her own way."

"That probably was *our* fault."

"That she was strong-willed?"

"No, that we gave in to it. In a sense we rewarded her rebellion."

Mrs. Pickering sighed. She didn't like to think about it.

"We should have insisted they spend more time with us," Mr. Pickering went on after a moment, "and they should have gone through some counseling. They didn't know each other well enough to get married. A year and a half wasn't long enough."

"They were just two good-looking people who looked even better together. Not much of a base to start a marriage."

"I sometimes wish they hadn't been involved in so many church activities. The church environment fed that wrong set of values."

"That's quite a statement from a former youth leader."

"Well, I wonder what good we did those kids all those years. Looking back, I think we in the church fed the boyfriend-girlfriend obsession in our passion to get them all matched with Christians. Half the kids who used to be in my youth group are divorced now. Our whole priority was to make sure the kids had a good time. We never asked whether we were giving them anything different than the world offers."

What Happened to Hal and Laurel?

Laurel knew immediately what they had done was wrong. She loved Hal but regretted going along with his plan. Down inside she knew she was the stronger Christian of the two and that she should have had the courage to stand up and say what she felt. But being afraid of losing someone you think you love is a powerful seducer toward compromise.

They struggled to make the best of it and put together a few things to add to Hal's one-room apartment. Without a shower or church wedding and the blessings of family and friends, their first week together was filled with awkward looks and half-smiles, and a gnawing sense of guilt in the pit of Laurel's stomach.

Within the first two weeks several friends tried to share with Hal and Laurel that they had made a serious mistake and that their marriage was based on rebellion against Laurel's father, a caring, godly man. More than one said they should have the marriage annulled so Hal and Laurel could submit themselves once again to Mr. Willard's parental covering, and thus reestablish their relationship and marriage on a sound footing. But they didn't listen.

Laurel cried off and on for the first month. Her mother cried almost as long. Hal was furious with their reactions. They were married. It was done. Why couldn't Laurel's parents accept it and go on? He didn't visit the Willards again for a very long time.

Laurel had been close to her mother for years and sorely missed that friendship. She went "home" for a visit now and then when Hal was at work. After three or four months, she apologized to her parents and they embraced her. Many more tears were shed, and the three are now attempting to rebuild a framework for trust. Hal, however, did not show an interest in developing a relationship with either of Laurel's parents for some time.

Hal and Laurel eloped less than a year ago at this writing. Hal has finally begun to come around to the Willard home. The young couple has been attending the Willards' church and are trying to establish a normal life together, though both are working and trying to finish school. They seldom see each other and finances are troublesome.

Hal and Laurel had just left after a Sunday dinner in the Willard home. Mr. Willard was helping his wife with the dishes. It had been a satisfactory visit, but, as always, seeing their daughter caused the pain to resurface.

Laurel's mother sighed. "Where did our plans get off track?" she said. "We tried so hard to do everything right. I thought it was going along smoothly."

"It **seemed** like it was going smoothly," replied Mr. Willard, "but courtship was so new for us. We made a lot of mistakes."

"I thought Laurel was committed to it."

"She wanted to date, and she wanted a boyfriend. She was never really behind us all the way."

"I know—she was with us one day, and against us the next. I tend to forget what a struggle it was."

"And we hadn't really thought it out thoroughly. It was too much for them to handle from the start, which I feel bad about."

"It wasn't your fault. Hal had no respect for either of us. I don't think he does even now."

"I suppose that's true," sighed Laurel's father. "As mature as he seems in many ways, he's never learned respect for authority. But I do feel that Hal and Laurel are right for each other."

"But how much stronger their marriage would be if they hadn't been in such a hurry."

"As it is, the foundation of their marriage is built on an angry, independent act. I'm afraid it may cast a shadow for a long time."

"They want to prove everyone wrong. What will happen when the real stresses of life together begin to emerge?"

"Hal will have to bear the responsibility for his actions," Mr. Willard said. "Along with Laurel, of course. No one forced her to go along. She knew it was wrong. But I share responsibility as well. I didn't see the danger in courtship. I saw only the benefits."

They were both silent for a time.

"Well," sighed Mr. Willard, "we need to pray for them every day, that their storms will be mild—until their weak marriage vessel develops more strength."

What Happened to Jerry and Michelle?

Jerry's last-minute hesitation about marriage disappeared the following day. He and Michelle were married in one of the happiest ceremonies their church had ever seen. When the pastor introduced them as husband and wife, the congregation applauded.

Once they were married, never were there doubts again. They faced plenty of hardships, but no doubts. They have had a rough marriage, with many unexpected circumstances thrown their way. All marriages have difficult patches. But the commitment Jerry and Michelle made to each other and before the Lord was true. They have remained solidly together . . . best friends for life.

They have been happy, productive, financially successful, and influential in the body of Christ. Theirs is a marriage that has worked.

They talk every once in a while about that night before their wedding.

"You know," Jerry said recently, "as awkward as I felt, I wouldn't trade that time in the car praying the way we did for anything."

"It was an important bond we entered into that night," added Michelle, "of prayer and trust."

"As much as you know I love you, it was not a bond built upon or sustained by passion, but because we knew our love was something God brought together."

"That knowledge really has helped carry me through some of the rough times."

"That knowledge . . . and our deep friendship," added Jerry.

Jerry wrote Michelle's father a very personal letter shortly before their twentieth wedding anniversary.

He really hadn't known Michelle's parents well before they married. He wished he'd known about asking a young lady's father permission to marry her, he told Mr. Jones. He'd never stopped to consider that it was a custom relevant for today, and he regretted that oversight. He was sorry to have missed out on that important opportunity. But he wanted to make it right, so he belatedly asked their forgiveness and went on to thank Mr. Jones, and Michelle's mother as well, for trusting him with their daughter and for encouraging and supporting them in their marriage all these years.

What Happened to Jerome and Kirsten?

A year and a half after Jerome and Kirsten married, they returned to the town where they had met to visit Mr. and Mrs. Raynold and Kirsten's other friends. Kirsten glowed with her first pregnancy and seemed happy. She talked about how great they were doing and their plans after the baby was born.

Jerome, however, was quiet and subdued. He dutifully followed Kirsten from place to place but remained mostly in the background, saying little. He stood beside his wife as a benevolent attendant while she visited and chatted with her usual exuberance. The Raynolds detected pain in Jerome's face, but he said nothing and they sensed no opening to inquire.

Six months later the telephone rang in the Raynold home. It was Jerome. "I'm sorry to bother you," he said, "but I need help. Frankly, I'm desperate." "What is it, Jerome?" asked Mr. Raynold.

"It's Kirsten," he replied. "Things . . . just aren't working out between us. Kirsten would be furious if she knew I was calling you, but I don't know who else to turn to."

"May I come see you?" asked Mr. Raynold.

"Please—I would appreciate it more than you can know."

Mr. Raynold drove the six hours to visit his young friends. Jerome was miserable. And he had been right about one thing. Kirsten **was** furious when she found out that he had called, and she did not appreciate the purpose of Mr. Raynold's visit.

Mr. Raynold stayed with them for two days. Jerome confided that the marriage was a sham. They went to church and gave every appearance of being a *contented Christian couple. Kirsten attended a women's Bible study every week. But at home, said Jerome, Kirsten ruled the roost. She expected him to love her and give to her but she didn't buy any of this submission stuff that was going around. In her zeal to be equal to him in all areas, she completely dominated the home. Whenever he suggested another way, she lost her temper and yelled that she would never be any man's doormat.*

The two men commiserated and prayed together, but without Kirsten's willing participation, what could they hope to accomplish?

Jerome made several valiant attempts to save the marriage, but Kirsten was headstrong. Within months of Mr. Raynold's visit, she was already talking of separation. About a year after their son was born, she filed for divorce.

Jerome has visited the Raynolds a number of times, and they have remained close friends over the years. More than once he has said, "I should have listened to you. You were so right—I didn't really know Kirsten at all. I should have **trusted** *that you were trying to do the right thing. I should have given it more* **time***. We should have found someone to* **pray** *with us regularly about the big step of marriage."*

Kirsten, like her mother, has been married and divorced three times, and has become a very successful businesswoman.

What Will Happen to You?

How do you imagine **your** *married life years from now?*

Thinking about what you want your future to look like can be helpful—not to build pie-in-the-sky dreams, but because nothing happens by accident. If you want to get somewhere, it helps to have a reasonable idea of your destination. If you want to enjoy a happy family life fifteen years from now, there are steps you have to take now.

As you envision your future, does a wonderful holiday dinner come to mind with everyone seated around the table enjoying one another? Everyone loves the Lord, and there is laughter and singing and open-hearted sharing, and no hidden animosities cloud the occasion. Do you see a trusting, happy relationship with your in-laws?

Can you, young lady, picture you and your husband working together in the yard while your small children make mud pies? Your parents drive up, and the children squeal with delight and run to greet their grandparents. Your husband stands to meet them, walks forward with a smile of welcome, and shakes hands with your father.

Your heart stirs because you know they mutually respect and love each other. You are thankful you and your husband allowed your parents to play an intrinsic role in your relationship from the very beginning. Your father never felt he was losing a daughter—he was gaining a son and a friend.

Young man, can you picture your wife working happily in your mother's kitchen? The two are chatting like sisters or old friends. Your wife pauses as she listens to your mother share a bit of wisdom with her. She is really a daughter to your mother. They don't know you're watching, but your heart is blessed to overflowing as you observe the truth of Titus 2:3–5 lived out in this relationship between the two women you love most.

Young people, allow your parents to be a part of your relationship—right from the start. Trust them. They want the best for you. Give yourself plenty of time. Be in no hurry to leave the safety of your parents' home and their counsel.

In the meantime, you have preparations to make now so these visions can become reality later on. Young men, make certain you can provide for a wife and family. Young ladies, develop the skills you will need to make a home and raise happy, obedient children.

*Parents, gently and prayerfully remain a part of your son's and daughter's lives so that they **will** trust you, and will **want** you deeply involved in their relationships.*

Ask God, "How can we most honor you in our relationships?" And, "How can we best help our children in this most important decision of their lives?"

*The specifics by which you young people carry out our suggestions matter far less than that you **trust** your parents and bring them into the process . . . that you take your **time** . . . and that you **pray** for God's guidance.*

*Then when your friends and family are watching **your** wedding ceremony, they will not have to cross their fingers and hope for the best. They will know where you and your best friend for life are bound!*

"But the one who received the seed that fell on good soil is the man who hears the word and understands it. He produces a crop, yielding a hundred, sixty or thirty times what was sown" (Matthew 13:23).

APPENDICES

Appendix A

"THAT'S ALL WELL AND GOOD . . . BUT WHAT ABOUT ME?"

You may have read the title of this appendix and asked just that question, wondering if this book has anything to offer you.

Obviously *every* book cannot be written to *everyone*. If a book is about downhill skiing, it's not really pertinent for someone in Florida who has never been snow-skiing in his life to complain that the book leaves him out—that it offers him no help on how to spend his weekends.

Similarly, we realize that people find themselves in many situations other than those we have addressed here. We have the utmost appreciation for the unique individuality with which God works in all of our lives. We can't address here every marital issue. We have written primarily to unmarried young people from Christian families and to their parents.

If you are a young person from a home where there hasn't been Christian training, we sincerely hope you too will be able to benefit from what we have offered. Perhaps you will be the first of several generations of strong Christian men and women, and a whole new direction in your family's history will begin with you. We write to you too!

But it is important for you to recognize that many of our comments have been directed toward Christian homes. Any book must be aimed more in certain directions than in others. There are primary and secondary audiences, and our readers will fall into both groups. You may need to adapt what we say to your situation.

Likewise, if you are already married, or if you have been divorced, or if you are fifty-five and preparing for marriage, we sincerely hope you will find much here that will be useful to you. We love you and care about your situation, even though we have not written perhaps as personally and specifically to you. Life throws us all unexpected curves. It is impossible to lay out a principle and then try to set forth a dozen slightly different applications: *If you have been divorced you will . . . and if you are over thirty you will want to consider . . . and if your upbringing has not been in a Christian home you will . . . or if your parents are divorced you will . . .* and so on. All our time would be spent on special cases.

We hope, therefore, that after every chapter you did not remark, "Yeah, that all sounds good . . . but what about *me?* My life isn't like that." We hope, rather, that you said enthusiastically, "That *does* sound good. My life doesn't happen to fit that pattern . . . so what can I do to adapt that principle in order to *make* it work in my situation?"

If the specifics of your circumstances are different than we have addressed, change the application to fit. That's *your* job.

In *whatever* situation you find yourself, there are worthy mentors—parents, relatives, friends, teachers, pastors—to whom you can make yourself accountable, and who would be happy to help you prepare for marriage.

Preparation for a best-friend marriage is worth the time and energy it will take, whether you're a teen and not contemplating marriage for ten years or whether you're in your thirties, whether your parents are Christians or not, and even whether you consider *yourself* a Christian or not.

Don't leave one of the most important decisions of your life to chance.

Find wise individuals whom you can *trust* . . . take your *time* . . . and *pray*.

Appendix B

SUGGESTED READING, AS WELL AS A FEW THOUGHTS

You may have noticed a singular lack of statistical references in this book. Many books on subjects such as those we have addressed—marriage, divorce, remarriage, sexual promiscuity, changing morals, etc.—go to excessive lengths to reference sources documenting what percentage of various segments of the population have done such-and-so by a certain age, that X percent of teens under the age of Y have engaged in this or that sort of behavior, which we would rather not mention.

We're not ostriches burying our heads in the sand. We *know* how bad the morals of our culture have become and feel no particular inclination to wallow in the evidence confirming it. We're confident you know how bad it is too, without requiring that we list all the statistics you've already heard from a dozen other sources that cite immorality and societal decay.

It is not the mere redundancy that we want to avoid. We feel there is far too much open and graphic discussion of sexual matters in reading material otherwise calling for purity and virtue. Though the ostensible purpose may be to alert readers to the crisis of our times, the way such material is presented to young people is seriously unedifying and cannot help but taint the overall effort.

When a parent wants to give a teen a book on purity and virtue but feels he must forbid him or her to read one of the chapters because of its graphic portrayal of *impure* behavior, it strikes us that perhaps something is wrong with the approach.

One of the books we have quoted from because we endorse its basic message makes the claim on its cover: "A vision for a generation . . . of . . . purity." On nearly every page, however, there are words like fornication or sexual activity, and more explicit phrases we will not mention. We began going through it carefully to see if our assessment was accurate, and in a half-dozen pages we had counted 37 sexually explicit words and phrases and not a single reference to purity. The book is far less a vision *for* purity than it is a diatribe *against* premarital sex.

To the innocent eyes and ears of a ten- or twelve- or fourteen-year-old, books like this—and many of the teen books in Christian bookstores—are nothing short of pornographic in their effect. Surely such is not their authors' intent, but to wide-eyed young readers who are not among the statistics of the "experienced," that is precisely their effect. One of our sons once said he learned what he knew about sex from the books in our own Christian bookstore! Now we actually screen youth books, magazines, and music from certain writers, artists, and publishers. Much of the material is not only inappropriate but downright polluting to young minds, despite the good the authors may be trying to achieve.

We believe the way to combat moral decay is by heeding Paul's words in Philippians 4:8: "Whatever is true, whatever is noble, whatever is right, whatever is pure, whatever is lovely, whatever is admirable—if anything is excellent or praiseworthy—*think about such things.*" And his words in Colossians 3:1–2: "Set your hearts on things above . . . *set your minds on things above, not on earthly things.*"

Do Christian writers and teachers need to preface every call for purity with twenty-five mind-filling, heart-distracting references to the distorted and sexually destructive things people in the world do?

We think not.

This preoccupation with explicit material so prevalent today among Christian writers makes recommendations difficult. We have stacks of books conveying great wisdom on the teen years and teen relationships. But we would be extremely hesitant to recommend most of them. And even with the few that are listed below, which we consider excellent, we caution both parents and young people that some of these books contain discussions of sexual matters we feel are too graphic for all ages.

With that disclaimer and explanation, we feel you may benefit from the following books:

On godly dating . . .

> *Dating With Integrity*, John Holzmann (Word Publishing Co.)

On preparation for marriage . . .

> *How Can I Be Sure?* Bob Phillips (Harvest House). Skip chapter 8.

On courtship . . .

> *Dating vs. Courtship*, Paul Jehle (Plymouth Rock Foundation, Fisk Mill, Marlborough, NH 03455). One of the best sources on courtship, though unfortunately one of the *most* inclusive of graphic sexual discussions and a great many "statistics" that we feel are unnecessary and that feed lustful fancies. Parents, please screen. Young people, for the sake of your own purity of mind, don't read this without parental supervision.
>
> *Of Knights and Fair Maidens*, Jeff & Danielle Myers (P.O. Box 88191, Colorado Springs, CO 80908).
>
> *Christian Courtship Versus the Dating Game*, Jim West (Christian Worldview Ministries, P.O. Box 603, Palo Cedro, CA 96073). Skip ahead to chapters on courtship!

On discipleship, dating, and courtship . . .

> *It's a Lifestyle*, Nathaniel and Andrew Ryun (Silver Clarion Press, 16718 Thirteenth St., Lawrence, KS 66044). Again, we're sorry to have to say, skip the statistics.

On friendship with the opposite sex . . .

> *What About Boy-Girl Friendships?* (Rod and Staff Publishers, Crockett, Ky. 41413).

On divorce and remarriage . . .

> *Marriage and Divorce*, John Stott (InterVarsity Press, Downers Grove, Ill., 1984).

On family relationships and the godly teen lifestyle . . .

> Audio cassette tapes by Jonathan Lindvall (Bold Parenting Seminars, P.O. Box 820, Springville, CA 93265):
> "Training Godly Teens"
> "Talk to Teens About Sex and Romance"
> "Preparing for Romance"

On the parental role in teen chastity and covenant talks . . .

> *Raising Them Chaste*, Richard and Reneé Durfield (Bethany House Publishers, Minneapolis, Mn.). This is a book for *parents* about teen chastity. Plain and simple, the subject is sex and there are graphic portions. Excellent for parents, we do not, however, recommend that unmarried individuals read this book.

On Christopher's Plan . . .

> *A Home for the Heart*, Michael Phillips (Bethany House Publishers, Minneapolis, Mn.).

Appendix C

STRENGTHENING THAT COMES FROM THE GREENHOUSE

(Excerpt from *The Eleventh Hour* by Michael Phillips, Tyndale House Publishers)

The following fictional selection may put some of our thoughts from Appendix B into perspective.

"You have no idea what a tonic your daughter is for my Matthew," said Thaddeus McCallum at length, as the three parents sat in the rose garden. "He has not had many quality relationships with young people his own age. It is one of the disadvantages of my work."

"He is very mature, though, Thaddeus," interjected Baron von Dort-mann, "which is certainly an advantage."

"Yes, he is. I am proud of him."

"I have not always been convinced that having children of similar age around is a great advantage in character development. In fact, my experience tells me just the opposite to be the case."

"I see your point. And yes, Matthew is a good, solid young man. But he expects a good deal of himself—too much I fear sometimes."

"He doesn't seem any the worse for it," commented Marion. "He is very grown up and personable, able to handle himself and converse easily with others."

"Being close as we are, and being my friend as well as my son, I have taken him everywhere with me. He's been around adults most of his life and has been comfortable with it."

"He seems able to enjoy himself here," said Marion.

"That is your daughter's influence," rejoined Thaddeus. "I can see that Sabina brings out the child, the playfulness, even an impulsiveness in him. He thinks a great deal of her, but mostly he finds her fun to be with. He has told me so. She brings a part of his nature to the surface that he has never had the chance to discover before now." He laughed again. "Though to tell you the truth," he added, "I can't help finding it humorous."

"What's that?" asked the baron.

"It's obvious that the two *aren't* children any longer. Your daughter is very much a woman."

"And your son is a striking young man."

"Exactly," rejoined Thaddeus, still chuckling. "I can see that Matt doesn't know when to be a boy or when to be a man when he's around Sabina. They both are very grown up and mature for their ages, and yet so young and innocent in so many ways. It's interesting to watch them work out the growing process, even as they try to figure out what they think of each other."

"I see the humor in it," smiled the baron. "It is a delightful thing to observe, because of who the two young people are."

"They are rather an unusual pair," added Marion.

"Now that you've told us all this, I do understand Matthew better than before," said the baron. "I thank you for sharing as candidly as you have."

"You cannot know how thankful I am for the times he's had to enjoy here."

"Your son is the caliber of young man we have hoped for Sabina to meet," said the baron. "But such come along rarely. We too express deep thankfulness for Matthew on behalf of our daughter. She will have a standard with which to measure other young men. Whatever your reservations, I would certainly commend you for the job you have done with him. He is clearly a young man of principle and integrity and fiber, and such qualities are not ingrained by accident. You have given him more of the mettle of manhood than perhaps you are aware."

"Thank you, baron," said Thaddeus humbly. "You are very kind."

There was a pause. It was the American who broke it after a few moments.

"Do you mind if I ask you a question?" he said. "About your daughter . . . yet, I suppose, not only about her, but concerning your whole way of life here."

"Not at all," replied the baron.

"All right," said Thaddeus. "Here it is: How are you preparing your daughter for a world that, it is all too clear, may not be pleasant? All this—it seems too perfect, too serene, too idyllic. Don't you fear that your daughter will be ill-equipped to cope with the realities of life, when she has been so completely protected from its harshness and cruelties?"

The baron nodded as Thaddeus spoke, deep lines of concern etched across his forehead and apparent around his eyes. He was obviously deep in thought. He continued in his reflection for a few moments after his friend was finished speaking. Then, "You cannot know how long and hard and earnestly we have discussed and prayed over this very concern, Thaddeus," he said. "Marion and I have spent countless hours asking ourselves that very question in a hundred different ways, quite literally since the day Sabina was born. Haven't we, dear?"

Marion nodded.

"There are times and seasons, Thaddeus," the baron said, "periods of life—now for one thing, then for another. God gives seasons of serenity at particular times, often with the purpose of preparation for difficulties that lie ahead. It is a mistake, in my view, to think that only hardship prepares one for hardship. There is, of course, a sense in which that is true. But in another sense serenity has equal strengthening value.

"Take plants, for example, such as any of a hundred we could examine growing in the garden here. Nurturing a tender young plant in a greenhouse and then too soon exposing it to the harsh winds and frosts of winter *could* kill it. On the other hand, if early in its life the plant is given sufficient care and time so that its roots go deep and its stalk and trunk and branches become strong and vital, then it can be a plant of such virility that it will flourish under any adverse circumstance. So, you see, the greenhouse yields two different possibilities of result.

"Likewise, imagine a tree having grown from a seedling high on the slopes of a rugged, rocky mountain where nature has done her best to destroy it. If that tree survives, it will indeed be tough and sinewy and hardy, and able to withstand almost anything. Yet most seedlings die on those fierce slopes before reaching maturity. Those that do survive are usually dwarfed and deformed and never as shaped and fruitful as they might have been had they spent their early years in a more protected environment.

"So which is the best way to grow a healthy and vibrant plant, Thaddeus?" laughed the baron. "In the greenhouse or on the mountain slope? Both contain inherent risks."

"You do enjoy making the earth's growing things into your object lessons, don't you?" said McCallum, joining in his laughter.

"If you only knew!" added Marion. "Positively *everything* in the mind of this husband of mine comes back to roots, soil, plants, and God's creation! He *loves* to find the lessons of nature for everything else in life."

The baron roared with good-natured laughter. "I confess to every word!" he said. "She is absolutely right, I do love it."

"I have the distinct feeling you are not talking about plants, though, baron," said Thaddeus.

"What are children but tender, growing *living* things?" asked Dortmann in reply. "I happen to be a strong believer in giving all things that grow a strong and healthy beginning in the protected environment of the greenhouse. Figuratively speaking, of course."

"Could you explain even more specifically?" asked Thaddeus.

"Yes, by example," replied the baron. "When I travel to Berlin to find a new specimen for my garden here, or to purchase seedlings, or when I visit one of my friends to obtain a cutting of some plant I want to try, I go to extreme lengths to give that plant all the help I can to make sure it gets a healthy start. Whatever strength it carries with it throughout the remainder of its existence depends on the help I give it in its first year or two. What I do the most at first is protect and shelter it from all sorts of effects that could kill it if left to itself—snow, frost, wind, pests, various fungi, rabbits, deer, snails, and so on. I am extremely protective of my young plants and often cover them with small shields until their root systems have taken hold well. I also fertilize and prune as needed. I spare no effort during the critical first two seasons."

The baron paused, glancing toward the eastern sky. "Do you see those dark clouds off in the distance, Thaddeus?" he said.

McCallum looked, then nodded.

"From the smell and the feel of the breeze that kicked up about twenty minutes ago, I can tell they are moving this way. There will be rain by this time tomorrow. I guarantee it. Possibly a severe rain. And if I had any plants or cuttings I had recently put in the ground, I would take the necessary precautions this afternoon to protect them from getting blown about or from the topsoil being washed away.

"You see, it is a matter of getting their roots to reach deeply into the good, rich soil so that the growth of the stalk and trunk and stems and branches and leaves above the ground is vital and healthy. Without deep roots, and with outside influences continually eating and destroying the first tender green sprouts, a long, healthy, and productive future is doomed.

"I believe the same protection is necessary in the care and nurturing of our children.

"*Roots*, Thaddeus! Roots must be nurtured carefully so that they extend deep into good soil. At the same time, pests and wind and frost and snails must be kept away so that the first tender shoots of life have sufficient protection to grow strong."

"There are many who would disagree with such a parallel," suggested McCallum.

"Yourself?"

"Not necessarily. Frankly, I've never thought about the things you are saying before. But I do know everyone would not agree with you."

"I run counter to the prevailing notions in most things, Thaddeus," laughed the baron. "Of course, you are correct—not merely would *some* not agree, I would go so far as to say *most* would disagree with the whole notion of greenhouses as being appropriate for children. But then all you have to do is look at a young man such as our neighbor's son, and you see all too clearly the results of a plant that is allowed to grow in any and all directions its sinful nature sees fit, without sheltering, without fertilizing, and without pruning. I feel sorry for the young fellow. In a way it is not really his fault," sighed the baron. "The tenders of his garden, I fear, let him go to seed early, and they are now paying the price."

"What about you, Frau Dortmann?" asked Thaddeus. "Are you of one mind with your husband?"

"Of course," answered Marion.

"Such was the Father's way with his own Son," the baron went on. "To insure Jesus' protection and nurturing, his Father chose the most godly woman of the time, young Mary, to act as his greenhouse, so to speak, to shield him from all that could thwart the Father's plan. If such was the Father's way, it is the example I for one desire to follow."

"But how long is such protection to last with children, Heinrich?" asked Thaddeus.

"Jesus remained at home with his mother for thirty years, so I suspect it is longer than most people realize."

The baron paused, then grew reflective. "As parents concerned for our daughter," he said, "we struggle frequently with this question. One can never anticipate everything that lies on the horizons of life. It has been our hope and prayer that by providing a serene life for our daughter, as you referred to earlier, and by giving her an environment where there is a minimum of internal conflict, she will be strengthened within to face the external conflicts that will come upon her later in life. It is exactly how I tend my garden. In a larger way, it is this very foundation upon which the ministry of *Lebenshaus* is built—by the peacefulness and serenity and harmony of our internal relationships and lifestyle and even this country setting we are blessed with, we are able to offer a retreat and peacefulness to others whom God sends us.

"There have been times we have wondered if we have created an unreal world here for Sabina. Will she be able to deal with life's stresses and conflicts and heartaches when they overtake her, as they inevitably do everyone? We do not have the answers to all these questions."

"Yet this is exactly what we set out to do in the beginning," said Marion. "We desired to show Sabina what life and relationships were *supposed* to be like, how they could and should function in an ideal setting, in order, as my husband has said, to give her the roots and strength necessary when later trials do come. You come to know the *true* and the *real* by being surrounded by it, not by going out into a world where *false* values and *wrong* attitudes and *shallow* relationships are the norm."

"I have always felt that the way to be strong for battle was not necessarily by being a fighter yourself but by being a person of courage inside," added the baron.

"So how long *do* you intend for the process to last with your Sabina?" asked Thaddeus, after a pause.

"Ah, you've put your finger on the most difficult question of all, my friend! Plants and children both must gradually be allowed to grow on their own, by degrees. With children it takes many, many years, steadily allowing more and more of their life to come from their own roots rather than from parental influence. Fertilization of those roots must, of course, continue, and even after twenty years there remains much nurturing to be done. Witness our own two—they have well-established root systems and are growing independently. Yet both are still children in so many ways. They are flourishing tall and strong and hearty, yet the full maturity of their adulthood has not yet fully come."

"It approaches rapidly, however," said Thaddeus.

The baron sighed. "Adulthood always approaches more rapidly than we think," he added.

A FINAL WORD FROM THE AUTHORS

If you know an individual or a family who would benefit from this book but who cannot afford one, please let us know. We will do what we can to get one into their hands.

As always, we would enjoy hearing from you, especially if you would like to share with us how you have put some of these principles into practice. You may write us at P.O. Box 7003, Eureka, CA 95502.

May the Lord bless you richly as you seek best-friend marriages!

Michael and Judy Phillips